A FIFTY-YEAR SILENCE

Miranda Richmond Mouillot was born in Asheville, North Carolina. She lives in the South of France with her husband, daughter and cat.

A Fifty-year Silence

Love, War & a Ruined House in France

MIRANDA RICHMOND MOUILLOT

TEXT PUBLISHING MELBOURNE AUSTRALIA

textpublishing.com.au

The Text Publishing Company
Swann House
22 William Street
Melbourne Victoria 3000
Australia

First published in the United States by Crown Publishers, an imprint of the Crown Publishing Group, a division of Random House LLC, a Penguin Random House Company, New York, 2015.
First published in Australia by Text Publishing, 2015.

Cover design by W. H. Chong
Page design by Lauren Dong
Maps by Meredith Hamilton
Interior photographs courtesy of the author

Printed in Australia by Griffin Press, an Accredited ISO AS/NZS 14001:2004 Environmental Management System printer

National Library of Australia Cataloguing-in-Publication entry:
Creator: Richmond Mouillot, Miranda, author.
Title: A fifty-year silence : love, war and a ruined house in France /
           by Miranda Richmond Mouillot.
ISBN: 9781922182586 (paperback)
           9781925095524 (ebook)
Subjects: World War, 1939-1945—France.
           Grandparents—France—Biography.
           Runaway wives—France—Biography.
           Family secrets.
           Families—France.
Dewey Number: 306.87092

This book is printed on paper certified against the Forest Stewardship Council® Standards. Griffin Press holds FSC chain-of-custody certification SGS-COC-005088. FSC promotes environmentally responsible, socially beneficial and economically viable management of the world's forests.

This book is for Anna.

What do you think? Do you also believe that what gives our lives their meaning is the passion that suddenly invades us heart, soul, and body, and burns in us forever, no matter what else happens in our lives?

—SÁNDOR MÁRAI, *Embers*
(translated from the Hungarian by Carol Brown Janeway)

Author's Note

A Fifty-Year Silence is a true story, but it is a work of memory, not a work of history. I relied on historical sources—primary, secondary, and historiographical—in the writing of it, but for the most part I based it on conversations and letters with my grandparents and on my own memories of and reflections about them. I have done my best to verify these memories and reflections by checking them against those of others and against historical documents.

As I dramatized key scenes from my grandparents' lives in the pages of this book, I sought to maintain the vertiginous sense of poetry that their silence provoked in my own life. In so doing, I have tried to be as faithful as possible both to their recollections and to the historical facts that informed those moments. Any inaccuracies I may have unwittingly introduced are due to the inherent difficulties of writing about a subject no one is willing to discuss.

A Fifty-Year Silence seeks to confront and illuminate a shadow that haunts every family: the past, which is at once sharply present and maddeningly vague. Indeed, I originally intended to call the book *Traveling Shadows*, after a line in *Speak, Memory*, in which Vladimir Nabokov compares the act of reconstructing the past to studying shadows on a wall. Shadow watching is a solitary and subjective practice, and my observations of my grandparents' shadows inevitably have been tinged by my own nature and experience; they cannot hope to be exact transcriptions of the people who cast them. As my grandmother said when I finally showed her a draft of this manuscript, "Mirandali, it's so long ago now, who can remember?" Grandma, all I can say is, I certainly have tried.

ANNA		ARMAND
Strasbourg •		• **Strasbourg**
Saint Hilaire du Touvet •	1937	
Hauteville •	1938	
	1939	• Montpellier
	1940	• Sète
Amélie-les-Bains •		• Agen
Caudiès-de-Fenouillèdes •		• **Caudiès-de-Fenouillèdes**
Saint-Paul-de-Fenouillet •	1941	• **Saint-Paul-de-Fenouillet**
	1942	
Lyon •		• **Lyon**
Col de Cou/Champèry •		• **Col de Cou/Champèry**
Lausanne •	1943	• **Lausanne**
Gams •		• Zurich
Saint Gallen Prison •		• Wald
Wesen •		
Engelberg Internment Home, Sumiswald •		• Arisdorf
Hotel Viktoria Internment Home, Montana •		
Bienenberg Internment Home •		
		• Olsberg
Winterthur •		• Sierre
Sanatorium Sursum •	1944	• **Geneva**
Finhaut Internment Home •		
Geneva •		
Montreux/Territet •		• Mösli Children's Home, Stallikon
		• Saint-Cergue
		• **Geneva**
Geneva •		
	1945	
Les Diablerets/Leysin •		
Geneva •		• Paris
Sierre •		• Nuremberg
Geneva •		
Les Diablerets •		
	1946	
Paris •		• **Paris**

Names in bold indicate places Anna and Armand were together.

ANNA AND ARMAND'S JOURNEY

France

Paris

Strasbourg

Zurich

Olsberg   Winterthur

Arisdorf   Saint Gallen
Bienenberg-Liestal   Prison

Rhône River

Stallikon   Wald

Sumiswald   Gams

Weesen

Switzerland

Montreux-Territet

Lausanne   Leysin   Davos

Saint Cergue   Les Diablerets

Geneva   Crans-Montana

Finhaut   Sierre

Alps

Lyon   Col de Cou/Champéry

Hauteville

Saint Hilaire du Touvet

Grenoble

Alba-la-Romaine

Pyrénées   Montpellier

Sète

Caudiès-de-Fenouillèdes
Amélie-les-Bains
Saint-Paul-de-Fenouillet

Germany

Nuremberg

France

Switzerland

ALBA-LA-ROMAINE

Bus stop

Castle

Mairie

The Camping

Alba

The Escoutay River

La Roche

La Roche

Anna and
Armand's house

PREFACE

In the ten years it took to write everything down, my grandmother died and my grandfather lost his mind. I got married and had a child. I abandoned my intended career, moved to another country, and spent my savings. And the house, which may or may not have started it all, continued to fall down.

But still I was afraid to begin, for this is a story about a silence, and how do you break a silence that is not your own?

I turned the question over in my head for what felt like an eternity. I wondered if I had any business—any right, even—to speak of it. And yet, unbroken, it was a burden, one that grew with every passing year. What would I do if I never succeeded in laying it down? Finally, I gave up and prayed.

Please, could you give me a hint?

The next day my daughter and I went for a walk behind our hamlet, in the shadow of Alba's castle, along the path that skirts the Escoutay River. It was the path I looked down the first time I saw this place, and thought, *This is my home.* The path my grandmother looked down in 1948, the first time she saw this place, and thought, *Someday this will be someone's home.*

And there, among the dandelions and primroses, was what the French would call a *clin d'oeil*—a wink. It was a clump of four-leaf clovers, a whole posy of them. Finding four-leaf clovers is something my grandmother passed down to me, along with ungraceful ankles and the ability to read fortunes with cards. We find them wherever we go, whenever we most need them. No doubt these days my grandmother, who always preferred agitation to tranquility, has taken up some position as parliamentary delegate or shop steward in the big social movement in the sky, so when I sent that prayer up, she didn't even bother to pass my petition along. She just made her signature noise, halfway between a snort and a sigh, the sound she always made right before she stepped in and sorted the matter herself, and rippled a message to me through the clover. Knowing her so well for so long, I understood it as clearly as if she had written it out for me in the mud of the riverbank: "Stop putzing around and begin at the beginning."

So here I go.

A
FIFTY-YEAR
SILENCE

PART I

The hamlet of La Roche and the Escoutay River, with Alba's castle in the background, circa 1960.

CHAPTER ONE

WHEN I WAS BORN, MY GRANDMOTHER TIED A red ribbon around my left wrist to ward off the evil eye. She knew what was ahead of me and what was behind me, and though she was a great believer in luck and the hazards of fortune, she wasn't about to take any chances on me, her only grandchild.

My grandmother had fled or lost countless homes in her lifetime, and though she never fully resigned herself to living in America, she was determined to die in her house in Pearl River, New York, to which she had retired from her job as a supervising psychiatrist at Rockland State Mental Hospital. She would tell me this with some frequency, because my grandmother viewed death as an interesting dance step she'd eventually get around to learning, or perhaps a pen pal she'd come awfully close to meeting several times—no doubt this intrigued equanimity was part of the reason she managed to live so long.

My grandmother told me many things over the years, in a jumbled and constant flow of speech. I hung on to her every sentence, fascinated and admiring. Each word she said was like a vivid, tangible object to me, a bright buoy, a bloodred lifeline:

MY Godt
musckle
VEG-eh-tayble
sourrwvive

That was her favorite word. She rolled it out of her mouth with Carpathian verve, inflected with Austro-Hungarian German and French.

You're like me, Mirandali, she'd say. *You'll sourrwvive.*

This was immensely comforting, because outside the reassuring confines of my grandmother's presence, I was never too sure about that.

When Grandma wasn't around, my life was bafflingly full of terror. I say bafflingly because my childhood, albeit eccentric, was outwardly perfectly secure: my parents divorced when I was small, but they'd done so amicably, and each remarried a stepparent I loved as fiercely as if they had all given birth to me. There I was, a nice little girl with two big front yards, climbing apple trees and peeling Elmer's glue off my hands at recess with my friends, except for the moments when my comfortably ordinary world incomprehensibly fell to pieces.

Take the day my friend Erin and I locked her little brother in the bathroom, and Erin began belting out a loud rendition of "The Farmer in the Dell" so her parents wouldn't hear him hollering for us to let him out: one minute I was singing along with her, and the next I was clutching Erin's arm for dear life, as if she might pull me out from under the avalanche of fear now suffocating me. "Stop," I begged her. "We have to stop. They played music to drown out the screams of the children when they were killing them." Years later Erin recalled that she'd been so upset by what I'd said that she'd run crying to her father.

"What did he say?" I asked her.

"He told me you came from a family of Holocaust survivors with a lot of bad memories to cope with."

All I could think was, *I wish someone had told me that.*

With the clumsy logic of a small child, I tried to protect myself from these episodes by constructing scenes of perfect domesticity in which everything was ordered and beautiful: careful dioramas I fitted into Kleenex boxes or arranged on the shelf beside my bed, elaborate habitats I squirreled away in hideouts behind the bushes of our front walk or tucked under my mother's desk. I would spend hours imagining myself away from the world and into these fictitious universes. If you had asked me, as a child, what I wanted to do when I grew up, I would have told you a career—ballerina, scientist, senator—but what I really wanted was my own home, a place to keep me safe from the lurking menace of destruction, the horrible crumbling feeling I knew was never far-off.

The habitats I created were of no use at night. I kept my shoes near the front door, so I could grab them quickly if we had to escape in a hurry, but then I'd lie awake and worry we'd have to use the back door instead. Biding my fearful time until I fell asleep, I would calculate how quickly I could jump out of bed and dress and count the places I might hide. I wished I were grown up and more graceful; I believed I was resourceful enough, but not tall enough, to survive. I grieved in advance for the loss of my cozy home with the books on the shelves and the bright bedspread, brush and comb on the dresser, fire in the woodstove, food in the fridge.

I would call out for my mother to come sit with me, hoping she could keep my nameless fear at bay, and pepper her with questions.

"Could someone steal our house?"

My mother always took me seriously, and she replied to my questions honestly, which meant her answers were rarely as reassuring as I wanted them to be. "No," she would say. "Not usually."

"But sometimes?"

"Well, if something happened." There would be a small pause as she considered what she would and would not explain. "For example, if you had to go away for a long time, someone could move in, or steal the papers saying you owned it, or make new ones saying it was theirs."

"What if you came back?" I'd press.

"Well, you would have to prove that the house really was yours."

"How could you do that?"

"Well, you could go to court, if the government were still intact."

There was also the question of fire. What if someone burned our house down?

"That's not very likely." Her calm, dry voice was silent another moment in the dark room. "Really. It's very unlikely."

But no matter how many times she reassured me with rational considerations of likelihood and risk (no one in our household smoked; we didn't have a furnace; we owned three fire extinguishers), my mother could not give me the gift of certainty that every child craves. What I longed to hear was *That will never happen.* But how could she say that? In our family, everyone had lost a home. The unspoken question that nettled me at night was not whether such a thing could happen but how many homes you could lose in a lifetime.

In my dreams, when sleep finally came, I'd pack quickly for my flight. Only the essentials. Coat, matches, pocketknife. I'd get bogged down as I tried to plan ahead, to think of all the things I would lack: change of underwear, soap, raincoat, antiseptic ointment, adhesive bandages, toilet paper, candles, shoelaces, string, a sweater, powdered milk, wool socks, long johns, tarp, hat, scissors. Pots and pans. A hammer. Stamps. Wallet. Photographs. Some sort of container for holding water. Rubber bands. Gloves, not mittens. A sleeping bag. Salt. Sugar. Towel. Needle and thread.

All the dreams were the same, except for the ones where they got me before I had time to pack. Sometimes I'd end up in a train, occasionally they'd shoot me right away, and always, afterward, I'd wake to a world drained of color, thick with a desolation so familiar I never even thought to mention it to anyone. I preferred the dreams of flight: in those, my grandmother would come back for me, wrest the excess baggage from my hands, and push me out the door.

Anna and Miranda in Pearl River, New York, June 1984.

Grandma and I were so close that when I shut my eyes, I can still count the spots on her aging skin, which reminded me of an almond in its smoothness and color. If I concentrate on my fingers, I can feel her silver hair, which even in her extreme old age was soft as silk and streaked with coal black. I can see her standing before her mirror in a pale pink slip, rubbing face cream on her high cheekbones and into her neck, all the way down to her graceful shoulders, doing "face yoga" to keep away the wrinkles, her gold and turquoise earrings quivering in her ears. They had been in her earlobes since she was eight days old, when her ears were pierced in the Romanian Jewish equivalent of a bris for a girl. I spent so much time looking at those earrings that their existence was more intense, more fully real to me than that of other objects. You could say the same of the way I saw my grandmother. She was so beautiful, even her dentures seemed glamorous, in my favorite shades of seashell pink and pearly white. "Your teeth fall out when you don't have enough food," she'd say in a matter-of-fact tone when I admired them in their little cup, secretly hoping she'd lend them to me one day. "So I got mine young. But maybe when you're very old you can have some, too."

My earliest memory was of her, of bouncing on her outstretched leg as she chanted a Romanian Yiddish nursery rhyme: *"Pitzili, coucoulou . . ."* Not on her knees but on her outstretched leg—my grandmother was the strongest woman I knew. She taught yoga to a group she called "my old ladies" and had a chin-up bar in the doorway of her bedroom. Lest you think she was some sort of health fanatic, I hasten to add that she also drank a pot of coffee a day and had a secret fondness for Little Debbie cakes. My grandmother's perfume was one of contradictions: she smelled of Roger & Gallet lavender soap, Weleda iris face cream, and raw garlic. Beneath that, her skin had a floral and slightly metallic scent, which put me in mind of roses and iron playground bars. When I open her papers, I can still smell it, growing fainter with the passage of time.

Her home in New York was like a ship pulled up onto an unknown shore, a bulwark she'd fitted out against the oddities of America, intensely personal in a way that indicated she knew she was here for the duration and was determined to make the best of her stay. Taste-wise, it was a mishmash: fine textiles; valuable etchings by her artist friend Isaac Friedlander; paintings by her psychiatric patients; furniture salvaged from the curb; rag rugs; giant plastic flowers in a gaudy ceramic umbrella stand from Portugal;

and the bits of Judaica and African art that are standard-issue home decor for left-wing Jews of a certain age. Her wardrobe was a similar jumble. Her dresses and jackets, custom-made for her by a couture seamstress she'd befriended in Paris, had been subjected over the years to endless alterations, additions, and improvements. She was devoted to a pair of flesh-colored orthopedic ghillies called "space shoes" that a retired figure skater had made for her in the 1950s to relieve the pain in her frost-damaged toes. Her preferred accessories were a child's sun hat with a bright blue splatter-painted band and matching sunglasses.

The year after I was born my grandmother bought the house next door to my mother's house in Asheville as a second home. It was the ugliest house in the neighborhood, but Grandma was extremely proud of it. It looked like a badly constructed pontoon boat had eaten and failed to digest a mobile home, then crashed into the mountainside. It had white aluminum siding and a flat tarpaper roof, with red aluminum awnings that made its doors and windows look like sleepy, half-closed eyes. But my grandmother didn't care. The house was hers, and that was what mattered.

Before she moved in, she shipped herself a coal-burning stove and a box of bricks from her house in New York. Grandma sent a lot of things to Asheville over the years, including a pair of fuchsia suede high-heeled sandals too large for anyone but my father, a fur wallet made by one of her psychiatric patients, and a kerosene lamp and cookstove, with live fuel included, "just in case."

A lot of things were just in case. Candles and cough drops, the woolen bandage she always carried in her purse. My grandmother practiced a peculiar and intensive form of self-sufficiency. She wasn't a wilderness type; she just knew that in the end, the only person she could truly rely upon was herself.

My grandmother lived alone in a way that seemed natural, inevitable, and inviolable, and for all our closeness, it never occurred to me to wonder with whom she had managed to produce her two children, my mother and uncle. She seemed perfectly capable of doing such a thing unassisted, and where in her life would a companion have fit in? Still, I remember a day when I was about five years old, and my mother handed my grandmother a photograph of me posed with my grandfather in a Sears, Roebuck studio, taken that summer on one of his infrequent visits to Asheville.

My grandmother examined the picture. "What a nice photo. Who's that with Miranda?"

My mother replied, "That's Daddy."

My grandmother's smooth forehead wrinkled into a map of sadness. She looked carefully at the picture, as if searching for a sign. Then she set the photo on the table in front of her.

"I would never even have recognized him." She sounded the words out slowly, shaking her head. "I wouldn't know him if I met him on the street." She picked it up and looked again. "May I keep this?" she asked.

"Sure," my mother said, sounding surprised.

Later I found the photograph tucked into a picture frame beside my grandmother's bed, where it remained until her death. At the time I wondered why she wanted to keep a picture of me with someone she didn't know. I was too young to put one and one together and realize my grandparents might once have been two, to discern they might ever have been anything but strangers to each other.

CHAPTER TWO

HOW COULD I, AT THAT AGE, HAVE THOUGHT TO match my grandmother to my grandfather? He wasn't apples to her oranges; he was pine cones or prickly pears: a remote and vaguely terrifying figure who noted corrections in the margins of his dictionaries, sent my letters back marked up with red pencil, and occasionally appeared in our house with tasteful gifts and an inclination to take umbrage in toxic doses. He was retired from the UN civil service and had been an interpreter at the Nuremberg Trials. I didn't know what the Trials were (we called them "the Trials," as if they were some kind of kissing cousin or family vacation spot), except that they added to his aura of prestige and authority.

Yes, he and my grandmother were more than opposites, or perhaps less; they were like the north poles of two magnets, impossible to push close enough together in my mind to make any kind of comparison, let alone a connection. The idea that they might be linked first came to me on the day we began addressing invitations to my bat mitzvah, and I pointed out to my mother that my grandfather hadn't been included on the guest list.

"I guess you could send him an invitation," she replied. "But he's not going to come."

"Why?"

"Think about it."

I could think of a number of reasons my grandfather would choose not to attend my bat mitzvah: for one, he was an avowed atheist; for another, he only came to America when work brought him here, never just to see his family. Or he might be taking silent exception to an undisclosed inventory of offenses and injuries suffered during his last visit. Really, the possibilities were limitless. I chose the most likely among them. "Is he mad at us?"

My mother shook her head. "He didn't come to your uncle's bar mitzvah. I didn't have a bat mitzvah, but I'm sure he wouldn't have come to it if I had. He didn't come to either of my weddings. He didn't come when you were born."

"Why?"

When my mother raised her eyebrows but didn't say anything, I realized I must have the elements of an answer that she was waiting for me to deduce for myself.

The response, when it occurred to me, seemed absurd in a contradictory, confusing sort of way: absurd because it was so obvious, or absurd because it seemed so unlikely—I wasn't sure which, but I ventured it anyway. "Because of Grandma?" My mother nodded, and I considered the two of them, Anna and Armand, holding them beside each other in my mind for the first time. I could easily imagine my grandfather being bothered by my grandmother, but when could they have met? "Have they ever been in the same room together?" I asked.

My mother laughed. "Well, look at me and your uncle."

"They were married?"

"Of course they were married."

"So they're divorced from each other? When did they get divorced?"

My mother couldn't say. She didn't know when they'd gotten married, and though she remembered her parents' separation, which had occurred sometime between 1950 and 1953, the divorce had dragged on for nearly two decades, until around 1970. All she could tell me was that they hadn't spoken in nearly forty years, since 1955.

Forty years seemed ridiculously, even impossibly, long to me. And like most children that age, my sense of my own importance in the world was inaccurately large. "But I'm his only granddaughter, and it's my bat mitzvah." My mother looked dubious. "Besides, if it's been that long, maybe they've forgotten about it. I'm going to invite him."

My grandfather responded to my invitation almost immediately, which was very rare for him. Though his answer had been written in haste, his words had the same dry and measured quality they always had, so that it was difficult at first to understand the operatic turn of events he was predicting—essentially, that being in the same place as my grandmother would cause them to have simultaneous heart attacks and die. In a postscript, he asked me to think about what I would like as a bat mitzvah present—what about a safari? We could go on a safari in Kenya, if I liked.

"Kenya would be about the distance he prefers to maintain between himself and your grandmother," I remember my mother observing when I read her the letter. Nowadays I marvel at how calmly she discussed a phenomenon that had wrought havoc on her and her brother's childhoods, but back then I thought it was the way all mothers discussed all things.

"What happened? What happened to make them be like that?"

"Who knows? No one has ever figured that out." My mother had only vague memories of her parents' marriage and separation. She recalled their passage from France to America on the USS *America* in December 1948, eating in the ship's nearly empty dining room with her father while her mother, pregnant with my uncle, lay suffering from nausea in their cabin, where all the furniture not bolted down slid back and forth across the floor as the ship pitched and tossed on the stormy Atlantic. Of those first years on Long Island, she remembered a kitchen table topped with red Formica, a red-handled grapefruit knife my grandmother took with her when she left, frequent fights, and not much else. And then, after the separation, the housekeeper, whom we'd now call the nanny, trying to persuade Anna to return to Armand.

"So why did they get married?"

My mother had no satisfying explanation for that, either: "Your grandmother was brilliant and beautiful, and your grandfather was brilliant and handsome. They met in Strasbourg, when they were students. I imagine it must have been quite electric."

I was left to flip through the few old photos we had from the years my grandparents had spent together, lovely little black-and-white windows from which a woman and a man named Anna and Armand looked out of the past, silent, enigmatic, and lost. The captions that accompanied my grandmother's photos were tantalizing: "Anna holding a cat whose leg she had splinted"; "Man on left wanted to marry Anna"; or, my favorite, written for a snapshot of her sitting in a field of narcissus, the flowers like wave caps in the grassy sea around her: "Anna picked bouquets for all 185 patients in the sanatorium." That was Anna all over. Her love of beauty was militantly democratic. The few pictures of my grandfather had no captions, or very cryptic ones, with no mention of his name, though I recognized his Roman nose, high cheekbones, and wry smile. There was one of him sitting at a desk, his arm flung over the back of the chair, his white shirt peeking out from under his suit jacket, at once elegant and diffident. Another showed him at the summit of a mountain, looking tanned, determined, and very thin. Brilliant, beautiful, and electric: what more could a young girl ask of her grandparents' long-ago youth?

But then a week or so later, my mother returned from the mailbox with an envelope for me. It contained a single photocopied page of text, with a note from my grandfather:

A friend sent me this poem, which reminds me of something in my own life. I thought you might like it.

It is late last night the dog was speaking of you;
the snipe was speaking of you in her deep marsh.
It is you are the lonely bird through the woods;
and that you may be without a mate until you find me.

You promised me, and you said a lie to me,
that you would be before me where the sheep are flocked;
I gave a whistle and three hundred cries to you,
and I found nothing there but a bleating lamb.

My mother said to me not to be talking with you today,
or tomorrow, or on the Sunday;
it was a bad time she took for telling me that;
it was shutting the door after the house was robbed.

My heart is as black as the blackness of the sloe,
or as the black coal that is on the smith's forge;
or as the sole of a shoe left in white halls;
it was you put that darkness over my life.

You have taken the east from me; you have taken the west from me;
you have taken what is before me and what is behind me;
you have taken the moon, you have taken the sun from me;
you have taken God from me, and my fear is great.

"Well, there you go," said my mother, when I showed her the poem. "He's not coming. He can't come."

~

Dramatic as that poem sounded, it would be inaccurate to say I was astounded by the discovery of my grandparents' marriage, divorce, and ensuing silence. Startled, yes, but at the same time, I'd grown up in a universe that revolved around an unspoken maxim: everything can fall apart.

As a child, I did not discern this principle ordering my life, though by the time I learned about my grandparents, I had begun to feel the contours of its presence. I knew it somehow related to my keeping my shoes by the door and thinking constantly about viable places to hide; to our always having candles and matches at hand; to my mother snapping off the radio or rattling the newspaper shut at the mention of certain things; and to my non-Jewish father remarking from time to time when I visited him and my stepmother, "This will all come down to you, Miranda. You're going to have to figure out how to carry it all."

But I digress in mentioning these phenomena, which I never thought to associate with my grandmother, not back then. I bring up this maxim only to say that in a world that revolved around the possibility that everything might fall apart at any second, the disintegration of my grandparents' marriage was neither surprising nor spectacular.

Certainly, my grandmother didn't treat her relationship with my grandfather—or lack thereof—as if it were anything special. If she deigned to talk about him at all, it was only very briefly, and then she'd veer off onto another topic entirely—obesity in household pets, or her thoughts on the U.S. Postal Service. I still remember the first time I tried to bring up the subject with her, the summer after I turned thirteen. If becoming bat mitzvah had made me a woman, then it was time for me to learn to tell fortunes. "Always have at least one skill to fall back on—it could save your life. It saved mine."

"How?"

"On my last journey home . . . I was taking a train full of traveling salesmen. They were eying me, and I pulled out my pack of cards. It kept them distracted all night."

I was too young to really comprehend the threat she was hinting at, nor how the skill she was offering me might guard against it.

"I remember another time," Grandma went on, "in my first year of residency, one of the other residents followed me back to my room, he invited himself in, and he kept moving closer and closer, so I pulled out my deck of cards and proposed a reading! Of course he accepted. It was the strangest combination of cards—I forget what-all, about his family, trouble with an inheritance, a lawyer, or I don't know what. He got quieter and quieter, and then he just left. Now pay attention, closely-closely, because I can't teach you. You have to steal it from me."

She pulled out a deck of miniature playing cards, with a pink and red Art Nouveau pattern on the back. Half of them were like new, their gilt edges still shiny. The other half, from the sevens up, were battered and worn. "These were your mother's cards. She foretold a bad fortune and got spooked and gave them back to me. Once you learn, you can have the ones my friend Cilli gave me before I took that last journey home. I used to eat at her house every day— she was a smart girl, at the top of our medical class, but then she had an affair with a doctor, a Romanian aristocrat, and got pregnant. He went home, he said he was going to sort of smooth the way with his family and then send for her, and she never heard from him again, except to send her the *pension alimentaire*. You know, the alimony—no, the child support. He was a nice little boy, the son, but she was so depressed. Always reading her own cards, which is bad luck, you know. Very bad luck. Never read your own cards." She tapped them with her finger and commanded, "Cut them, twice now, with your left hand, toward your heart."

Everyone in my family had some complaint about my grandmother's incessant talking—"She's not hard of hearing, she's hard of listening," my father once grumbled after a particularly long disquisition—and I was just old enough to have begun feeling embarrassed by it, by the way she jumped from topic to topic, by her extremely spotty sense of tact, by her refusal to pronounce her *w*'s correctly. But I still hung on her every word as she zigzagged from one memory to another.

For hours we counted out the cards together, my grandmother reading and me observing until I had memorized the different steps and layouts and begun to grasp the cards' many meanings. "Very good," she said. "You have to keep practicing, though. So you should have something to fall back on," she repeated. "In case you need money, or what—you never know."

She swept the cards off the table and shuffled. "Cilli, I don't know what happened to her. I think she became a *collabo*." I didn't know what shocked me more, the story ending that way, or my grandmother's casual use of that terrible word. Now I also wonder how I could already have been familiar with the term—and its implications—at such a young age.

It suddenly occurred to me that my grandmother might have known my grandfather then, so I ventured, "What about Grandpa? Did he know Cilli?"

"He met her, Cilli. But he didn't like her. Maybe he's the one who told me she was a *collabo*."

"Did you tell his fortune?"

She laughed. "He never wanted me to. He said it was superstitious, or it made him nervous, or what—he never let me."

"Were you together then?"

"Together . . . well, you know, I knew his sister, Rosie, and his mother—can you imagine Rosie had never washed her own hair until she got married? I ask you. The only girl of the family. Your grandfather was the baby. Do you know what he told me when we first met? He said he hated his father. Could you imagine, hating your father? I couldn't believe it. Hating your father. He wouldn't even say goodbye to him when they were evacuated. Never saw him again. But he was brilliant. Everyone said so. I was taught to admire brilliance."

I tried to sift through all of the information tumbling at me, but Grandma was already in Samarkand, or maybe Australia, stressing the importance of "just talking to people," a skill she claimed my grandfather did not have. "He never could get comfortable. Me, I always just got on a bus and there I was. Like in Russia, in the sixties, visiting the insane asylums." She made air quotes around those last two words and chuckled. "Boy, did they get mad about that." Vainly, I tried to steer her off the bus and back toward my grandfather, but she'd already flitted away on another tangent. "I've even been to see the—oh, what is it called—the fancy Hitler vacation house."

I abandoned my efforts and blinked. "The Hitler vacation house?"

"You know, where he went on holidays. Famous! Big gardens, paintings, sculptures . . . it's on a lake . . . what's the name . . . Berghof? Berchtesgaden? The Adlersnest? You know what I'm talking about. Ah ha!" This last comment was directed at the cards. "See, travel!" She pointed at the nine of diamonds. "And family." She tapped the ten of hearts.

I ignored the ten of hearts. "Did you go inside?"

"Sure not!" She looked at me incredulously. "Go inside? With guards everywhere? Of course I didn't go inside. But I did rent a little rowboat, and I rowed across to have a look at it. I got real close. I could see the guards. Pick a card," she interjected, and I obeyed, imagining my grandmother in a little rowboat, the water reflecting on her milky skin and the wind blowing her black curls, watching tiny silhouettes of guards marching like toy soldiers up and down a tree-lined shore, more taken with the image of her than with the geographic location, expecting her to switch courses again and tell me some other tale. "Go inside," she scoffed instead. "What do you think—he was going to invite me in?"

"Who?"

"When I got back I read in the papers that he was in the house at the time."

As usual, it was hard to say whether she was ignoring my question or merely answering it sideways. "Hitler?" I persisted. "You mean this was while he was alive?"

She didn't even give me a sideways answer this time, just looked at me as if to say, *Excuse me, but why else would I go see the fancy Hitler vacation house?*

I could never tell whether these digressions were a reflection of her overly busy mind or a clever feint to distract me from topics she preferred not to discuss.

CHAPTER THREE

I DID NOT BEGIN TO APPRECIATE WHAT AN EXPLO-sive topic my grandparents' marriage might be until I visited my grandfather on my own for the first time, a few months after I turned fourteen. He had forgotten about the safari but not about me, and he invited me to come stay with him for ten days over my spring break.

As a child, I saw very little of my grandfather. The summer after I was born he'd had a linden tree planted in my honor in our front yard, a gesture typical of him in that it was not on time, required

*Armand on one of his rare visits to Asheville, in June 1982
(carefully timed to avoid crossing paths with Anna).*

more work of other people than it did of him, and was the poetic vehicle for a painful memory he kept secret from the gesture's recipient. (In this case, the lindens that lined the Boulevard Tauler, the street he grew up on in Strasbourg—which were destroyed, along with his home, during the war.) For years I associated my grandfather with that linden and not much else: I posed there for annual photographs so he could mark the growth of me and the tree; we'd pose there together on the rare occasions he visited us from Geneva.

My grandfather, even by my family's standards, was a uniquely difficult character. He thought nothing of making you peel all the chickpeas in the dish you were preparing because he had recently read that chickpea skins were disruptive to the digestive system. Or of asking you to replace the buttons on your shirt before he left the house with you because he felt they were too gaudy. Or of snubbing you forever if you served him bad wine. He kept binder notebooks on members of the family of whom he particularly disapproved.

The last time he had come to Asheville was in 1990, when I was nine years old. He cut short his stay with us because he thought the guest room smelled of something ineffably and unbearably noxious. When pressed, he compared the scent to mothballs but would say no more than that. He declared it impossible to sleep with such an odor. My mother could not smell it, and that made him even more aggrieved.

This was the man I set off to visit in 1996, having seen him just once in the years following his abbreviated stay. A friend once asked me why my mother let me go see him alone, knowing as we did his extensive capacity for unpleasantness. What can I say? The vicissitudes of my family's fortunes meant there weren't many of us left; he was the only grandfather I had.

~

His apartment in Geneva was like a tiny museum, lined with books and curios, smelling cleanly of bergamot, rosemary, paper and pencil, and pipe tobacco. It was full of clear light that poured in from big picture windows, the ones in his dining room overlooking the Jura, the ones in his living room overlooking the Alps, the Lac Léman, and Geneva's old town. When I arrived, my grandfather showed me where I would sleep, a daybed in that living room, which also served as his office and guest quarters, and then went to make tea. After tea, he gave me a sponge, blue to match the color scheme in the kitchen, with which I was to wipe away any stray drops of water I might accidentally let fall on the tile floor. There was another one just like it in the bathroom. A mini-vacuum cleaner sat in the corner of the dining room; he pointed it out so I could clean up any crumbs I might drop while eating. He showed me how to brush back the carpet pile where I stepped on it so I wouldn't scuff it.

I realized quickly that my grandfather was not a maniacally orderly man; he was just intensely territorial. He needed me to cover my tracks.

During those ten days, we grew almost easy with each other, and perhaps I became overconfident, lulled into believing I had gotten the hang of my grandfather and his carpet pile, for one morning at breakfast, when he reached across the table for my hand and asked about the amethyst ring I was wearing, I said, "Maybe you recognize it." He shook his head, and I added, "It belonged to my grandmother."

A certain dark stillness settles into the air before a rainstorm bursts out of the sky and sozzles you. In the stillness I noticed my grandfather's face looked white and drawn, and it occurred to me that perhaps I had made a mistake. "Your *grandmother*? Your *grandmother*. May I ask"—he could barely bring himself to say the words— "may I ask whether you . . . whether you see her regularly?"

I nodded. Abruptly, he pushed himself away from the table and snatched up our breakfast things. He set them in the sink, jerked the faucet on, and began washing. "And what do you think of her?"

"Well," I began, trying to be prudent, "she's my grandmother, and I—"

My grandfather snapped off the water, and the sentence faded in my mouth. He turned to face me. "You'll have to be forgiven for that, I suppose. You do not know her as I do."

That was certainly true, so I shook my head.

"Do you know what I call her?"

I shook my head again.

"Seraphina. In irony, of course." He jerked the faucet back on and resumed rinsing the dishes. I did not know what to say. "*She* left *me*, you know," he fumed.

"Yes, is that why—" I started to say, thinking of something my mother had told me recently about my grandmother taking the children to Israel at the last minute instead of moving back to Europe when my grandfather's transfer from the UN's New York headquarters back to Geneva came through. But he did not seem to hear me.

There was only one small teacup left to clean, but he left the water running, and it poured out of the faucet and landed in the sink with a harsh, metallic sound. "Of course you may think she is just a nice little old lady in a ruffled apron serving you cookies, but you do not know what poison she hides. For years, she has been trying to ruin my life. Horrible woman."

I sat still. I had never seen my grandmother wear ruffles. Or bake cookies.

"The last time I saw her she had come all the way to the United Nations to try and get money out of me via the personnel office—to try and *ruin my reputation*. And of all things, I happened to be walking past the office when she came out. And do you know what she did?"

I shook my head.

"Do you *know* what she did?"

I cringed and kept shaking my head.

"She came up to me, said hello, and *asked me for a ride to the train station.*"

The water still splattered angrily against the sink's metal sides. That did seem exactly like something my grandmother would do, but I refrained from saying so.

"Do you know what that is like?" He set the teacup in the dish drainer in a way that made me fear for its well-being. I shook my head again.

"*That* is like *shitting* on someone's doorstep, ringing the door-bell, and *asking for toilet paper.*"

He rinsed the soap out of the sponge and wrathfully threw it down. "I should never, ever have married her."

"Why did you?" I regretted it as soon as I said it and sat waiting for I knew not what fury to descend on me.

He turned to face me, the open faucet forgotten, hands drip-ping water all over the floor. "I couldn't . . . and the war . . . what else could I do?" He looked helpless, shipwrecked, lost. "She was beautiful," he said, his voice bewildered, almost dreamy. "She had beautiful hair. Beautiful coal-black hair."

CHAPTER FOUR

As I entered the thick of adolescence, the closeness my grandmother and I had once enjoyed became far less enjoyable. It still existed, somewhere, but we had trouble finding our way into it, and when we did, it was often to have an argument. Grandma may have spent a good deal of her career treating adolescents, but outside her office it was a phase of life for which she had no patience. In her mind, the teens were just another mystifying and wasteful American invention, like colored bathroom tissue or instant pancake mix. "That's American teenagers for you. No respect," she'd grouse if I failed to clear a plate from the table or wore glitter and mismatched socks to dinner. "Go and change. Someone will think you're an escaped mental patient. Slovenliness is a dead giveaway."

Indeed, I believe she decided to send me back across the ocean to check—or at least temper—my objectionable slide into one of the parts of her adoptive culture she liked the least.

When I announced I was bored in school and wanted to try something new, my mother phoned my grandmother for advice.

Grandma didn't hesitate. "Send her to Geneva," she instructed.

"Isn't that far?" my mother objected.

Grandma brushed her off. After all, at sixteen she had moved from Romania to France to pursue her medical studies, a fifty-six-hour train ride from home.

"It will be good for her." Her voice left no room for argument. "Your father will help pay for it."

"What makes you think Daddy would want to help Miranda with her studies? It's not like he ever helped you with mine."

"You'll see. He'll be glad to have his granddaughter with him."

As though the decades had been minutes and she could still predict the motions of his mind.

∼

On the day of my departure, Grandma accompanied my parents and me to the airport. Sitting in the backseat and holding her hand, I felt sentimental and very grown up and, though I would have been loath to admit it, a little nervous. Seeing my smooth hand cupped in her brown-speckled one, I felt moved to say something about how much she meant to me, how I adulated her strength and wisdom, how I had all the spots on her skin memorized, how I would miss her. "*My Godt*," she said, pulling her hand away with a little snort of irritation, "don't talk like that. It's bad luck."

∼

The less said about my life at boarding school, the better; it was lonely and largely uninteresting—Grandma's convenient excuse, I am now convinced, to get me where she intended me to go. Every Friday I'd pack my overnight bag and walk the three miles that separated the boardinghouse from my grandfather's apartment, where I'd spend the weekend experiencing a second, albeit more interesting, form of loneliness, for you can get only so close to a compulsively solitary and excessively punctilious eighty-one-year-old.

He certainly made an effort: he filled the wooden bowls on his honey-colored dining room table with my favorite fruits, found recipes for us to try together, read Proust aloud to me over linden blossom tea and madeleines, and picked out poems for me to memorize to perfect my French. But settling into a routine together was not easy. I was always making mistakes. Once I spilled ink on his dressing gown and spent a fearful evening convinced he would ask me to leave and never speak to me again. He thought I held my pen wrong and mentioned it so often that I taught myself to position my fingers differently so I could do my homework and write letters at his house without irking him. I quickly learned it was best to avoid the Shakespeare authorship question. I kept my hair up at all times because he didn't like it left loose. But worst of all was the day I came back from a walk with a handful of four-leaf clovers. I was pleased to know that my gift for finding them functioned on both sides of the Atlantic and thought it would be nice to share it with him. I had forgotten the provenance of this gift, but my grandfather hadn't.

I walked over to his desk, where he was correcting an article for a friend, and held the clovers out to him, a little offering cupped in the palm of my hand.

He peered at it and recoiled violently, pushing himself back in his chair, as far away from me as he could. His face drained of color. He looked so pale and horrified, I checked the clovers to make sure they weren't harboring some dangerous insect.

"Witches," he croaked. His voice was strangled and low, his gaze mistrustful, as if I might pull some other awful trick. "You're all witches."

~

Noticing differences between my grandparents became a kind of hobby that year. Cooking was the first to stand out: Grandma improvised her dishes with whatever she could find—stale cookies, squishy kiwis, a half teaspoon of leftover oatmeal. Grandpa, on the other hand, excelled at ornate dishes that required precision timing and ingredients you had to go out of your way to buy. Grandma could not bear to throw away food—waste gave her nightmares. She even fished the bay leaves out of her stews, washed and dried them, and put them back in the jar for later use. My grandfather tossed things out with something approaching relish: a lettuce leaf with a tiny spot, the green middle of the garlic clove, the white flesh in the not-quite-ripe tomato—all of it went into the trash with less than no regret. Grandma favored bright colors, and Grandpa wore only muted ones; she preferred flowers, and he preferred leaves; she liked Rilke, and he liked Baudelaire; she watched TV, and he listened to the radio. Unlike my grandmother, who clung to her Austro-Hungarian-Romano-Franco-Yiddish accent as a last link to a lost world, my grandfather's English was impeccable, spoken with more heed and purity than any BBC announcer. Where Grandma divined my sentences before I even spoke them, Grandpa pretended not to understand me at all unless I enunciated as he did, removing all trace of America from my words.

But their biggest difference was the war. My grandmother's war seemed almost friendly, almost enviable. I loved to hear her tell of that perilous era and all her near misses. She called the war "the university of my life" and took a zestful, triumphant pride in all the ingenious ways she'd figured out how to survive. Grandma believed everything in life came with a lesson, and the lesson she conveyed as she told of her encounters during the war, from the gendarme who'd kept her off the deportation lists to the woman who took her in for the night just to keep the Nazis from requisitioning her spare bedroom, was that everyone she'd met was just as luckless—or lucky, depending on how you looked at it—as she. My grandmother surged through life armed with a lid she clapped over her memories when they got out of hand, keeping discipline among them with a battery of axioms and aphorisms. If she had survived, it was because whatever comes, comes for the best—as she reminded me over and over. Grandma had deep faith in a God whose goodness she'd accepted she would never comprehend. If everything happens

for the best, what right did she have to question? What right had
she to founder in grief?

My grandfather did not believe he was lucky. God had not been
good to him, and in retaliation, he had become an atheist, a revenge
he exacted daily on the Holy One, lest the Holy One forget. My
grandfather spent his days remembering; after all, if God did not
exist, then someone had to do it. His house was filled with books
and articles on the persecution of the Jews during World War II,
and he regularly attended conferences and films on the subject. The
only Jewish holiday he observed was Holocaust Remembrance Day,
when he forced himself to sit through at least three hours of Claude
Lanzmann's *Shoah*. But much like the God he didn't believe in, he
did his remembering in silence. He never said anything about what
had happened to his parents, and I never dared to ask him. I knew a
little from hints and slips of stories I'd picked up from other people
in the family, but broaching the topic with him seemed as foolhardy
as exposing pure sodium to air, as if it could spark a grief strong
enough to deafen and blind us, a white-hot sadness that would stun
and burn us beyond remedy.

Once a week though, on Shabbat, I would strike a single, dangerous match. The first time I asked if I could light candles I was
merely homesick and hadn't considered the implications of my
request. Grandpa, in his perfect, measured English, reminded me
of them immediately: "You understand, I hope, that I no longer
believe in God after what happened. During the war, you know."
Then he added, "If it makes you happy, please go ahead. But I shall
not participate."

Nevertheless, he retreated to his room and returned with a pair
of candlesticks. He set them in the middle of the dining room table
and rummaged through the hall closet until he found a box of candles. Then he stood back and looked at me a little defiantly. "There's
no challah," he observed.

"I'll just use ordinary bread." I took some from the kitchen, set it on a plate, and covered it with a paper napkin. We stood there awkwardly.

"I can open a bottle of wine," Grandpa suggested. "I shall go get one from the cellar."

When he uncorked the bottle, I unfolded another paper napkin and covered my head. Outside it was already dark, the blue night stained green by the streetlamps and orange from the floodlights gleaming off the soccer stadium across the street. I scraped the match against the box and it puffed into a flame; I lit the two candles, gestured the light toward me, and cupped my hands over my eyes. The apartment grew even quieter. I wondered, as I said the blessing, whether Grandpa had slipped out of the room. When I uncovered my eyes, I looked through the dim glow of the candles and saw he was weeping, his shoulders shuddering, just barely suppressing sobs. He looked up at me with wide eyes I could hardly bear to meet.

"My mother," he whispered hoarsely.

The next week he asked me to come on Saturday morning. Then I went back to showing up on Friday night, and every time he would pause in our dinner preparations to ask, "Are you going to light candles?"

And with some subterranean instinct that it was necessary to shine at least a wavering beam across the darkened plane of his past, I would always answer in the affirmative. Weeks went by in which every Friday night was the same: I would touch the match to the candlewick, and he would begin to weep, and I would weep with him, and we would eat our dinner in near silence.

Then one Friday night he appeared at the table wearing a *kippah*. "I found this," he announced, as if he'd picked it up off the ground in the park. "I thought I didn't have one anymore." He wore it every Friday after that. A few weeks later a braided loaf appeared on the table. By spring, we made it through the ritual without crying, exchanging a tiny smile once the candles were lit.

And one day he led me into his bedroom to show me something new: a glass frame he'd hung over his bed. In it were the only photographs remaining from his childhood, a posed portrait of him with his parents and siblings and a snapshot of his young mother.

"You see," he said, and though I waited, he said no more. He smiled and touched my cheek, and we left the room without another word. That was all he ever told me about his parents.

Despite his forbidding silence, living with my grandfather finally allowed me to put words to the fears and nightmares from which I had suffered for as long as I could remember. His vast library taught me many things, including that I was part of a community of people coming to terms with a genocide. And if his library taught me the vocabulary and the history, he himself taught me to recognize the landscape in which the survivors of destruction live their lives, to see that minefield of guilt and sadness for what it was. Hints of the people and the world lost were everywhere, waiting to blow holes in his fragile hold on the present. Just as I vacuumed my crumbs and wiped up my water droplets, I did my best, for his sake and mine, not to disturb the minefield. Little did I know, he was still suffering from the fallout of a single explosion, the one that had originally blown him and my grandmother apart.

～

"You can come home," my mother offered, when I relayed the details of this life to her over the phone. "Maybe you should come home."

But I didn't. I wanted to prove to myself that I could tough it out. My grandmother kept writing me encouraging letters about how much I was learning, how much character I was forging, and I didn't want to disappoint her, either. But more than that, I felt that I was not finished, that there was something else for me to discover, though I didn't know quite what.

And if President Chirac hadn't dissolved the National Assembly that spring, perhaps I never would have found out.

~

One week in May 1997, my grandfather phoned the boardinghouse to say I should not come to his apartment that Friday night, that instead he would pick me up at seven a.m. sharp that Sunday, because he had to go vote in the early legislative elections. He didn't explain further but promised to take me out for a celebratory dinner if the Left won a majority.

On the appointed day, I waited in the vestibule of the boardinghouse until his car rolled up the Chemin de Verey, turned around, and parked outside the gate. He disliked my housemistress intensely and refused to park on school property in case he ran into her. I got into the car, and we drove south in silence, over little highways that wiggled precariously through the mountains, on main streets through half-abandoned villages, on back roads past quiet factories with dark eyes shattered into their windowpanes, past geraniums and lace curtains and dingy cafés. My grandfather pointed out monuments to the Resistance along the way, sad gray stones tucked up onto the banks of the road, where bands of men had been denounced, discovered, shot down. Entire villages, he told me, had been massacred because they wouldn't surrender their resistance fighters. Women and children had been burned alive because they would not speak. As I listened, I thought of all the times my grandmother complained to me that Americans had no sense of history. Now I understood that she meant Americans had no sense of *her* history, of *our* history. Here the past was everywhere, an entire continent sown with memories. For the first time, I wondered if she had sent me back so I could learn what it was like to live in that punishing landscape. I cracked open the window a tiny bit; I felt suffocated. The wind pierced the silence inside the car, whose pneumatic suspension system I imagined pumping more air into itself to hold the weight of those stories. I wondered what life would be like without that load to carry.

Then my grandfather rolled his window down, too, and we left the back roads for the highway. For ten minutes we went delightfully fast, and suddenly everything felt lighter again. Without slowing down until he was well into the curve and pulling up hard against the tollbooth, my grandfather exited the highway, and there we were in the suddenly hotter, yellower, greener South of France.

Over the centuries many people have written about this warm and wonderful region, the dark trees on the pebbly hillsides, the sassy tango of pink flowers peeping out from behind the oleander's bottle-green fingers, the villages made of stones the color of honey. At fifteen, however, I had not read a single one of these accounts and was unprepared for all that beauty.

Even as we crossed the river and sped through the gray town of Le Teil, which looked as if it had seen better days, I was intoxicated. The road began to snake up the side of a mountain, which dropped away to reveal precariously perched farms and garden beds, and clotheslines dangling pants and bedsheets at unexpected angles into the ravine below. Up and up, around a big bend, past stone farmhouses, an abandoned filling station, an elderly mammoth hulk of a factory, an abandoned train station, an abandoned hotel, and then grapevines, stripes and stripes of them, marching away toward the hillsides. Ahead of us and to the left, beyond the vineyards, I saw a castle, of the fairy-tale kind, with one half of its quatrefoil shape fallen to ruin. That was Alba, though I didn't know it yet.

Aerial view of Alba with the mairie *(town hall) in the foreground and the castle in the background, circa 1960.*

We turned left with the regiments of vines, which seemed to march beside us along a flat stretch of road, and then I really saw the village, draped over its little hill like a somnolent moth with drowsy terra-cotta wings speckled in mushroom gray, crowned by that mournful, fanciful castle.

We arrived just after noon on a wide main street, parked beneath the plane trees, and emerged into the heat of the May afternoon. "Stay here," my grandfather instructed, and went inside the town hall to vote.

I sat in the car with the door open, my legs sticking out the side, and watched the town. Sometimes, even now, when I walk through Alba, I try to reason out just what it was that made me fall in love with the place. It was not the first intact medieval village I had ever seen, nor even the most beautiful. The stones in its walls were dark and ungainly, shaped by time and the river and placed every which way. The little church was austere and uninteresting. The buildings had little to nothing in the way of embellishment. No particular effort had been made to charm the outside world: no window boxes, no awnings, no brightly colored shutters. There were no endearing establishments selling snacks or souvenirs, just the necessities: pharmacy, grocery, tobacconist, bakery, bar. Alba's attraction seemed deeply private, homey and homemade, beautiful for itself, not for passersby.

I want this place to be my home. It was an odd, disorienting thought to have, but I could not make it go away.

When he returned, we drove a short way down a hill, past mulberry and fig trees, and turned into the gravel parking lot of a tiny hamlet. We left the car and walked under a low archway, onto a medieval street cool as a pool and cellar-dim. Everything was built from anthracite-colored stone, the street itself and the houses that

The house in La Roche (on the right), circa 1960.

crouched along it. Across from where I stood, a cherry tree perched on a rock wall had dropped its dark red fruit in a gooey, shadowy circle. The air smelled of old dust and dry grass.

"Look up," Grandpa said.

I obeyed and saw an enormous rock, a prehistoric creature, tufted with clumps of grass and crowned with a sort of stone fortification. Here and there a tree or a bush slanted off it in an unruly tangle. "That's La Roche," he told me. "There used to be a castle at the top."

To our left, the street dropped down in wide steps toward an arched portal in a fortified stone wall. We descended the steps and stopped in front of a recessed door, made of wood that had weathered to nearly the same gray as the stones. The lock creaked, and the door groaned open across an uneven floor. A chilly hush emerged from a whitewashed hall. We stepped inside. Gray light, slow as an old man, filtered through a dirty transom. "Wait here." Grandpa took a key from a hook and disappeared. In a moment, a light appeared. We stepped forward into a room furry with dust.

The furniture, arranged around a gigantic hearth with a stone mantel, slept under sheets of cobwebs like a royal retinue under a spell: to the left, a table and a motley assortment of chairs; to the right, a bed with metal curlicues at its head and foot, a green basket chair, and a rustic stool. The mantel was crowned with an odd assortment of objects: a coffee grinder, a hurricane lamp in pale green glass, and a sailing ship made from some sticks and a Pelforth beer carton. I looked through the dirty windowpanes of the door on the opposite side of the room and saw a terrace covered in weeds, bordered by a stone wall. Beyond it, a path led from the hamlet toward a small river a few yards away. A cloud blew over the sun as I stood, transfixed, watching the wind brush over the earth and grass. That was when the bomb my grandmother had hidden so many years ago went off. My ears buzzed. I felt butterflies in my stomach. It echoed through the rational part of my brain, blinding me to the fact that the house was primitive, dusty, and cold inside, and flashing an alternate image of the place in my mind's eye: fixed up and cozy, with me shelling peas on the terrace. *I want to live here,* I thought. *I must live here.*

I heard my grandfather calling and followed his voice to the hallway, where he was dragging open another door into a huge space. "The *magnaneraie,*" he said. "This is where they raised silkworms." He pointed out a rudimentary stone niche he said had once been used to build fires to keep the silkworms warm. The room was wide and lofty, with ceilings two stories high and windows overgrown with vines. A petrol stove enameled in two shades of brown hunched in one corner. There was a large lumpy bed beside it; at the other end of the room were two twin beds and a round table with heavily carved legs. A wooden structure, like a loft but with no floorboards, overhung the lumpy bed and the stove, and a narrow walkway ran along the inner wall of the room, connecting the loft to two doors on the upper floor. The only way up was a crude ladder handmade from splintery scraps of wood. Grandpa gestured to it. "Climb up."

I acquiesced. Not daring to forsake the relative safety of the ladder for the rickety walkway, I leaned far enough to one side to catch a glimpse of a room with a dirt floor and a sloping wooden ceiling. Through the door of the room, I could see a Turkish toilet squatting crookedly below a length of green hose attached to a faucet.

"You see?" he called up to me. "This house has all the modern amenities. I even put in a second toilet just in case the first one was ever occupied and someone had an urgent need."

"How practical." I tried to imagine a need so urgent I'd use the Turkish toilet. The scenarios were all unpleasant, so I climbed back down without anything else to say.

Grandpa had already left the room. When I found him, he was

back in the entryway, unlocking another door, located to the right of the front door. He yanked it open, and I winced as the wood groaned across the concrete floor. We crossed into a structure that seemed wholly separate from the part of the house we'd just explored. "The tower." He gestured up to the high ceiling. To our left, a poured concrete structure that resembled a bunker took up half the tower's floor space; the remaining space in front of us and to the right was a dusty, cobwebby mess. "This is the wine cellar." Grandpa indicated the bunker, whose walls were more than a meter thick. Inside, a bare bulb shone on empty wine racks and a few elderly-looking bottles. "There used to be wine here, but it was all stolen."

"By whom?"

"By people here. The neighbors are thieves."

I was eager to leave the wine cellar, which looked a little Bluebeard-ish, so I backed out into the light. Grandpa locked the door behind us.

He pointed up to a small opening in the wall, with what looked like a miniature window seat set into it. "Do you see that?"

I nodded.

"Once, long ago, a lady sat there with her handwork, watching for her knight to come home from the Crusades."

"Really?" I had never heard my grandfather voice a flight of fancy before, and this only added to my love for the place.

He pointed again. "You see that little ledge? That's where she would set her sewing so she'd have enough light." This imaginary woman would have had to be elf-size to fit in the niche, but my grandfather's authority was absolute and the idea was delightful, so I forbore to comment.

We looked, and then suddenly that was enough. Grandpa sent me back out to the entryway while he went to turn off the electricity. I stood in the doorway and gazed up and down the stone street, the vines making green curtains over the power lines, the young trees growing out of abandoned stone walls, the gray-green and yellow lichen and the tiny succulents creeping over everything. It was warmly, thickly silent.

Through my daze, I tried to understand the strange spell that had enveloped me. The house had a *thereness*: people had come and gone from its rooms, but the house itself had not moved or changed. It had a presence so palpable, I felt I could grip it with my hands. Its walls felt safe, cool, and beautiful, as if no memory or sad event could ever perturb them. In my mind's eye, living there would be like diving into a still, subterranean universe immune to the changeful, hot, dry, catastrophic world above. I imagined its stones were a plain, strong exoskeleton into which I could fold my soft and confusing existence.

I was startled by the sound of my grandfather's voice. Reluctantly, I stepped outside; he moved forward and turned the key twice in the lock; and we left.

"What do you think of it, my dear?"

"It's lovely." I searched for adequate words and failed to find them. I didn't dare say that walking into the house made me feel like I was coming home. "It's the most beautiful place I've ever seen," I told him instead.

"It might have been lovely," he conceded. "I'll tell you about it someday. Come along now."

~

I left Geneva just a month later. I was so happy the year was ending, I didn't realize until the day I departed that I, in all my isolation, had constituted nearly the whole of my grandfather's society. My grandfather hated separations and usually picked a fight the day someone left to distract himself from the pain of parting. There was none of that this time. *"Il y aura un vide,"* he said as we got ready to go to the airport. *There will be an emptiness.* He embraced me, then pulled back and touched my cheek. He had tears in his eyes. I imagined his deep green carpets with no more scuffs, his polished wooden bowls with no more fruit in them. The breadth of his solitude frightened me. As my plane took off, I wondered, *Had my grandmother known it would be like this? Was the loneliness that replaced me when I left a form of revenge? Was I sent to teach him a lesson, to show him all it is to love?*

CHAPTER FIVE

WHEN I CAME HOME FROM GENEVA, AT FIFTEEN and a half years old, I was eager to set aside the rigidity and lonesomeness that had defined my life there and have a real go at being a teenager, that useless and wasteful American contrivance my grandmother so deplored. I relegated the house in Alba and my grandparents' mysteries to the back of my mind, bought a fake fur coat and purple high heels, and dyed my hair blue. I learned to drive and pasted bumper stickers all over my '86 Toyota Cressida. I made new friends, drank coffee downtown, and skinny-dipped in the Warren Wilson pond; I dated boys, stayed up late reading aloud bad poetry, and tasted my first White Russian.

But the past is not so easily set aside. I began to suffer from panic attacks and depression. I'd be sashaying along just fine in those purple high heels when, with no warning, sinewy fingers of sadness would reach up from some old, dark part of my consciousness and clamp down on me with strangling force. Once the invisible hair trigger for those panic attacks was tripped, I'd hurtle at warp speed through a cosmos of despair; I tapped into the grief aorta of the entire world. I'd come to and find myself slumped in the bathtub, or covered in scratches, or driving on the wrong side of the road.

No one in my family thought to connect these incidents to our family history, not immediately at least. "Hot shower," my grandmother advised when I came to her hoping she'd prescribe an antidote to my misery. "When my patients seized up like that, I always put them under hot water. Very hot. Relaxes the muscles. And then go to bed."

Then one of my friends started working for a man who claimed to be a psychic and a medical intuitive. He spent an evening showing off his skills on me to a group of friends. I don't remember exactly what happened, except that the room went dark and I spiraled down into my pit of desolation. "Your past is calling you," he announced when I recovered, as if we were both connected to some sidereal switchboard. "Did you have a tragedy in your family? Something to do with the Holocaust, I'd bet." He looked smug and unremorseful about the terror he'd just caused me. "Check into that."

"This will all come down to you," my father said to me, when I visited him in Knoxville and brought up my panic attacks and my encounter with the psychic, just as he had when I was younger and woke up from those nightmares or voiced one of my odd fears. "Each of us has our own ways of connecting with the world of the dead. You're the only grandchild. You're the one who's going to have to carry it." I wondered how a locum tenens pathologist who subscribed to the *Skeptical Inquirer* could make such pat statements about the world of the dead. And I wondered how I could possibly carry a thing whose outlines I couldn't even see.

～

On May 23, 1998, two years almost to the day after my grandfather first showed me the house, the phone rang. We were celebrating my stepfather's birthday with a Sunday brunch on the back porch, eating sticky buns from the farmer's market and watching the carpenter bees chew holes in the rafters.

My mother, as she told me later, was surprised and a little nervous to hear her father's voice when she answered the phone, in the way we were always surprised and a little nervous when he called. She wondered whether he might be calling for my stepfather's birthday but dismissed that as unlikely, and when she heard the casual tone he reserved for discussing potentially controversial things, she braced herself. He opened with a few niceties, then cut to the chase. "You may recall I have a house in the South of France?"

My mother did her best to sound extra polite and extremely neutral as she searched her memory for a house. "Only vaguely." She thought she recalled a conversation from a visit with him in 1979.

I doubt Grandpa cared one way or the other, but he paused in acknowledgment of her response. "Well, I no longer go there myself—it needs too much work—but I often lend it to people of modest means who could not otherwise afford a vacation."

"How nice," my mother said. "How nice for them, I mean—how nice of you."

"Quite so," allowed my grandfather. "Well, in any case, a nice Dutch woman I know would like to buy it from me, and I would like to sell it."

My mother searched for a response my grandfather could not interpret as offensive in any way and settled on "Ah."

"Yes, well . . ." My grandfather paused. Doubt and regret filled my mother's mind: Should she have been more enthusiastic? Or less so? Was *ah* too casual? Too inarticulate? She was still pondering the prudence of elaborating on her response when my grandfather resumed talking. "The thing is, it turns out that your *mother's* name is on the deed, and I need a power of attorney from her." His voice dropped all pretense of pleasantness when he said the word *mother*. It slid out of his mouth, acrid and bitter, and hovered in the ether while my mother held her breath. "So I just wondered if you might call her and explain to her that I need her signature. I cannot think why—no, even *she* could not possibly cause trouble. *I* took care of it all these years. The bills, the taxes. A frightful expense."

"Yes, all ri—yes, of course," my mother said, perplexed as to what my grandmother could have to do with a property in France—and even more as to how the most loquacious person any of us knew could have failed to mention it before.

"Very good. I'll have my *notaire* send along the appropriate documents. *Je t'embrasse.*" He hung up.

When my mother returned to the table and related the conversation to us, memories of that Sunday with my grandfather flooded over me, and I remembered my deep desire to live in La Roche.

"I know that place," I told my parents. "That's where he took me to vote." I searched for words to describe it to them, feeling slightly panicked as I recounted my day there. What if La Roche really was my home, and what if I never saw it again?

~

Later my mother sat down in her blue velveteen chair and called my grandmother. "Oh yes," Grandma said. "I remember I bought that house."

"Really? Why have I never heard about any of this? He says it's his."

"That's just like him," my grandmother sighed.

"Well, now he wants to sell it. He says he needs you to sign a power of attorney." I sat at my mother's feet, leaning against the arm of the chair, trying to decipher the muffled voice of my grandmother through the mouthpiece, trying to picture how she would react to this information. Would she say yes and make the house go away forever?

"Why would I do that?" Grandma asked.

"Well, I don't know," my mother replied. "You tell me! How on earth did you end up with a house in the South of France?"

My grandma emitted one of her peppery rhetorical noises that made it sound like she was picking up a story she'd left off a few seconds ago in another dimension. "I read an article in *Combat,* or *L'Humanité*—one of those left-wing newspapers—by some artist, talking about this old village, falling apart, with beautiful houses you could buy and fix up. You know, start an artistic, intellectual utopia, a new life after the war. And I love history."

When would this have been? My mother searched for a question that would connect this explanation to a fixed point in the space-time continuum, but Grandma wasn't one to pause and wait for you to catch up. "So I went there—on the way back from Marseille, taking my parents to the boat to Israel, you know." My mother didn't, but my grandmother had already taken off down another path. "Your father had a little money saved up from the Trials and thanks God I was there to do something sensible, otherwise . . . *my Godt.* You know what he bought with his first paycheck? A silk tie. With a baby at home. Real silk. Yellow. Can you imagine?"

Not for nothing did my mother write her doctoral dissertation on the insanity defense. She pressed on. "When was this?"

"November."

"November what?"

"November. Your father had already gone to New York. He came back to help us move to America in December but got real sick; he made me call a doctor. You imagine? Me a doctor, and he makes me call another one. He said I was trying to poison him."

The story about the time my grandfather got the flu and accused my grandmother of trying to poison him was legend in our family, and my mother pounced on it. "So that would have been in 1948?"

My grandmother ignored her in a way that, after a lifetime of interpreting her speech, my mother took as assent. "I was pregnant with your brother, and so sick. The lady in the inn I stayed in was so nice—she could see I was pregnant, she didn't say anything, kind of just looked me over and gave me a *bouillotte*"—the term *hot-water bottle* had never made it into Grandma's vocabulary—"and of course the only reason I got to sign that day was it turned out the *notaire* was the cousin of a friend of mine from Hauteville. I had to wait for him to get out of Mass. Then I got back to Montélimar for the train. You just have to *talk* to people, you know?"

"That's when you brought me the nougat!" my mother exclaimed, allowing herself to slide down one of Grandma's tangents. She caught herself, though. "So are you going to sign?"

"Why would I do that?" Grandma asked again. "I'm the one who bought it."

"Did you ever see it again? Did you ever think about it?"

My grandmother's high-wire chatter slacked off into silence for a fleeting moment. "What do you think?"

"Honestly? I think you should do whatever you want."

"I'll think about it," Grandma concluded. "'Bye." As always, she hung up immediately, the second she decided the conversation was over. Then she called my mother back.

"No," she said.

~

After a few more phone calls with my grandmother, my mother summoned her courage and telephoned my grandfather.

"Of course," my grandfather fumed, "that woman has been trying to ruin my life from the moment she met me. After the money, I daresay."

"Well, no. She says she'll think about selling if you send her a copy of the deed and an appraisal." My mother took a deep breath before uttering the next sentence, which she knew would send my grandfather into a rage. "She says it's her house, too, and if it's going to be sold, she thinks the profits should be divided evenly between the children." This was meant as a jab from my grandmother to my grandfather, one last attempt to strong-arm a man who had refused to pay child support and disinherited my mother and uncle. But my grandfather was too furious to notice.

"*Her* house?"

"That's what she said."

"Very good. I see she still has no compunctions about *lying*."

"Do you have the deed?"

"Of course I do."

"Well, maybe if you showed it to her, to prove you were the owner, it would solve the whole question."

Some people manage to write exactly as they talk, but my grandfather is the only man I know who manages to talk exactly as he writes. "I did not spend *decades* trying to obtain a divorce from that woman to have to *prove* something is my own. If she would like to reimburse any of the *myriad* expenses I have undertaken—taxes, the roof, the walls, the windows, electricity, running water; I shudder to think how much money I have put into that house, money thrown away—should she choose to contribute to *any* of that, I might consider her in some way owner of the house.

"Not to mention, of course," he added, "that buying it was my idea in the first place—I read about it in *Combat*."

"That's interesting—" my mother started to say, *She says she was the one who read about it.* She thought better of continuing and closed her mouth.

"What's interesting? That she wants to *steal* something that was purchased with my money? It was my money, you know. She may have gone down there, but it was my money. Can't you do something about this, Angèle? The woman is impossible, you agree?"

My mother was silent. Finally, she conceded, "I'll phone her again."

"I knew you'd see reason about this," my grandfather approved.

I watched with a kind of horrified fascination as my mother went back and forth between her parents, trying to broker some kind of deal. I remembered the awestruck, infatuated feeling that had overtaken me upon my arrival in Alba, remembered the castle and the town hall and La Roche with its strange volcanic excrescence, remembered my daydreams of cooking dinner in that old kitchen, shelling peas on the terrace and watching the river and the trees, painting those battered shutters and that creaky door. Mostly I remembered how beautiful it was. I had been amazed to discover the house was actually—if only partly—my grandmother's, and terrified to think she might let it slip away. I could not bear to believe that such a beautiful place would disappear from my life.

That summer I visited my grandfather and, as tentatively as I could, broached the subject of the house, venturing to inquire about why he wanted to sell it.

"It's been so long since I spent any time there at all," he sighed. "It's been nothing but a source of unhappiness and worry to me for a long time. It will be a relief to sell it." He began cleaning out his pipe. "That is, if *that woman* ever decides to stop making trouble about it." Holding his pipe above the crystal ashtray on the dining room table, he tapped until the burnt remains of yesterday's tobacco landed in a little black pile. "I'd give it to you," he added, "but I'm afraid it would be more of a burden than a gift."

I hesitated. I didn't know how to describe everything I had felt in the few hours I had seen La Roche. I was afraid to tell him I had fallen in love with the place; asking him for a house seemed like the kind of thing that would send him into a blinding rage. Certainly, he had cut people out of his life for less than that.

"*That woman,*" he groused again.

I tried to head him off at the pass. "But I thought—they said—if you faxed the deed—"

"It's very nice of you to care." The scary saccharine note in his voice spelled trouble. "I know you probably think she is a sweet old lady with white hair who bakes cookies." *Again with the cookies,* I thought. Was it because she'd decided to live in America that he thought she baked cookies?

"Seraphina—I call her Seraphina, ironically, you know."

"Yes, I do, yes." For as long as anyone could remember, Seraphina had been the epithet my grandfather employed in situations where he would not otherwise have been able to avoid uttering my grandmother's name. Once I had looked it up in one of the big dictionaries he kept by his desk. I'd found no entry for Seraphina, but under *seraph* I read, "A seraphic person, an angel." I wondered whether the nickname had once been earnest and loving. Under *seraphic* the dictionary said, ". . . worthy of a seraph; ecstatically adoring." I strained to picture Anna and Armand ecstatically adoring each other. "The presumed derivation of the word from a Hebrew root *saraph* to burn, led to the view that the seraphim are specially distinguished by fervor of love." The ominous silence in the kitchen reminded me that my grandfather's current fervor was anything but loving.

"She's spent years trying to ruin my life." His angry voice shattered the quiet.

"But she—"

He ignored me. "Do you know what she's doing?"

I shook my head, no.

"This is all part of her plan. She is waiting around for my pension." He paused to let this sink in. "Now she wants the house, too."

I had been doing my best to remain neutral, but this seemed so silly, I felt compelled to protest. "Grandpa—" I laughed, thinking about my independent grandma relying on anyone else for anything at all, let alone income. "She isn't waiting for your pension. She has her own pension. Besides, didn't she tell your *notaire* that she would agree to sell, as long as the money went to the children?"

His jaw tightened. *"The money?"*

Oh no, I thought. *What have I done?*

"Does she think I care about that? *I don't give a damn about the money!*" His face quivered with indignation.

We were silent. His face had that washed-out, shipwrecked look again. A year spent scuffing his carpets and dropping crumbs under the dining room table had not made me any less frightened of incurring his wrath. I waited. Finally, he spoke. His voice had lost its anger, and he delivered each word in a strange, even tone.

"You know, she was the reason I had to stop coming to your house."

"I'm sorry?"

"I could smell her, you know. I could smell her in the bed. I couldn't bear sleeping with her there."

I didn't know how to tell him that my grandmother had never once slept in the guest room of my mother's house.

⌒

When I returned home to Asheville, I got out my mother's old photos and thumbed through them again, past my great-aunts and -uncles and my beautiful young grandparents. There were only two pictures of Armand and Anna together in the whole album. In both, they were standing on a ledge at the top of a building. In the first picture, my grandfather was posed behind my grandmother, his hand resting on her shoulder. Her black hair was combed back into a neat bun, and she wore a fitted blouse and a dark skirt. She gazed directly at the camera, smiling. He, in a shirt and tie, was looking sternly at the sky. I was rather taken aback by this photo, not because it showed them together but rather because I had never seen my grandparents look so ordinary.

In the second picture, my grandparents appeared to have been blown apart by a strong wind. They leaned as far away from each other as was possible in that narrow space, he up against the wall, she against the railing. My grandfather's hair, smooth just a moment before, now stood on end; my grandmother's, too, had escaped from its bun and frizzed away from her head in unruly tendrils. Their smiles had turned tiny and grim. I looked back and forth between the two pictures: tidy and pulled together in the first, messy and blown apart in the second. Or was it messy and blown apart in the first, and tidy and pulled together in the second?

Anna and Armand in Geneva, 1944.

A loose photo fell into my lap. It showed my grandmother on another balcony leaning on an iron railing, her head tilted toward her shoulder. A single curl had escaped from her bun. Her dark dress with its lace collar hung from her body, still thin from starvation, making her look like a child playing dress-up. Her eyes looked terribly tired, but the expression in them hovered somewhere between shy and girlish and intensely passionate, so intimate that I felt slightly embarrassed meeting her gaze or looking at the picture at all. In the bottom left-hand corner was a blur, the photographer's finger—my grandfather's finger, I surmised. As if he could not bear to keep all of himself behind the camera, separated from her. There was an inscription scrawled across the back of the photograph in my grandmother's spiky handwriting: "Geneva 1944. Cours de Rive, where Angèle was conceived." Angèle is my mother.

～

At first, no one could figure out why my grandfather wouldn't send her the deed. This made my grandmother furious. Now it was she who phoned my mother: "Do something, Angèle." My mother consulted a family friend with a law firm in town. He referred her to a lawyer in Atlanta who specialized in family property law. The lawyer in Atlanta referred her to a lawyer in Paris, who specialized in international property disputes. The words swam around the family: power of attorney, deed of sale, joint ownership, sole proprietor, communal property, pre-nup, a sea of solutions and laws and stipulations. Marriage license, divorce papers, property deeds—all of it secret, locked away, hidden, lost. Storms of phone calls and opinions flared up and died away as various legal professionals faded in and out of the picture, their advice ignored, their ideas dismissed, their letters unanswered, their requests unheeded.

Time passed. And the question became, why are they holding on?

CHAPTER SIX

MY GRANDPARENTS WERE SO MASTERFUL AT stymieing each other from afar that any possibility of actually selling the house in La Roche quickly foundered and was lost in the deeps of their inscrutable silence. Life went on. To no one's surprise, my grandfather did not attend my high school graduation.

I left for college, which was a revelation: I wasn't bored, and I didn't feel like a misfit, though I probably was the only person on campus who wore an Uzbek silk tea cozy and a feather boa instead of a hat and scarf. Martha Beck describes the Harvard experience as "heady, exciting, even thrilling, but . . . laced with heavy doses of fear and misery . . . like having lunch with a brilliant, learned, witty celebrity who liked to lean across the table at unpredictable intervals and slap me in the mouth—hard." And since that is an excellent description of life with most members of my family, I thrived there. I adored it. For the first time in my life, I felt as if I had emerged from the all-too-interesting shadows of my quirky relations and could become my own person.

The house in La Roche faded from my mind in the tumult and excitement of my new life, but it lay in wait in a corner of my memory. One clear winter day I was standing in front of Hilles Library with my friend Helen and chatting about our bluestocking daydream of creating a sort of artists' colony somewhere, and a vision of the house, the stones and the sunlight and the castle on the hill above it, surged back to me. Perhaps if I occupied it with a group of friends all working on various academic or creative projects, my grandparents would see its utility, and they would decide conclusively not to sell.

My feeling of removal from the labyrinthine complications of my grandparents' relationship must have been pretty complete, or else my *coup de foudre* for the house had deprived me of my reason, because during my sophomore year in college, I wrote to both of them to ask whether my friends and I could spend the summer in Alba. My grandmother, who was always enthusiastic about any project I embarked on, said yes right away. "But I think you should go there alone," she cautioned. "Get to know people. You don't want the villagers to get the wrong idea about you." My grandfather took longer about it, but he, too, assented. "Just don't go there by yourself," he warned. "The people there are all drunkards and thieves." I set about applying for a summer grant from the Harvard College Fund to study village life in medieval France and turned my attention to other things, lulled into a temporary belief that things could ever be so simple in my family.

～

Then one morning, not long before spring break, my mother called, sounding slightly harassed, saying that my grandmother wanted to go to Alba. "What for?" I asked.

"I'm not sure." She sounded worried. "She's really, really stirred up about it for some reason. She says she absolutely wants to see the house."

Not yet comprehending what the whole affair had to do with me, I said, "I guess it's only fair—she did buy it, after all. She must feel kind of cheated about it, that she never got to see it again. It makes sense to me."

"Well, your uncle thinks it's a terrible idea. He says she's too old to travel, and she shouldn't go."

"What do you think?"

"Well, she is eighty-seven, and I certainly think she shouldn't go alone—you know how hard traveling has gotten for her. And I can't go with her. But she's totally set on it."

"I'll go," I volunteered, feeling a rush of excitement. In my mind, I was still fully the child and she the adult. I loved traveling with my grandmother, and I felt nostalgic for the easy camaraderie we had shared when I was younger. I was always on the lookout for ways to reconquer the distance that had settled in between us when I entered adolescence—especially ways that didn't involve my being a faithful correspondent or spending too much time just sitting and being with her, which would have been the best solutions but were beyond the ken of my nineteen-year-old self. Besides, I wanted to see the house again, too.

"I don't know," my mother wavered. "I'm just not sure it's such a good idea."

"It's her choice to make, isn't it?"

"Yes, of course it is. And she says she really wants to go to France one last time. But I don't know—even getting down to Asheville is an ordeal for her now."

"Well, tell her if she wants to go, I'll go with her, and then she can make up her own mind."

I had seen changes in her myself, but I had not yet realized it was possible for my grandmother to actually diminish or weaken in any way. The grandmother in my head still did headstands and hung from a chin-up bar. The last time we'd both been in Asheville together, she'd invited me to a topless bar with her friend John, an adjunct professor at the university where my mother taught.

"John? A topless bar?" I'd squeaked.

"That's what I said, but he told me it's the fashion for dinner these days. God knows what they'll serve, but I figure I can brush up on my anatomy. Why not? You should try anything once."

"Where is it?"

"Downtown somewhere—it's called Zamba or Saba or some-thing."

"You mean Zambra? It's a tapas bar." I dissolved in giggles.

"Well, that makes more sense," Grandma reflected. "He didn't strike me as the type, but you never know." I couldn't help thinking she sounded disappointed—she'd already tasted Spanish food, after all. How could I have believed that the strength of such a woman was fading?

~

If I had, as a child, been saved in my nightmares by my grand-mother hustling me out the door, her hurriedness now drove me crazy. She had booked an evening flight to Lyon, and I, wanting to spend at least one night of my spring break hanging out with my friends and my boyfriend, decided to arrive at her house on the morning of our departure. Grandma was hysterical. My uncle, who was supposed to drive us to the airport, excoriated me for making her anxious, for wanting to go to France with her, for getting in-volved with the house in La Roche. "This house is like a beautiful, poisoned dagger," he fulminated. "It's brought nothing but trou-ble to this family. You shouldn't have anything to do with it." He started to say more, but my grandmother surged into the room, and we hustled out the door.

We arrived at the airport with five hours to spare before our flight. With great satisfaction, Grandma settled in for the wait. Traveling must be too much like fleeing, I thought. The waiting calmed her: you know where you are; you know where you're going; there's nothing more to be done; and if you've forgotten something, too bad, in fact, so much the better, you'll just have to exercise your ingenuity. I watched her observing a couple of parents fail to make their hyperactive children behave. Any minute now, the river of words would start—I could already see her mind putting a story to-gether, crackling with intelligence and her peculiar sideways logic. She laughed and shook her head. "The children in my ward were always loud. Always running around, screaming, shouting, crying. But when they went into my office—" She grinned and halted the remembered children's noise with a wave of her hand. "Silence."

"You mean at Rockland State?" For years she'd run the Female Adolescent Unit at the large state mental hospital near her home in Pearl River.

She ignored me. "The nurses were always asking, 'Dr. Munster, Dr. Munster, how do you make them be quiet?' So I looked at them, and I'd say, 'I strangle them.' " She cackled. So did I.

"What did you really do?"

"The children would come into my office, blubbering and cry-ing." Here she gave the mocking imitation of babyish sobs I remem-bered from my own childhood—still, to this day, the only person I have ever met who could sob with an accent. "So I looked at them, and I would say, 'If you want to be loud, you can go and sit over there in the loud chair.' I had a little child-size chair in front of a little table, with crayons and paper and what. And then I would say, 'But if you want to be quiet, you're welcome to sit in this big chair next to me. But don't do me any favors. If you want to scream, go ahead and sit in the loud chair.' "

"What did they do?"

"Oh, children are very symbolic. They always stayed next to me."

I wondered whether her chair technique would have worked without the special sort of sorcery she exercised on children, and I squeezed her hand. "You're such an extraordinary person. I'm so glad to be going on a trip with you."

"*My Godt.*" She pulled her hand away. "Go walk around or something."

~

Somewhere in the dim roar of our nighttime flight to Lyon, I realized I had no idea what Grandma and I were going to do once we landed. We had no hotel reservations, no contacts, and no idea of how to get to Alba. Despite my passionate feelings for La Roche, I couldn't have located it on a map, even if it had been big enough to show up on one. I looked at my grandmother, who didn't seem at all bothered by these trifles. She was probably the only adult on the plane tiny enough to find the seats comfortable, and she was sleeping peacefully. I tried to settle down and get some rest, too, but I couldn't. I was beginning to suspect that this trip might be a bit more complicated than I had anticipated.

When it was time to land, Grandma awoke refreshed, drank two cups of airplane coffee, and gathered her things around her, impatient to be on the move. When we got to the gate, she strode down the gangway and brushed aside the wheelchair we had ordered to meet her. Suddenly she tripped and went sprawling onto the floor, wincing like a tiny boxer with the breath knocked out of her, as the wheelchair attendant and I rushed to pick her up. She refused a doctor but grudgingly sat down in the wheelchair.

"Take us to the bus stop," she commanded.

The wheelchair attendant set off, and I hurried along next to her.

We had been traveling for twenty-four hours. While we waited for the bus, Grandma pulled an elderly bandage out of her purse and laid one end of it on top of her injured wrist, which had begun to swell. "What do you know about wrapping a bandage?" she snapped when I offered to help. Her face was pale and drawn from the pain, and her age suddenly showed. So did mine. I was beginning to feel extremely young and slightly panicked.

The subsequent hours were a blur of worry and exhaustion. We made it to Lyon, and the next thing I remember clearly was standing at the ticket counter in the Lyon Part Dieu train station asking for two tickets to Alba-la-Romaine. The ticket agent clicked the keys on her computer keyboard, then leaned down, opened a drawer, and pulled out a book that looked like an outlandishly thick and yellowed parody of a bygone era. She thumbed through it for a while, then looked up at me. "Mademoiselle, there hasn't been a train to Alba since 1913."

"Nineteen thirteen?" I had already been feeling queasy and ashamed of the stupidity of our quest. Now an irrational fear gripped me. What if Alba didn't even exist?

The woman jabbed a finger at the yellowed page, and I stood on tiptoe, trying to get a look at it, but the print was too small.

"What did the lady say?" Grandma asked. "I can't hear her." I relayed what the ticket agent had told me, and Grandma shook her head, no. "That's not true."

"What do you suggest we do?" I asked the ticket agent, ignoring Grandma's last statement.

"The farthest I can get you is Montélimar. Then you'll have to take a bus, or maybe a taxi. I don't know. I've never heard of the place."

Grandma was whacking my arm with her good hand, so I turned to her and repeated what the lady had said.

"Montélimar . . . Montélimar. I think that's where I took the bus from last time."

This was cold comfort to me, given that the last time had been in 1948, but I bought the tickets to Montélimar, since that seemed better than staying in Lyon.

Once we were on the train, Grandma unwrapped her bandage and inspected her arm.

"I don't think it's broken," she announced.

"Great," I said, though I knew sarcasm was on the list of failings she ascribed to American teenagers. "You don't *think*? Shouldn't we call a doctor?"

"Doctor?" She brushed me off. "What doctor? I am a doctor." She winced as she rewrapped her bandage, and I felt even more frightened as I realized I had never seen her betray any sign of physical pain or suffering. Scared we'd miss our stop, I struggled to stay awake while Grandma dozed. I watched the cherry blossoms and vineyards and the view of the Rhône River out the window and wondered how they could seem so beautiful in the midst of my terrible anxiety. When the conductor with his warm southern accent called out, "*Montélimar, ici Montélimar,*" Grandma snapped into action and rushed me off the train like a drill sergeant.

When we walked out of the train station, Grandma looked around her, and her eyes widened. She inhaled sharply and took a step back, reeling as if someone had knocked the wind out of her.

"*My Godt,*" she said softly, as if speaking to herself. "It looks so different."

I took in the louche-looking young men with puffy jackets and slicked-back hair loitering in the plastic chairs outside the station café, the cars, the park with its fountain, the nougat factory. "What do you mean?" I asked. To me, Montélimar looked timeless and old, a nineteenth-century resort town gone to seed.

"It was all bombed out," she went on, sucking her breath in through her teeth and shaking her head. "All black and broken."

"Where?"

She gestured with her uninjured hand to take in the whole town. "Everywhere." She straightened up. "The cherry trees are the same, though. Come on, let's go." She started walking toward the taxi stand.

"Grandma," I protested, "Alba is miles from here."

She waved her good hand and kept walking.

～

Despite my fluster and enervation, as the taxi drew up to Alba, I thrilled at the sight of the little stone village, the castle peering shyly off its hill over the rows of green vineyards. We drove through the village and down the hill, and then the driver waited for us in the parking lot of La Roche while we walked under the low arch into the shady street. My grandmother's movements were slower and more painful with every step, but we finally made it to the house. We didn't have a key, so there wasn't much to see: the dark stones, the weathered shutters closed tight, the dim street, and the stone passageway.

I was lost in a tired reverie, thinking how extraordinary it was that we were here, standing in this particular spot on earth, in this tiny, far-off, and extremely old place, when I heard my grandmother say, "Well, I don't think I'll go back."

I plunged into panic again. Grandma's English always got a little erratic when she was tired or unhappy, and seeing her defeated and diminished and visibly suffering was so inimical to anything I had ever associated with her that I interpreted her words as meaning she was going to die on the spot.

I tried to arrange the thoughts racing through my head. How would I explain to the taxi driver? What would I do with the body? The funeral? The tickets home? Was there a special body ticket? I felt overcome with guilt for having accompanied her.

"Miranda?" Grandma's voice interrupted my flow of macabre thoughts.

"What? What can I do?"

She looked at me oddly and beckoned with her good arm. "Come on. I think we can do everything we need to do up in the village. There's no reason to come back down here to the house."

I felt ridiculous and relieved as we slid into the taxi and drove back to Montélimar. The driver deposited us at the Hôtel Dauphiné Provence, traded a few jokes with the owner, checked us in, carried our bags up to the room, and charged us a preposterously small amount of money for the three hours he'd just spent with us.

"You take good care of your grandmother," he told me as he left. I wanted to cry.

My lack of sleep had given the whole world nightmarish proportions. It's bad enough to have made it possible for your grandmother to fly across the ocean and injure herself, but I can assure you that arriving in a hotel room covered in wall-to-wall carpeting makes everything feel worse. It was everywhere: the floor, certainly, but also the walls, the headboards of the bed, the toilet seat, the little alcove sheltering the sink. In the twilight, it gave the room, and me, a feeling of tawdry, muffled desolation.

My grandmother was breathing laboriously and having trouble walking. The mute relief with which she lay down on the bed was almost immediately dispelled by the sharp pain that creased her normally smooth face. I felt terrified, haunted by the thought of her dying in this creepy hotel.

It was the first time I had ever cared for an adult. Grandma sat up again, and gingerly, I pulled down her socks, unlaced her shoes, took her hearing aids out of her ears, slid her blouse over her head. For a second, as I undressed her, I leaned my head against her good shoulder and breathed in her scent of roses and iron, wishing I were still a little girl and could have my invincible grandmother back, with her hot milk and strong opinions.

Then I pulled myself together and ventured out to buy dinner for the two of us, since we hadn't eaten all day. It was Sunday, and Montélimar was conclusively shut. The city had sucked itself up behind shutters and rolled-up awnings and gave away nothing but chipped paint and stone buildings whose stucco was grayed from years of grime or bleached off-white by the sun. All I found were crepes, warm and savory, a comforting weight in the stomach, but too much food, too greasy. After we had eaten what we could, Grandma wrapped the scraps in napkins. "Maybe we can use these later . . . No refrigerator . . . They won't be very good after . . . Maybe we should throw them . . . No, I'll just put them in my bag for tomorrow."

When she was in the bathroom, I threw the crepes away, hiding them under the other debris in the wastebasket, hoping that she was tired enough that she could forget them tonight and that she'd feel better enough to keep forgetting them in the morning.

Once we were both in bed, I lay listening for each of her breaths, reminding myself of her resilience, her bravado, watching the Hôtel Dauphiné Provence's green neon light flash on and off, on and off, bright and dark through the slats of the shutters. How could I have been so naïve? How could I have believed that any of this would be easy? Difficulty was my family's reality: fights and bitterness, illness and injury, trauma, bad memories, and crazy grudges. Restful trips to beautiful houses in the countryside were not our stock-in-trade.

⁓

My grandmother awoke the next morning feeling much better and agreed to let me send breakfast up to her in bed. After some strong coffee, we both felt reinvigorated, and I resumed trying to take care of her.

"I'm going to the pharmacy," I announced. "I'm getting you a new bandage and some cream for the swelling."

"No!" Grandma exclaimed. She sounded as if I had offered to stab her in the leg.

"You know the bandage you have isn't big enough for you."

She shook her head. "It's fine. It's a good wool bandage. I've had it since the camps. They don't make them like this anymore."

She undid the bandage awkwardly and held out her wrist. It was shiny and puffy, the normally wrinkled sags pushed out by the pressure under the skin. "I'm going to the pharmacy," I said again, slowly and clearly, "and I'm getting you the cream and a better bandage."

"I'm going with you. It's dangerous."

"Grandma, Montélimar is tiny. It's safe. Don't worry."

"Listen," she said fiercely, as she rewound the bandage. "I read about it in a magazine. There are North Africans here. It's very dangerous. They could try to kill you."

This announcement silenced me completely. It startled, even frightened, me. It was akin to her telling me that Montélimar was full of Martians, or anthrax, or Elvis impersonators. She'd been all over the world. She'd been to Russia with one of the first groups of American doctors ever to see the inside of a Russian mental hospital, back when Russia was Communist and its mental hospitals were sinister, scary places. She'd been to Japan. She'd been to Mexico. Come to think of it, she'd been to North Africa and enjoyed herself immensely. Her sudden fear of North African murderers was completely out of character.

"I'm going with you," she repeated. "And then we'll take the bus to Alba and present ourselves at the *mairie*."

"What do they care about us at the *mairie*?"

"You never know. You should always talk to people. Make yourself known."

I gave up on arguing with her. As we walked out of the hotel room, she snapped at me, "Where's your passport?"

"In my suitcase."

"Don't you *ever* leave the room without your passport." Sensing it was best not to protest, I retrieved the passport and put it in my purse.

"What will you do if your purse gets stolen?" she quizzed.

I slipped it into my bra and was about to lock the room, when she snapped at me again. "Hide the bags," she commanded.

"What?"

"Hide the bags."

"Hide the bags? Hide them where?"

"Put them in the closet." I obeyed. "Cover them with those blankets."

"Grandma, why—"

She cut me off. "They look through the bags when you're not in the room."

"Who looks through the bags?" I asked her, but she was already out the door.

Once I had shut the door and locked it, she hissed, "Hide the keys."

When I failed to satisfy her by putting them in my pocket, I stuffed them into my bra next to the passport.

"It's a good thing I'm wearing a loose blouse," I quipped.

She gave me a pained look, and I thought of what she'd said at the train station yesterday and of her face as she looked at the countryside around her. "You haven't been back here since 1948?"

She nodded. Arriving in Montélimar had clearly unleashed a flood of emotions, the shock of which was just as great as the one to her wrist when she fell at the airport. I wondered what exactly it was that she was remembering.

~

On the third day of our trip to France, Grandma and I had regained confidence in her resilience and mastery of any and all things, and I made an appointment with a *notaire*, Marie Frizet, who had told us she could help us find records and figure out my grandmother's legal questions. She had a soft brown bob that framed pink cheeks, quick, sympathetic eyes, and a ready smile I suspected hid a robust sense of humor.

"I will tell the story," Grandma announced, after Maître Frizet had shown us into her office and we had all sat down. She pointed at me. "You take notes."

I pulled out a pad of paper, and Grandma began. "When I left my ex-husband, he took the children's passports—he wanted to intimidate me, in case I changed my mind." She paused. "And I guess he was right, because I did change the tickets . . . but I couldn't go back."

Maître Frizet looked nonplussed. "Back where? What tickets?"

"Grandma," I said softly, "you're not making any sense. She doesn't even know why we're here." Raising my voice and turning to the *notaire*, I added, "We're here about a house. My grandparents bought a house together in 1948, in Alba-la-Romaine."

Maître Frizet made a note.

I was about to go on, but my grandmother interrupted me. "I know what I'm talking about." She plunged ahead with her story. "Now, I understand he was angry, but it wasn't fair of him to take it out on the children. He wouldn't send the child support, he said he forgot, or he said he was only sending half because everything cost so little in Israel, or saying he would only support one of them or the other. I had very little money. Nobody had any money back then. So if you think about it, he owes me quite a lot of money. Can you imagine, from Israel I had to sail all the way to Nice, take a train to Geneva, so I could go to the UN family office and beg them to make him pay—because I knew they paid him a dependents' allowance, it was called, I think. I put them through college, graduate school, I sent my son to boarding school, all by myself. He didn't help with any of it."

Maître Frizet had given up on taking notes early in Grandma's speech. Now she glanced down at her notebook as if she regretted her decision. "So you are owed money by your ex-husband."

"No, no—" I interrupted. "They bought the house right before they moved to America. And they divorced a few years later. Well, twenty years later. The house wasn't mentioned in the divorce settlement. Now he wants to sell it, but he can't."

Maître Frizet looked skeptical. "Back then everything went to the husband. Unless the wife's name was the only one on the deed. Do you have the deed?"

I shook my head. "He won't send it to her. But his *notaire* says he can't sell without her power of attorney."

"Well, her name must be the only one on the deed, then. Was it a French divorce or an American divorce?"

My grandmother shook her head. "I think he was seeing another woman. A sculptress, or something. He was really very nasty to me those last few years. The fights . . . terrible. And then he claimed it was my fault, because I left. I walked out one day when he was at work because I really didn't want any fuss, and I took the children. And the typewriter. He had another one, in his office."

I interrupted. "No one seems to remember whether it was French or American."

"Well," Maître Frizet reasoned, "by French law, if there's no prenuptial agreement, everything is automatically divided evenly in the case of a divorce. So I think that really, especially if it wasn't mentioned in the divorce, you own half of the property."

My grandmother had already been told this by several other lawyers. She nodded emphatically. "And he's trying to sell it!"

"Couldn't you speak to him about it?"

Silence. Now it was my grandmother's turn to look nonplussed.

"I mean, to explain your side of things—"

I interrupted again. "They haven't spoken to each other in about fifty years."

Maître Frizet sat back in her chair. "Oh."

"He claims that it's his property because he's paid taxes on it and repaired it since the beginning," I explained. "My grandmother only saw it the one time, when she bought it."

"He rents it out, I hear," my grandmother added.

I could see the *notaire* writing "rent" on her pad of paper. She stared at it as if it might offer some clarity. "Do you need the money? I could contact his *notaire*, and we could probably make him give you half of the rent money, and you are certainly entitled to half the money from the sale." She sounded relieved to have figured out a solution. "In fact, if you sell it, I could arrange for the money to be paid to you monthly, as a pension."

Again, my grandmother looked nonplussed.

"No, no," I clarified hastily. "My grandmother doesn't need the money. It's just that she—" I trailed off. I wasn't sure what she wanted.

The conversation limped along for nearly an hour. By the end of it, I had a headache, but my grandmother looked more than satisfied. We shook hands all around. Grandma took Maître Frizet's card and promised to send her a sheaf of documents. It seemed to have done my grandmother a world of good to tell her story to a neutral party, and I suspected Maître Frizet could see that, since I couldn't for the life of me figure out what she would actually do with the documents. Back in the taxi, Grandma squeezed my arm triumphantly. "That was very successful."

⌒

That night we ate dinner in the hotel's yellow dining room. Grandma seemed jubilant after her visit with the *notaire*. "You know how to keep from getting drunk?" she asked when the wine arrived.

I shook my head.

"At least that's what my sister—your great-aunt Alma—says: before you drink, you take a tablespoon or so of olive oil, like that." She raised her injured hand, stiffly, and brought it to her mouth, throwing her head back as if she were drinking a shot of neat whiskey. "You know how she learned that? She used to be a nightclub singer."

My eyebrows went up. Grandma nodded, pleased to have surprised me. I knew Alma as a tiny, tough old lady living outside Tel Aviv. It was hard to imagine my gin-rummy-playing, ex-elite-athlete (she'd beat national records in Romania and represented her country in the 1932 Maccabiah Games) great-aunt singing in nightclubs.

"You know my father had the biggest, fanciest restaurant in Czernowitz but no head for business. He had the best chefs, always, and people loved the big, round dining room with the red carpet, gold everywhere. But one year he heard about this new thing, an automat."

"An automat?"

"You know, you put the dishes in one side, they put in a coin and open the door and have a meal, which they had in the big cities in Western Europe. So, what did he do?"

A rhetorical question.

"He took all his savings and went to Berlin and bought an automat! The first in the region."

"Was it a success?"

"At first it was a sensation; everyone came to see it. But then there was the depression—big failure. All that money, and no one liked it anymore."

"That's terrible."

"Well, if you think about it, when people went out to eat, they wanted a real restaurant, with waiters, and the chefs didn't like it either! But he always kept the house running the same way, and he paid for everyone's education. This, because he had the best wine in Romania. He even had a title, he was a purveyor to the

Austro-Hungarian emperor. And it was because of this that he saved Alma's life."

"How?"

"The chief of police was a big drunk—always was. When the Nazis came, they were rounding people up into the trains. They got her." Grandma took a sip of her wine. "So here she was on a cattle car, in the train station—the train was going to leave. So my father ran to the police chief and collared him. He said, 'Listen, I've been giving you wine since you were this high.'" Grandma held her good hand to the height of the table, and I imagined a tiny drunkard. "'Twelve years old! Not even tall enough to see over my counter.'"

She paused.

"What happened?"

"Eat your dinner."

I picked up my fork but put nothing in my mouth.

"The police chief says, 'So what?' And my father shouts, 'So? So now the best runner in the history of Romania is on that train, and you are not going to let her be sent away.' They went down to the train station and went through all the cars and found her and pulled her off the train."

"Really?" I glanced around the warm yellow dining room. I felt as if I had been swimming and were coming up for air, as if time were fluid and it could be any year, then or now.

As if she had read my thoughts, Grandma said, "Back then, the regulars would have had their own napkins that they kept in a cubby near the bar." She took a bite of food, a sip of wine, and dove again. "The second time the Nazis came, Alma was still at home."

"Why didn't they arrest your parents?"

"They were too much a part of the community. Everyone loved them. My father gave something to everyone. My mother, too. And she wouldn't leave them. They told her and told her to get out."

"Where would she have gone?"

My grandmother gestured to somewhere far away. "The day they were supposed to come, the neighbors had warned my parents, and my mother woke Alma up at four in the morning and said, 'It's time to go.' Alma wouldn't. She's very stubborn, you know her."

"I certainly wouldn't argue with her," I agreed. Alma had once hurled a mantel clock out the window at a neighbor who suggested it was unladylike to participate in international athletic competitions.

Grandma laughed. "Well, just imagine our mother. She was even more stubborn. Finally she just threw Alma out onto the street, told her to run."

I tried to imagine this.

"So she worked her way to Bucharest, as a barmaid, and singing in nightclubs, and dancing. The country was full of Russians. The Russian officers loved her!"

"Was that a good thing?"

"Exactly! It was dangerous. Every night they would come and buy her drinks. You know they get very mean if you don't drink with them. So, every night"—she made the shot glass motion again—"she would take some olive oil before she began to work. They wanted her to go to Moscow and sing for the big generals."

"What happened?"

"She knew that if she went she would be dead before long. So she ran away."

"What about your brothers?"

"Arnold was in Siberia; Werner went to a labor camp when he was fourteen, and then he walked through Turkey to Israel—you know, he could just survive . . ."

Her reminiscences drifted further back in time, to her own maternal grandmother. "She knew all about herbs, took care of the sick in her village—the smartest woman around, the best educated. The Orthodox priest would come around every Sunday afternoon, and they would pull the big religious books with the gold edges on the pages off the shelf, and they'd argue for hours in the salon. Such a lovely house," Grandma continued dreamily. "But when I was a child all of that was gone. We sat on rough wooden benches."

"Why?"

"During the first war the Russians came and burned everything. A tribe of mercenaries. Kalmuks. They took everything outside in a big pile and set it on fire. They loved the books best, the golden sparks the gilt pages made when they burned. Then they went to live in the barn."

I blinked, clearing smoke and sparks from my eyes. "The barn?"

"Sure. They liked it out there. They helped with the animals— they were herders, not professional soldiers, you know. They made the most wonderful cheese."

Grandma's memory had overflowed like a springtime river escaping its banks, and her stories lapped over me. They say a flood makes the world look as it did in the beginning, before the dry land emerged. It seemed to me that her outpouring of memories had dissolved the wide gulf between us and the past, that beside her I could glimpse her grandmother, and her grandmother's grandmother, and all the worlds each of them contained. I had understood how the war severed my grandmother from her everyday life, relegating it to the bygone and the lost, but now I saw it had also carried away her past—not only loved ones but also advice and instructions, proclivities and inside jokes, books and recipes, trinkets and keepsakes, all her rightful inheritance. For a split second, I saw an infinity of forgotten details dancing across history's dizzying expanse. Folded into remembrance is the knowledge of all that cannot be recalled: I realized that when my grandparents passed away, I would carry within me not only the memory of them but the memory of their memories, on and on over the horizon of being, back to the tohu-bohu before the waters parted.

∼

It was our last night in the Hôtel Dauphiné Provence. The carpet didn't seem so awful now. I closed the shutters and dimmed the lights, and the green neon sign outside the window flashed on and off through the slats, casting a murky pond-colored glow onto the floor of our room. I helped Grandma undress and slid her night-gown over her head, and we climbed into bed, side by side like two peas in a neon green pod.

I began to fall asleep. The room, and the carpet, and the green glow receded.

Then I heard Grandma whisper into the dark. "Camps . . . you know . . ."

I held my breath.

". . . they wanted to put us in camps."

The silence pressed in, and I felt my old, familiar panic and de-spair rearrange themselves into compassion and love for the woman who'd really lived those feelings. I reached under the blankets and took her hand. She held on to me lightly, her fingers soft and cool and familiar, her quiet, sober voice completely different from the ex-uberant certainty I knew so well. "They killed so many people . . . we were so frightened . . . we wouldn't make it . . . I was so fright-ened." I stroked the smooth skin on her hand, and her grip tight-ened, almost imperceptibly. "Some words you can't even say."

"I know," I said, though I was only beginning to, only a little bit. We lay there in the dark together. I imagined the house in La Roche, somber and empty in its shadowy hamlet. *Maybe they never meant it to be lived in,* I thought. *Maybe it's just a place to hold their ghosts.*

CHAPTER SEVEN

I T WOULD BE AN UNDERSTATEMENT TO SAY THE TRIP to France was a sobering experience. It was hard to feel the same enthusiasm about spending a summer in Alba after seeing my grandmother's reaction to the place. If life had taught me from an early age that the world was sown with land mines of memory, I now realized that the house in La Roche might be the biggest land mine of them all. But it was too late—our miniature and slightly dweeby artists' collective, which in the end consisted of two friends and me, had already collected their grants and purchased their plane tickets. I can't deny having chosen my subject of study—village life in the Middle Ages—a bit as a lovesick teenager chooses a bus route that might take her past the object of her affection, as if reading Georges Duby and the Rule of Saint Benedict could somehow bring me closer to La Roche. But when we got there, I realized once more that it wasn't just a repository for ghosts and shadows—it was the place my heart had inexplicably and incontestably named as its home.

Cleaning the house took a day of hard labor, and then it was a pleasant, if primitive, place to live. We had no car, no Internet, and no telephone. To get into or out of the village, we had to walk almost two miles to a bus stop on the side of the highway. I could wax rhapsodic about the passionflower vines growing over the stones, and the breeze blowing off the river, and the forbidding, mysterious view of the castle—all reasons I love Alba, but what I loved best, and still do, was that ineffable and odd sensation of comfort and security I derived from living somewhere that had existed for so long. That, and the isolation, made everything about La Roche seem to exist with more intensity, a kind of potent vitality I had only ever associated with my zestful grandma. Was that why she'd chosen to buy the place?

La Roche in the summer was blissful. The world seemed far-off and blurry beyond the tiny universe of the village, reminding me of the little habitats I used to construct as a child, not so long ago. It was as if I'd finally managed to enter one of them, and everything around me seemed magnified to a gritty, wonderful complex of simple things, an infinity of details to notice, examine, and enjoy—the taste of bread, the smell of grass, the color of sunshine. I remembered sitting in my grandfather's car that Sunday I'd first seen the village, wondering what it would be like to take part in the homey beauty of Alba, and now here I was. There was even a gray tabby cat who came around for snuggles from time to time; I gave her milk and imagined myself a life there that was permanent enough to include a cat.

But I knew, deep down, that I didn't really live there, and that made me sad. At times I felt as if I'd never been so at home, and at times I felt like a beggar at a window, dazzled by a thing that wasn't mine. Already, I was plotting my return. I couldn't help believing that if I came there for good, I would be freed from the weight of my history, that I could escape the past by living somewhere that embodied it.

My friends and I drank wine, cooked big dinners, and lazed around on the terrace, and that was grand, but intellectually, the summer was deeply frustrating. I traveled to hot dusty archives and found snippets of information about deeds and titles and marriages and fealties and charters, but they revealed little about the people who had felt hungry and angry and happy and tired within the thick rampart walls of Alba and La Roche. Medieval studies had revealed a world of historical scholarship that I loved as much as my grandparents' house, and I dearly wished to link the two together in some sort of grand unified field theory of the past. I'd applied for the grant with this modest hope in mind, but as I scrubbed stone floors, listened for footsteps in the street, or squished my laundry around in a tub, I began to see the cracks in my plan. All the fantasizing I did about what life might have been like for the people who had once lived there hardly amounted to history or even explained why I felt such a deep connection to the village. Many were the days I abandoned the archives and retreated to the ruined part of the house, staring at the rubble of old newspapers, dusty lumber, and brambles pushing in through the windows, feeling completely baffled that life had propelled me to this improbable, run-down place. I knew my grandparents and their silence were at the root of it, but the more I pondered it, the more mysterious I found the connection between their outsize personalities and the house in La Roche. My grandparents' story was like a fairy tale whose particulars had been forgotten, glamorous in its details and secrets. I liked to imagine their love as dizzy and spectacular, with an ache behind it I couldn't identify. I felt like an archaeologist, or an undersea diver, certain that if I picked through the debris in the house I would find something terrible, or something wonderful, or maybe both, that would provide me with a key, or a hint at least, to the story of their love and separation. Or so I sensed, but the truth was far-off to me then. Little did I know how far. Nor did I realize how long it would take me once I began to dig.

PART II

*Anna, circa 1934, found in
an old wallet of Armand's.*

*Armand in 1937, the year
after he met Anna.*

CHAPTER EIGHT

M Y TRIP TO ALBA WITH MY GRANDMOTHER and the summer I spent there in 2001 left me feeling spooked and embarrassed about my strange, immature obsession, and for a time, I tried to convince myself that there was more to life than my grandparents' story. But even as I resolved to follow my own path, Armand and Anna exerted an undeniable influence over my decisions. Switching out of medieval studies (away from the house) and into early modern history was, I told myself, a dispassionate choice. I was interested in the origins of political ideology and national identity, and if I studied those topics in France, it was simply a matter of geographical continuity, of linguistic convenience, of the unique historical moment that was the French Revolution. But I just as easily could have chosen England, or Italy, or Germany. France was and wasn't my grandparents' home: it was the country where they had met, studied, fallen in love, been hunted and hidden—the country they both regretted and refused to live in, where they'd bought and abandoned an ancient stone ruin. Circuitously but irresistibly, I kept returning to the place my grandmother had picked out for me.

Their influence was not immediately detectable in my thesis topic—Jacobinism in rural France—until you examined a map and noticed that the archives in which I chose to do my research the summer before senior year were in Avignon, which just happened to be an hour south of Alba. Even my accommodations in the Papal

City were evidence of my grandmother's persistent interference in my fate: when she heard I was headed to Avignon, she excitedly recalled that a friend of hers, the poet John Allman, had a close friend there named David Mairowitz, a respected American writer who taught at its university. I ignored this information, but without asking me, she wrote to John to get me an introduction to David. I'd intended to stay in a youth hostel, failing to notice that my research project coincided with the Avignon theater festival, when all lodging in the city is booked months in advance. Thanks to my grandmother, I had a doorstep on which to land when I arrived for the summer. David took pity on me, with my lopsided braids, thrift store tuxedo pants, and rumpled blouse, and let me stay in his guest room. I made it to Alba just once in 2002, for a weekend that I mostly spent trying to fix a broken window in the house, which only made me feel more passionate and protective of the place.

~

Devoted though I was to doctoral studies and Jacobins, my grandparents' story seemed more urgent than my chosen field. The French Revolution was over and could wait; Anna and Armand's adventures, on the other hand, felt burningly alive. The more I contemplated it, the more I felt I had no right to go on with my own life until I had learned what had happened in theirs. Such a love story demanded recording. I thought it wouldn't take very long, that I could compact the process into a gap year between college and graduate school. Getting to the bottom of their mystery would be a bit like crafting a Penelope tapestry: I would write everything down, present it to my grandparents, and they would cry, "No, that's not what really happened!" Then the process would begin again, with me running back and forth between them, weaving and unweaving a story that tended asymptotically toward the truth, all the while approaching the zero of their death, but never touching it.

~

I would go to La Roche because I believed the very act of living there wouldbe a kind of listening, that it would help me see my way to the truth. But there were holes in my plan. Two, to be precise: Anna and Armand. There was no reason to think my grandmother would submit to becoming the protagonist of a tale of love, loss, sadness, and survival; my grandfather promised to be even less co-operative. Nevertheless, I once again asked their permission to live in the house.

Over the phone, my grandfather warned me, as he had before, to steer clear of the drunkards and thieves he was certain populated the village. "I shall draw you a map of the people you can trust, when you come to get the key," he reassured me.

"So it's all right? You don't mind if I go live there?"

"Why not? There are sure to be scorpions," he added. "It will probably be infested, by now."

~

"Of course," said my grandmother, as if she were merely confirm-ing a plan she'd made herself.

I had gone to visit her in Pearl River; we were walking together in her neighborhood, and Grandma, never one to follow the path laid out for her, cut a corner across the grassy embankment between two sidewalks. When she'd gone half the way, she stopped still. "Just promise me one thing," she said. I stopped, too, and waited for her to catch her breath. Her trip to France with me had indeed been her last. Now she avoided airplanes and generally strayed no farther than the ShopRite a couple of blocks from her house, or down to the park and the library, and then only by foot.

"What?"

"Don't come home."

"Don't come home? Of course I'm coming home—"

"For my funeral," she cut in, "or, you know, if something should happen to me. Stay where you are."

"Don't say that," I protested.

"What? I'm in my ninety-first year." My grandmother was the only woman I have ever known who made herself sound older than she actually was. "I didn't come to my grandmother's funeral. I saw her before, and we said what we needed to say to each other. A grave is nothing. Just the ground they put your body in."

"I guess. But please, I hope you stick around. I'm only going for a year."

I offered her my arm. She shook me off. "What do I always say?" she reprimanded. "Never help an old person. We need to stay in shape."

"You're in great shape," I countered, as if I could change her mind about being old. "Look at you. You get around just fine. You still do your yoga."

She flicked these observations aside with a wave of her hand. "My eyes are going." She'd stopped under some oak trees, and the afternoon sun filtered through the branches and lit the leaves as if from within. I wondered what she saw, or did not see, with her aging eyes. "Four-leaf clovers," she replied, as if I'd asked the question aloud. "You know I used to find them all the time."

I nodded, thinking of my grandfather and that handful of clovers I'd tried to give him. I also remembered a winter visit to my grandmother when I was four or five. Grandma had let me go outside to play in the snow on my own, and I had stepped right out of my galoshes, which were too big for me, and kept moving through the snow in my stocking feet. In the time it took me to realize what had happened, my grandmother had darted outside, swept me up the stairs, stripped off my wet clothes, wrapped me in a wool blanket, and dumped me in front of the woodstove, muttering angrily about frostbite. That eagle eye and that swiftness contributed to the witchiness I so admired in her and that my grandfather found so unsettling.

Grandma still hadn't moved. "I can't see them anymore. I can't see that far." She sighed, and then she shrugged. "It's all right, though," she added. "I know they're there. I tell myself someone else will find them now." I looked at her with great love and a little sadness, unmoving and resolute in her neon-splatter-painted denim children's hat and funny-looking shoes, a pint-sized figurehead on a grassy knoll in the New York suburbs.

Then I looked again. At her feet was a halo of four-leaf clovers, neatly lined up around her toes.

"Grandma!" I exclaimed, kneeling to pick them. I held them out to her, but she pushed my hand away.

"You keep them." Still clasping my hand, she closed my fingers around them. "It's your turn for luck. I don't need them anymore."

When we got home from our walk, Grandma sat down and rested for all of thirty seconds, then popped out of her chair again. "I have something for you." She left the room and came back with a three-inch stack of photocopied pages.

"What are these?"

"My refugee files. I ordered them from the Swiss archives. Can you imagine? They kept such records of us, and they still have them."

"What's in them?"

Grandma shrugged. "I didn't look too closely. It brought back memories."

I flipped through the pages, which blew a little breath of air on my fingers as they settled back into the stack. "Thank you."

"Sure, well, you're always asking me questions, and I'm getting too tired to answer them." Grandma sat down again, heavily this time. "You want something to eat?"

I shook my head.

And then, apropos of nothing, she said, "It's good you'll be close to your grandfather. You can keep an eye on him. He needs you."

⌒

In February 2004, when I arrived at my grandfather's apartment in Geneva to pick up the keys to the house in La Roche, I noticed that the usual perfect order of his apartment seemed subtly disarranged. I had written and phoned to remind him of my arrival time, but he appeared surprised, though not wholly displeased, to see me.

"That's quite a lot of luggage," he remarked, with a disapproving gesture at my bag.

Automatically, I assumed his forgetting was a kind of reproof. "It's for the whole year," I pointed out.

"Really? Well in that case, I suppose it's not that much. Would you like some tea?"

"Yes, please." I trundled my suitcase into the sitting room, taking care to smooth out the scuffs on the green carpet. Usually when I visited, Grandpa placed a neat stack of sheets and blankets on the chair at the end of my bed. This time there was no bedding, just a pile of papers.

Grandpa appeared in the doorway. "I don't know, Miranda, how you prefer your tea. Do you like it weak, medium, or strong?"

"Medium, please." I straightened up and smiled. Something about him seemed milder than usual, which put me on my guard.

From the kitchen, I heard him call, "Pardon, I didn't hear your answer. Weak, medium, or strong?"

"Medium's fine—I'm just going to wash up."

"Miranda," Grandpa summoned.

I hurried back to the kitchen.

"Ah, there you are. Now, how do you like your tea? Weak, medium, strong?"

"However you like," I replied. Was this some sort of test? "Medium?"

Tea making, once a plain, established ritual, had become strangely chaotic. Grandpa's electric kettle sat abandoned on the edge of the kitchen windowsill while water boiled down to nothing in a saucepan on the burner. Grandpa chose a tea at random from the cabinet, and I saw that the regiment of carefully labeled jars he'd always kept on his shelf had disbanded into an aimless group of stragglers. "How do you like your—"

"Medium, please."

"Ah yes"—there was his triumphant slyness—"but is that medium-strong or medium-weak?"

"You choose," I told him, my worry easing a bit.

"I don't remember—do you take milk in your tea?"

"Yes, I do, please."

"I'm not sure if there is any," he said, looking thoughtful.

"I'll go and have a look." I opened the refrigerator and found a mess that confirmed my suspicions. The shelves overflowed with a seemingly endless repetition of the ingredients Grandpa appeared to be buying every day and then forgetting and buying again— Gruyère cheese, endives, butter, olives, eggs, and potatoes, over and over and over again.

I spied an unopened carton of milk in the door, checked the expiration date, and carried it into the kitchen.

"You don't take sugar in your tea, do you?" Grandpa asked.

"No, no."

"Milk?"

"It's right here." I took two rice-ware bowls from the cabinet and set them on the tray.

"We'll have tea in the dining room, I think," he suggested, "if you'd like to bring in the tray." When we got there, I waited while he moved stacks of papers to the end of the table to clear out a space for us. He looked up. "Do you like milk in your tea, Miranda?"

"It's here, Grandpa."

"Ah, yes. I'll go and get the teapot."

"It's here, too."

"Ah, yes. Silly of me. Sugar?"

"No, thanks."

"Me, neither." He looked ruefully at his little bowl of sugar packets, many of them open and half empty, all pilfered from various Geneva cafés.

We sat down.

"May I pour you some tea?"

We sat in silence and sipped. He smiled at me.

"It's good to be here," I offered.

"I'm glad you came. How did you get here? I'm sorry I couldn't come pick you up—perhaps I told you I gave away my car," he explained. "To a young couple at the UN."

"Why?" I asked.

He shrugged. "I don't need it anymore. It's too much trouble. I'm getting too old to have a car. I can take the train or the plane anywhere I need to go."

I didn't know what to say. This was the first time I had ever heard my grandfather admit to aging. We finished our tea in silence, and then I stood up.

"If it's all right with you, I'm going to clean your refrigerator," I said, waiting for him to fly into a rage at such a presumptuous proposition.

"If you would like to," he said. "I don't think I've cleaned it in quite some time."

I hid a smile. "I don't think so, either." Grandpa stood and watched me work for a while, then drifted away to the living room. As I cleaned, I tried to figure out what to do. My grandfather was eighty-eight, and other than a kindly couple across the hall, he had no one to help or look after him. He had alienated nearly everyone in his life. He did not appear to have any plans for his old age, either. The fact that he was still clean and tidy and put together seemed to be enough for him. How much help was he going to need, and how soon? And how was I going to give it to him? When I had finished with the refrigerator, I went to find him. He was sitting in the living room with a stack of books, staring off into space. "I have to take the trash out," I announced. "And then I'm going to buy some rubber gloves and some cleaning materials. Also some things to eat for dinner."

"What for?"

"Well, I've been cleaning the refrigerator. It's really quite filthy." I choked on my impoliteness, my peremptory tone, my impropriety, but he did not seem to notice. "And now that I've thrown out all the rotting and expired food, we don't have anything to eat." He looked skeptical. "I'll show you." He got up, and we walked to the kitchen.

"I see." There was a silence. "All of this was from the refrigerator?" He counted the trash bags waiting in the vestibule to be carried downstairs. "You've really done quite some work, here, Miranda. I feel really guilty."

If I'd been surprised Grandpa would admit to aging, I was downright taken aback that he would voluntarily name anything he was feeling. "It's not your fault," I reassured him. "You just don't remember."

We ended up eating dinner out that night, and I watched my grandfather dither over what to order. He noted his choice on a little piece of paper, slipped the paper into his shirt pocket, noted a different dish on the place mat, and then ordered something else entirely when the waiter came. The night had turned very cold by the time we left the restaurant; I said so, and Grandpa offered me his arm. We moved along in companionable silence.

"I hope you find the bed comfortable," Grandpa said, as if he had been meditating upon the matter for quite some time.

"Of course. I love that bed. It's like an old friend."

"Really?" Grandpa's voice sounded as if I had said something truly bizarre.

"Well, I've been sleeping there since I was a child," I reminded him.

"Really?"

"I slept there every weekend when I was at the International School." I felt a small, thready sensation of alarm.

"But where did we meet?" That was Grandpa the gentleman, puzzled, but always polite, always patient with strangers.

"Do you remember who I am?"

He shook his head.

"I'm your granddaughter."

He stopped and looked at me.

"Do you know who my mother is?" I turned my face to him. *How cold it is outside, how bitterly cold,* I thought. I wanted to keep going, but he held me still, my arm tucked firmly into the crook of his own. "Angèle," I told him, "I'm Angèle's daughter."

His blue eyes grew wide and sad. "Of course. *Tu vois? Tu vois comme je suis devenu idiot.*" We started walking again. When we got home, we wished each other goodnight, and I sat down on my little bed and cried. I would have given anything to have my bitchy old grandfather back.

⁓

The next morning I awoke to a quiet apartment. I could hear my grandfather's radio murmuring from his bedroom, so, timidly, I knocked on his door. "Come in," he called. I opened the door and realized I had never seen my grandfather supine. He smiled at me, the old cautious smile and soulful blue eyes. "Ah, Miranda."

I felt such tremendous relief, I thought I might turn into water. "You remember who I am?"

He looked mildly offended—wonderful! "Of course I do," he remonstrated. "I may be getting old, but I'm not *so* doddering as all that."

I spent the next few days in a flurry of phone calls to various senior citizens' service providers. I arranged for a visit from the social worker in charge of retirees' affairs at the UN, and my grandfather received her cordially. He accepted the pamphlets she handed him about retirement planning, assisted living, and home health aides, offered her tea repeatedly, and shook her hand twice as she was leaving. "She seemed quite pleasant," he remarked when she was gone. "But I can't imagine what she thinks I need all this for." He indicated the pamphlets.

I proceeded with caution. "You've been having some trouble with your memory."

"I know *that*. But it's hardly a reason to treat me like an old schnook."

I didn't answer. If he couldn't keep track of tea and groceries, what was next? What else would slip away?

My grandfather did not seem bothered by such questions at all. "Did you see I rearranged my library?"

"No, I hadn't noticed." My grandfather had so many books, he had to store them in double rows on his bookshelves, except in the dining room, where he kept a wall of white shelves only partially full, a promise to himself that there would always be room for more.

"Well, not the whole library," he amended. "I just rearranged the shelf behind you."

He gave me a little tour of the books there, explaining how he'd placed his leather-bound editions of Lessing and Mendelssohn side by side, since the two men had been friends in real life. I ran my hands over the gold-embossed spines. On the next shelf I saw an anthology of contemporary poetry whose brightly colored paper cover clashed with the other volumes around it. I picked it up and thumbed through it.

"Which is that one?" my grandfather inquired. I handed it to him.

"Oh, yes," he said. "I bought that in a St. Pancras bookshop because of the name of one of the poets."

"Which one?"

He smiled. This was exactly the kind of guessing game he liked. "Which do you think?"

I looked through the list of authors. None of them seemed familiar. I shook my head. "I don't know."

He pointed to a name: "Fraenkel."

"Who was he?"

My grandfather closed the book and put it away. "I had a friend by the same name. Fébus Fraenkel. An Austro-Hungarian medical student. He played chess—he made money by writing chess problems, actually. A truly extraordinary chess player. We used to play together. He'd let me open with one extra move. A clever man." He sighed. "He's the person who introduced me to your grandmother."

"Really?"

He nodded.

"When was this? When did you and . . . my grandmother meet?" Grandpa had by now acquired the faraway look on his face that often preceded his rages about my grandmother, and I tensed, waiting for the inevitable explosion.

"In the mid-thirties."

"Nineteen thirty-five? Thirty-six?"

"I don't remember. It must have been after 1935—I had entered the university. She wanted me to edit her thesis." He went silent.

"Did you?"

"A bit."

"How did your friend introduce you?"

"Oh, Fraenkel was very clever—very clever. Much cleverer than I—if I had known . . . He was looking to get rid of her, you see."

"And?"

"Well, he knew he could escape her clutches more painlessly if she had someone else to latch on to. Quite the dirty trick, no?"

I wasn't sure what to say.

"I was very naïve at the time. Have you read Proust?"

I nodded, feeling a little wounded. "Of course I have—you used to read Proust to me."

"Really?"

"Right here at the dining room table. You'd give me linden tea and madeleines and read aloud to me."

He looked pleased with himself. "How clever of me."

This wasn't the first time he'd compared his affair with my grandmother to that of Swann and Odette, and I'd already searched *Swann's Way* for passages that seemed pertinent:

He was introduced . . . by one of his old friends, who had spoken of her as stunning, a woman with whom he might be able to start something up, but he had made her out to be more unattainable than she really was, so that his introducing them would seem even nicer than it really was.

"Did she look like Odette?"

"Who?"

I tried again. "What was she like? What did you like about her?"

"She had beautiful hair. Coal black. Pale, white skin. Blue eyes."

"Like Snow White?"

"Yes. Like Snow White."

We were both silent. Eventually, my grandfather's dry, clean voice startled me away from my thoughts. "Does she visit you, Seraphina?" I looked up. He leaned forward. "I call her that as an ironic nickname, you know."

At least that's one thing he hasn't forgotten, I thought. His voice had taken on that dangerous edge I knew so well, but this time relief mixed with the nervous tension that gripped me when he skated to the edge of a rage about my grandmother.

"Does she still visit you, Miranda?" Grandpa queried again.

I chose my words carefully. "She's getting older, too. It's difficult for her to travel."

He puffed on his pipe, which made the dining room smell rich and warm. "You don't have much to do with her, do you?"

I shifted in my seat, tucking my feet onto the beam in the middle of the table. "I write to her," I replied warily. "I see her."

His voice was wound tight as thread on a spool: "You don't know her as I do."

"No," I conceded, feeling the limpid beauty of his airy apartment constrict around us. "I don't think I do."

"I should have known even then."

"Known what?"

He gave me a baleful stare. "Once I came to fetch her to go work on the thesis. And she wouldn't let me into her room. She just stuck her head out and said, 'Wait,'" he adopted the high, mincing voice he used when imitating her. "Then she closed the door again. So I waited, and I heard noises, and then she sidled out a crack in the door—like a crab," he waved imaginary pincers, "and closed it behind her, and smiled," his mouth formed a treacly smile, "and said, 'We can go now.'"

"What does that mean?"

"It *means*," he said, leaning across the dining room table again and looking over his glasses at me, his pale blue eyes wide with anger, "it *means* she was hiding a man in there."

CHAPTER NINE

SINCE THE HOUSE IN LA ROCHE HAD NO HEAT, I returned to the guest room in David's apartment in Avignon, which he had offered to rent me if I ever wanted a place to stay. I would live there until the weather got warm enough to move to Alba, I decided. Initially, I thought I would use the cold months to sort out what I did and didn't know about my grandparents, to begin sketching out their stories and figure out what questions I needed—and dared—to ask them. My temporary new home, with its tall windows and crowded bookshelves and richly colored carpets, felt like a reprieve from my nascent worries about my grandfather—and it offered the additional advantage of being an easy train ride to Geneva.

The U-shaped apartment occupied the entire floor of a building in a neighborhood just inside the rampart walls of the old city. I inhabited one leg of the U, with a bathroom and an office to myself. It was exactly what Virginia Woolf meant by a room of one's own, a beautiful, quiet space in which to write—and just as important, in which to be myself unhindered by the outside world.

When David wasn't off consulting with radio stations in former Soviet bloc countries, unearthing odd facts about dictators, collaborating on opera libretti, or collecting prizes in Italy, he would retreat to his half of the apartment and write. We gave each other a wide berth and avoided chitchat, but in the kitchen, our common territory, we developed an odd kind of intimacy. David wasn't my professor, my peer, or my mentor, and he did not try to be any of those things. As a result, he became a little of all three. He gave me books on the era I was researching, listened to me musing about my grandparents' past, and read drafts of my first book chapters. I observed the discipline and rigor he applied to his own work and tried to follow his example. I didn't know anyone else in the city, but it didn't matter to me. I was there to write. In many ways, I didn't feel as if I was living in an actual place. France felt like a giant mnemonic device to me: if Fébus Fraenkel and the date of my grandparents' first meeting could pop out from a random book on my grandfather's shelf, I had to be constantly listening, constantly vigilant, on the lookout for even the tiniest hint.

~

In Avignon, the breadth of my ignorance dawned on me: I knew almost no facts, no chronology, no geography. I tried to sketch a timeline of my grandparents' relationship and realized I didn't even know what year they had been married. As if she'd foreseen this snag in my plans, my grandmother sent me a package the week I arrived with a collection of her notebooks and loose papers. *"I thought you might find these helpful,"* she wrote. The stories and essays, most of which she had written in creative writing classes at her local senior center, were arranged in no particular order, and she'd included multiple drafts and copies of the same pieces. If Grandma's spoken words were a river, her writing resembled a dense jungle of information, only some of which had anything to do with the questions I was interested in answering. I read it all, hoping for a glimpse of my grandfather, or at least a glimpse of an empty space or silence where he might have fit.

My grandmother began medical school in Strasbourg in 1931, at the age of eighteen.

I loved it. There was a very active and intense cultural life. . . .

During my time in Strasbourg I attended Wagner's whole Ni-belungen. . . . Every spring the English Shakespeare plays, concerts, theaters galore, to have my fill when, I initially dreamed, I'll practice in my grandmother's village or nearby.

Interwar France was a heady place to be young, though its freedom, creativity, and tolerance were tinged, even in my grandmother's memory, with the darkness that was to come:

I did so well in pharmacology that the examining professor invited me to join his research lab. It never came to be as Hitler had already started to raise his head, and we saw Jewish students crossing the Rhine, seeking refuge. For a few days I hid a [male] Jewish medical student in my room at night. Females were allowed to visit, but even fathers or brothers weren't allowed in the rooms.

Reading this, I recalled my grandfather hissing, "She was hiding a man in there." I wondered if he was suffering from a seventy-year-old misunderstanding. Nevertheless, I began to comprehend his seething jealousy. Not only was he completely absent from her writing, he appeared to have had a lot of competition.

One paragraph meandered through an argument with a bacteriology instructor who had failed her for helping another student, a man named Rosenfeld, who passed the course thanks to Anna's assistance, and ended with a proposal: *"In our graduation year he asked me to marry him and settle in Montreal."* I couldn't help wondering if she regretted declining Rosenfeld's offer and the safety she could have had with him across the ocean in Canada, or any of the others she'd turned down, for that matter: the son of the Egyptian consul, for example, or an Indo-Chinese student she'd met at a Sunday afternoon tea.

I combed through her accounts of classes and suitors and social events, looking for an opportunity for my grandparents to have met during the year she wrote her thesis, but it seemed to me they barely would have had time for a cup of coffee. In her last year in medical school, Anna traveled to England to represent her lab director at an academic conference (where, she loved to tell me, everyone compared her to Princess Marie of Romania) and made her last journey home to do research for the dissertation her M.D. program required, the legendary train ride on which she'd told the traveling salesmen their fortunes. Upon her return to France, *"A particularly vicious pneumonia with very high fever sent me to the hospital, where, I was told later, I spent the first week in a semi-coma, in isolation, with no visitors allowed."* Her friends, inquiring about her at the hospital reception desk, were given a prognosis so gloomy that they took up a collection for a funeral wreath, a fact my grandmother found endlessly amusing. *"Only the presentation of my doctoral thesis was delayed,"* she exulted. Possibly because I was feeling rather discouraged myself, I imagined my grandfather walking disconsolately home from the hospital and dropping a coin into the collection box for that flower arrangement. And if he (or I) had hoped that her convalescence would afford some time for them to spend together, further reading revealed that Anna had gone on a rest cure in the mountains once she was released from the hospital.

The lack of concrete evidence of my grandfather's presence in her life only reinforced my belief that the best way to uncover my grandparents' secret was to imagine my way into it. I identified with my grandmother so deeply, and I knew my grandfather so well, that I was sure I could figure out what had happened, if I only could set all the facts around me like one of those Kleenex box dioramas I'd made when I was a child.

By letter, Grandma answered my questions in her usual sideways fashion. *"I forgot in which medical year I met your grandfather but know where. In a very popular café for students not far from the university.*" She mentioned in passing that he was taking German literature courses at the university, despite not having earned his baccalaureate—a war profiteer, I remembered her calling him, since he'd later managed to get a university degree through a refugee aid program in Switzerland without ever finishing high school. A joke to her; an insult to him. *"When I became friends with Armand . . . I started research for my doctorate [and] he helped,"* Grandma owned, *"but not as much as Prof. Larousse."*

I pictured Armand and Anna sitting and staring at each other surreptitiously in the din of a big café. He would have been annoyed by her expansive, candid chattiness; she intrigued and exasperated by his reticence and his scrupulous attention to every word he chose. The more I thought about it, the less I believed it was, as my mother had said to me when I was thirteen, simply electric. Or rather, I suspected the electricity had been there only as an undercurrent.

They disliked each other on sight, I decided. It was the autumn of 1936, and Anna had bold eyes and a smile she directed at you like a search lamp; her black hair would have been pulled into a loose bun at the nape of her neck, just ready to unravel. It would have taken her some time to sit down, since she would have stopped to say hello to half a dozen people, giving everyone her lit-up smile, or creasing her forehead into a worried pucker, or laughing in a manner Armand would have mistrusted.

Armand would have been sitting with his friend Fraenkel, waiting for Fraenkel to finish his conversation so they could start their chess game; perhaps Fraenkel was talking politics, and Armand was not in the mood for sincere, high-minded discussions. He didn't have much repartee; he would have sat quietly, smiling a little when someone turned toward him to include him in the talk. He would have had trouble not looking at her. Every time she spoke I bet he stole a glance around the table to see what the others thought of her, half-hoping someone would catch his eye to share a bit in his disdain.

Anna would have noticed Armand staring—she always noticed someone staring at her—and noted how he was making a show of ignoring the things she said. Anna liked a joke that was on her, so maybe she told the story about the time she got arrested in a cabaret for laughing too loudly. Then Armand would have murmured something snide to Fraenkel—"It seems her charm is so formidable it requires an officer of the law to be appreciated safely"—and Fraenkel would have introduced them.

Grandma, of course, revealed nothing of this sort. In her letter, she'd abandoned my grandfather almost immediately for her thesis adviser, Professor Larousse, concluding with an enigmatic memory: *"Because he was* 'fiévreux' *I went evenings to his home and this became an intense period of learning in all sorts of ways for me."* Again, I couldn't help sympathizing with my grandfather's wild insecurity over my grandmother's affections.

I had a copy of my grandmother's thesis, so I knew she'd presented it in the spring of 1937 and left soon after for postgraduate training at the sanatorium of St. Hilaire du Touvet, near the Haute-Savoie region of France. If she'd still been conducting thesis research in the fall of 1936, the actual paper wouldn't have been available to proofread until the end of the year at the earliest. The window in which they could have met seemed tiny—maybe six months.

I thought of all those men who'd wanted to marry her, and then of my difficult, diffident grandfather. Had she chosen Armand because he *didn't* pursue her? *Not that falling in love is really an active choice*, I thought, and went searching for more facts to add to my diorama. *Were you and Grandpa dating when you left Strasbourg for St. Hilaire?* I wrote to Grandma.

While I waited for her answer, I returned to the scene of their meeting: in the lost Strasbourg of my imagination, the plaza near the university was always lit, always full of people spilling out of cafés, scraping seats up to tables balanced tipsily on the cobblestones, their arms flung over the backs of their chairs, arguing, speechifying, playing games, making eyes, saying grandiose things about international politics and the menace of war beyond France's borders. I conjured Anna and Armand getting to know each other as they worked on that thesis, sitting side by side in the café, leaning toward each other as they went over Armand's corrections, their eyes meeting perhaps a little more often than was absolutely necessary. Somewhere in that time the distance between their bodies became noticeable, bridgeable.

A sudden, devastating love for Anna—if it was indeed comparable to Swann's love for Odette, then such devotion and desire must have swept over my grandfather. Swann had made Odette into a work of art in his mind; perhaps Armand had done the same with Anna. Perhaps what made Anna so fascinating to him was that she, like a great work of art, was possessed of a changing beauty. In the photographs in the album on my mother's shelf, sometimes my grandmother was stunning, so beautiful she didn't seem real, like a naiad or a dryad or a sylph—one of those unearthly creatures. And sometimes, to the contrary, she seemed somehow too earthy, disturbing, uncontrollable. It was easy to imagine visions of that beauty twisting around in Armand's mind when things went bad, transforming Anna into the hellion enchantress she was to him now, surging through his life on a sea of hurly-burly and mischief.

~

My grandmother's answer to my question seemed like no answer at all, and I sighed with frustration.

In 1937 . . . a famous "Prof" in whose lab I had volunteered pro-
cured for me an unpaid post, but permitting specialization in
phthisiology at St. Hilaire du Touvet in the Alpine "massif de
la Chartreuse," down the main road from Grenoble. I spent my
24th birthday in Grenoble invited by the Dentist, only other Jew,
a Sephardi from North Africa and colonial France. . . . We left
on an early [funicular], visited old and new parts of the town,
had lunch at the Bastille . . . [the] fanciest and most expensive
restaurant in Grenoble . . . and I wanted to return when Sam-
ama [the dentist] said he had counted to see a show with me and
spend the night in town. . . . No way! We had a few sharp words.
I returned on my own.

I sighed a second time: if my grandfather flew into a rage every
time my grandmother was mentioned, and my grandmother responded to questions about my grandfather by gliding off onto
other subjects, how would I ever pin down the facts? Returning
to the letter, I realized Grandma had at least given me a hint of an
answer to my question: she and Armand must have been dating,
but not seriously enough to preclude her being taken out for a fancy
lunch with another man. They couldn't have been terribly attached
to each other, I surmised—at least not officially.

With her letter my grandmother had sent more papers. They
turned up a single sentence:

My boyfriend, who later became my husband . . . was a longtime
resident of Strasbourg, and so I attempted to find a residency in
sanatoria in the region without success.

At that point I did what I usually do when I feel overcome with
contradictory thoughts: I called my mother.

As it happened, she had just returned from a visit with my grand-mother. "You'll never guess what's in Grandma's living room!" she crowed.

"What?"

"A little silver dish. It's been hidden in plain sight all these years on the big brass tray she keeps tchotchkes on. Like maybe a coaster you'd put under a very small stemmed glass—or maybe a dish a waiter would bring your change in, I don't know."

I had spent hours of my childhood examining those tchotchkes—and asking my grandmother for the stories of their origins—but I had never noticed there was anything special about that tarnished little dish. "Oh yeah, there was a branch of white coral on it that Vladimir brought her from the Red Sea."

"Yes, and there's a word stamped inside it. Do you remember that?"

"No."

"You'll never believe what it says," my mother repeated.

"Tell me!"

" 'Aubette.' "

"What's that?"

"Grandma said it was from the café where she met your grandfather."

"What? Really? Did she say anything else?"

"Not a thing. She said she can't remember why she has it, and then she changed the subject. I couldn't get her to say anything else about it."

"Can you imagine? Can you imagine how far it traveled?"

"I guess it survived the war because it was so small. It's just the size to slip in a pocket."

"I bet Grandpa stole it," I wagered.

"That's true. He has that whole collection of teaspoons." My grandfather had an elegant set of Georg Jensen stainless-steel flat-ware, but all his teaspoons had been snitched from various cafés, restaurants, hotels, and airlines.

"But then how would Grandma have gotten it? Wouldn't she have had to steal it from him? Do you think she took it when she left him?"

"I don't know," my mother owned. "But it certainly says *something* that they held on to it all those years."

To me, it said everything: whatever mystery persisted in the particulars, whatever details my grandparents had hidden, lost, forgotten, or obscured, that dish existed. One of them—or both of them—had made sure it survived. A tiny silver dish, carried all over Europe, across the ocean and back: its silence seemed far more elo-quent than any love poem I had ever read.

～

"Do you remember a café called Aubette?" I asked my grandfather, the next time we sat down at his table for our ritual teatime. Silence flooded the room.

"How do you know that name?"

"My grandmother told me . . ." I lost my nerve. "She says you liked to spend time there, when you were students." I held my breath.

"Liar," Grandpa hissed.

"Liar?"

"That's not where I went. I used to play with Fébus in a place that was much more modest, on the upper floor of one of the build-ings that lined the square."

"With Fébus—not my grandmother."

"With Fébus, of course. *Your grandmother* was a lousy chess player."

"So it's possible you could have met her in the Aubette?"

"Of course it's possible," he sniffed. "Just the kind of pretentious, showy place she would have enjoyed."

That night, after I had gone to bed, there was a knock on my door.

"Come in," I called, and my grandfather pushed the door open. He stood at the foot of the bed, his lips pressed together in a thin white line. I waited.

"That woman," he said. "You must know—that woman . . ." He trailed off with a strangled, desperate sound. "How could I? How could I have been so foolish?" He tightened his palm into a fist and gestured wildly. *"That woman,"* he repeated, spitting out the words. "She would love to see me undone. I won't have it. Do you understand me? I won't have it."

CHAPTER TEN

ONE EVENING IN AVIGNON I WANDERED INTO the kitchen to make myself dinner and found David pulling a stockpot out of the cupboard. "I'm making soup," he announced. "I picked up a chicken carcass from the butcher's. Care to join me?"

"Sure," I said. "Can I help?"

David handed me some carrots to peel. "I don't mean to interfere, but don't you want a little more company? People your own age?"

I shrugged. "Kind of. I guess. I don't know. I just want to work, I think."

David cocked his eyebrow. "I don't know, when I was your age—you just seem awfully serious all the time. Aren't you lonely?"

"I barely have a year to finish this," I countered. "And I'll be in Alba soon anyway. I don't have much time to meet people."

"True," he agreed. "Here, can you chop the celery, too?" He opened the refrigerator. "I don't know, Miranda, when you talk about your grandparents, who are, what, ninety now?"

I nodded. "More than ninety, actually."

"Well, more than ninety, long divorced, separated by an entire ocean—what's extraordinary about them is that they're more emotionally involved with each other than most married couples who have been living together for that long." He pulled out the chicken carcass and a bag of onions and set them on the counter. "There's no room for 'kind ofs' with a legacy like that."

"What do you mean?"

"Well, here you are, going off to live by yourself in an old dilap-idated house in the Ardèche, and—"

"I love that house," I interrupted.

"I know you do, but is it enough? Is it strong enough?"

"What does that mean?"

He chopped some onions and added them to the stockpot. "You know I hate psychoanalysts with a passion, but I read somewhere that houses are symbols of the human psyche." He turned to face me. "What are you going to do once you get to that house? What are you going to do once you figure out where all the feeling comes from? What are you going to do about you? Where's your love story?"

I couldn't muster a reply. Even though I had begun to realize I could choose my own way to live, every path I had found led me back to the past. I couldn't conceive of a better use of my time than waiting for a hint to come booming out of the silent chambers of my grandparents' memories.

⁓

The next time it was dried figs.

"Do you want me to soak them?" I offered, when Grandpa set out figs to eat with our tea.

My grandfather was as particular about his figs as he was about everything else: before eating them, he ran them under warm water and massaged them gently until they regained something of their original shape and consistency. I would never soak my own figs, but with my grandfather, one did not have a choice about such things; I ate them without question and found them good. But this time Grandpa said, "No need," and I felt a twinge of nostalgia for his fussiness.

We each took a fig. Maybe the seeds between his teeth made a sound like boots crunching over pebbles in the South of France. "I think the first time I ate fresh figs was in the army," he mused. "We were always hungry."

"Didn't they feed you?"

He shook his head. "The food was lousy. And young men are always hungry. It was fall, in the south. There were figs all around." He finished his fig and held his hands in a circle the size of a large dinner plate. "The *chasseurs à pied* had big berets, like this, and I remember filling mine with figs to eat."

"What else happened?"

"Then I lay down under a tree and had a nap."

"I mean, what else did you do while you were in the army?"

He marched his fingers up and down the table. "That. And I learned to take apart a gun, and put it back together, and clean it."

"That's all?"

"More or less."

"Wasn't it the war?"

"Yes, but nothing had happened yet. And the Germans were up north, anyway."

Emboldened, perhaps, by his lenience with regard to the dry figs, I pressed a little further. "Why did you enlist in the south if you lived in Strasbourg?"

"I bicycled down there."

"You bicycled? Wasn't that far?"

"I liked cycling," my grandfather said, taking a sip of his tea. "And when they evacuated Strasbourg, when the war broke out . . ." He looked off out the window. "The trains and wagons were all crowded . . . I was able-bodied. It seemed only fair to leave the seats to the people who needed them. And I was curious to see what the city looked like when it was empty." My grandmother had told me my grandfather had been fighting with his father when they parted ways. Had that been the real reason he hadn't left with his family? That was a corner of the minefield in which I didn't dare tread.

To my surprise, my grandfather kept talking. He saw his family off—mother, father, sister-in-law Rose, nephew Paul—on the second of September and waited to leave until the next day, or possibly the next. When the time came, he took his bicycle, attached the panniers, and stood beside his apartment building looking around the empty street. Bits of paper and empty cans rattled down the sidewalk; stray cats mewed; abandoned dogs wandered forlornly in the street. Before he left, he went back upstairs for one last look at his family's home, now emptied of their most important possessions. Everything else was swathed in dust cloths. The shutters were closed, the stove was cold, and the kitchen was bare, except for the glass crock of pickles Armand's father put up every year. They were still curing. On impulse, Armand reached up, took the crock off the shelf, and carried it down into the street. He couldn't possibly take it with him, he realized, but he didn't want to abandon it, either: he didn't want to leave anything the German soldiers might enjoy. So he smashed it, lifting it as high over his head as he could and dashing it against the sidewalk. The glass tinkled, and the little pickles rolled everywhere. The ocean smell of brine seeped up into his nose as it sank into the pavement. He thought he heard footsteps, and quickly he straddled his bicycle. He pushed off, then stopped, listening. The sound of footsteps was louder now, closer, accompanied by a little creaking sound. Armand held his breath. An old man in a ragged suit and bedroom slippers emerged from behind a building, pushing a baby carriage. There were two neckties and a tin can on a string around his neck. A pack of sad-looking dogs followed after him, looking hopeful. Spooked, Armand pushed off and biked away as quickly as he could, headed south.

"Why south?" I asked again. I was hoping for a mention of my grandmother, for I knew he'd gone to see her.

"I wanted to join the navy," Grandpa said. "I didn't know how easily I got seasick," he added wryly.

"Why the navy?"

"Because the Germans had a weak navy. Everyone was saying that the war would happen on land, not at sea." He laughed, full of regret and self-deprecation. "Of course everyone had had the same idea as me, and . . . how does one say, *j'ai traîné les pieds*—ah yes, I had dragged my feet to enlist, and the navy was full." He described the recruiting officer, a large, jovial man who rocked up and down on his feet and smoothed his handsome naval officer's jacket over his belly and called my grandfather *"mon petit." "Mon petit"*—my grandfather imitated the man's booming voice—"we aren't even taking fishermen's sons." Then the officer wrote the name and address of a friend who was a recruiting officer on a little piece of paper that he tucked into the breast pocket of my grandfather's jacket and sent him off to Sète, where he signed on with the *Chasseurs alpins,* an elite infantry in the French Army. In ordinary times, Armand would have learned mountaineering, cross-country skiing, and survival skills—possibly even how to build an igloo—but now the entire French Army was in a confused frenzy of disorganized preparation for a war that wasn't happening as they'd thought it would, so they all just sat around and waited instead.

This was the opening I'd been anticipating. The trail of my grandparents' love went cold in St. Hilaire du Touvet, but I knew my grandmother didn't stay there for very long. In November 1937 she was hired as chief assistant to Dr. Joseph Angirany, the head of a private sanatorium halfway between Lyon and Geneva, in a TB station called Hauteville. I knew from my mother's blue photo album that he had visited her there and from my grandmother herself that they had taken a vacation together before he enlisted. "Did you go to Hauteville?" I asked.

My grandfather looked startled, as if I'd made a rude and un-

Anna (front row, second from the right) with the staff of the Hauteville sanatorium in 1939. Dr. Angirany is seated beside her, in the center.

pleasant noise in the quiet of the dining room. "Whatever do you mean?"

"She—my grandmother—I thought—did you go to visit my grandmother in Hauteville?"

"Indeed I did," Grandpa said haughtily. "Once for my birthday and once when the war started." He sighed. "She gave me a travel blanket for my birthday, and she *berated* me when I lost it. Unbearable." His face darkened, and for a moment I worried he would crush his teacup in his hand. He set it down, though, and snarled, "No one could stand her. Even her precious Dr. Angirany threw her out. Of course, he was an anti-Semite."

"He was?"

"Everyone knew it."

"You knew him?"

"Yes." He leaned toward me. "Not the way she knew him, of course." He raised his eyebrows. "They had a relationship that was distinctly *hors professionnel.*"

"What does that mean?"

"I believe you're old enough to know what that means."

He poured himself some more tea and glared at me, daring me to ask another question, but I had run out of courage.

～

Back in Avignon, I looked up the distance. Five hundred kilometers he had bicycled to be with her. More than three hundred miles. I called my grandmother. "Did you expect you'd marry Grandpa, when he came to visit you in Hauteville?"

"What? Speak up. You know I can't hear a thing over the phone."

I raised my voice and repeated the question. To my surprise, she laughed. "Not really, no. Dr. Angirany was always trying to introduce me to other people. He didn't like your grandfather. I was a little surprised when he said we should go on vacation together."

"Did you share a hotel room?"

"Of course we did." From across the ocean, I heard the little creaky birdlike sound she made when there was something unresolved on her mind. Were they thrilled to see each other? Distracted by thoughts of war? Did they feel a bit awkward at first? But that didn't seem to be the unresolved question. *"Patron,"* she said. "That's what we all called him. He threw me out when the Germans came—I always wondered why. Your grandfather said he was an anti-Semite."

"Did he say anything to make you think that?"

"Angirany? No. But why else would he have thrown me out?"

～

Dr. Angirany had been my Grandma's professional role model, her hero, and her champion. *"In my later career,"* she wrote, *"I always compared my skill as a physician to his, and wondered whether I was as good as he was."* The two of them learned new diagnostic skills together, consulted with each other over difficult cases, and coauthored at least one paper. When the war broke out, every other doctor in the sanatorium was drafted, and Anna and Dr. Angirany ran the entire two-hundred-bed hospital by themselves.

These circumstances alone, I thought, would be enough to make my grandfather wild with jealousy; it was easy to imagine him try-ing to talk Anna into a bad opinion of her *patron* when she was sent away. But why *had* he sent her away? In my room, among the cold stones of Avignon, I tried to picture Anna and Angirany in the win-ter of 1939, exhausted and never warm enough, making the rounds of their frightened, displaced patients.

> *Despite our special allocations as a tubercular hospital every-*
> *thing became more difficult. The winter 1939-1940 was harsh*
> *and the "patron" was frequently ill from overwork and too lit-*
> *tle rest, so was I. My worst task was my mandatory presence at*
> *all funerals. We never had any before the war. Prognosis was*
> *quite precise and we summoned families of very sick patients*
> *and advised them to remove their family member to local facili-*
> *ties so they could be buried in family plots and local cemeteries.*
> *[Now], of course, evacuees were the sickest, [and] we had more*
> *work with less personnel and many, many losses. All this winter*
> *I attended the funerals, representing family and hospital . . . in*
> *freezing rain or snow on the windblown hill cemetery above the*
> *village . . . always a sad ordeal. . . . To this day I could perform a*
> *Catholic burial service and sometimes did so in my dreams.*

A memory returned to me of my grandmother sitting on the back porch of my parents' house one summer in Asheville and star-ing into the bottom of a dessert plate, across which was smeared a streak of bloodred raspberry juice. I asked her what she was think-ing about, and she said, "I had a patient, a student. A Belgian, a relapse who escaped to France. He survived a firing squad because when the bodies fell, one of them fell on him and they left him for dead. A miracle." With that word she pushed down hard on those dangerous memories and rushed on. "That winter Dr. Angirany—he was a former tubercular, like me, like most TB specialists—one day he looked at me and pulled me aside into an empty examining room and started unbuttoning his shirt." She smiled. "I always told him it was my real specialization certificate—he'd been coughing all winter, and he wanted confirmation."

I compared this rather incoherent version of the story to the written one I had before me. It was easy to see why my grandfather might have thought she and Angirany were having an affair—surely the idea of a man undressing in front of Anna, particularly someone she so admired, would have made him boil with rage.

The high point of my collaboration with [Angirany] was when one day, during the first war winter, he asked me to examine him. We were overworked and cared for many more patients than the sanatorium was built to carry because patients from around Paris had been evacuated to our region at the approach of the German troops. The patron started losing weight and coughed. I could hardly believe it when he asked me (and none of the venerable physicians of the other sanatoria) to examine him. I still remember how I was almost touched to tears, and told him that this gesture of his was my real specialization certificate.

～

Despite my grandmother's professional closeness with Dr. Angirany, I could find no evidence of any personal friendship with him. Nor could I find any logical reason for him to send her away. He began urging her to go south when the war broke out, more and more frequently as it became clear France was headed for defeat. *"A Jewish assistant didn't look right"* was how my grandmother explained it. *"Not really knowing what went on with my fellow Jews, I had never planned to flee, considering my place was with the patients."*

Fleeing may never have been her intention, but the pressure of the war kept mounting: the Nazis surged through the Ardennes and began pushing toward Paris. One day in June 1940 Anna happened to pass by the house of an acquaintance, a German-Jewish woman named Madame Rollo, who had been renting a cottage in Hauteville. Anna had dined with Madame Rollo and her parents multiple times before the war had made her too busy for socializing.

> *I found her, ready, packed to leave for Amélie-les-Bains, where the Paris Government had removed itself, as well as many Embassies and Consulates. She had some extra gas to last for the long journey. She invited me to join her and I did after picking up a few things to take with me.*

It looked like Dr. Angirany hadn't thrown Anna out; she was the one who decided it was time to go. Moreover, in my grandmother's Swiss refugee files, I gleaned an interesting fact: Joseph Angirany had my grandmother's work permit renewed on the very day France capitulated to the Germans. I cannot help but wonder—cannot help but hope—that he pressured her to move south because he feared for her safety. He would have been of an age to remember all too clearly the carnage of the last world war. Perhaps my grandfather's venomous jealousy was somewhat founded: perhaps Dr. Angirany truly cared for Anna and wished to protect her.

They must have parted on reasonably good terms because Dr. Angirany promised to send along Anna's trunks as soon as she had a forwarding address. He must also have promised to forward letters to her; indeed, maybe it is thanks to him that my grandmother and grandfather stayed in touch. However amicable their parting, though, it would have taken superhuman maturity and remove not to feel betrayed and abandoned by her *patron* for casting her out into chaos.

The journey, once we hit the main roads in the valley, is dimly remembered. We passed slowly through crowds of Belgian and Northern refugees with many children and old people. Some walking on foot, others in all sorts of cars, carts drawn by asses, horses, mules, and everyone carrying most prominently the gas mask canisters which had been distributed to the population at the outbreak of war. Overhead the constant noise of the German airplanes.

Where and how we spent the night I can't remember but do clearly the blackout. Everywhere in trains and roads, streets, only blue light bulbs, even in flashlights, were allowed. On the second day, toward dusk we arrived in Amélie-les-Bains. Streets were ultra crowded, everyone appeared frenzied. We spent the night in the small apartment of [Madame Rollo's] friends. No lodging was available anywhere. Our hosts were gloomily agitated. Food had become scarce and they had no news of their families. We had to register right away for ration cards. After a day or two I was assigned another residence north of Perpignan because I was Romanian. I was put on a Bus for Perpignan, where I had to change for another bus to Caudiès-de-Fenouillèdes. I remember walking around under a blue sky in unbearable heat dressed in a woolen blue coat (saving thus a garment by wearing it) and often crying in self-pity, while waiting for the right bus. I had very little money, I felt all alone in the world of the South, being a Northerner and mountain-dweller. I was too tired, also hungry and dehydrated to think of the frightening unknown ahead.

I always had idolized Grandma, but in Avignon, I began to learn all the reasons there were to worship her, beyond her charm and beauty and intelligence and witchiness. Now I saw the moment in her life when, alone in a place she'd never been, with little money and no resources, she'd rolled up her sleeves and become heroic.

> *At this point, Madame Rollo lived with [her mother and step-father] while trying to get visas through Spain and Portugal for her way to Alexandria Egypt and her husband. Being certain of the Germans' occupation of all of France, [Madame Rollo's parents] disappeared into the surrounding mountains to commit suicide, so as not to be in her way. She [came to Caudiès and] appealed to me to help find them.*

By this time, I had learned enough about the war not to be shocked by this fact; indeed, my grandfather had translated an entire book about suicides related to the political situation in Austria and Germany in the late thirties and early forties. My grandmother, with her usual resourcefulness, found the nearest army unit.

> *I approached the Commandant of the Senegalese troops, who were, at the time, stationed in the region awaiting their return to Africa. . . . [They] willingly sent several groups into the hills in all directions to search for the old couple. One group found them and brought them into the village. The woman was dead, the man in a coma but still breathing. A burial ground and hospital were needed, only to be found farther [away] in Perpignan. The daughter . . . [took] it for granted that I'd accompany her, which I did.*

My grandmother's matter-of-fact tone, I thought, very nearly hid the astonishing bravery of this act. *"The transport of dead people by unauthorized persons,"* she noted dispassionately, *"was punishable by law, as I well knew."* Had they been discovered, Anna and Madame Rollo would have been arrested and deported immediately. Nothing daunted, Anna had the Senegalese soldiers carry Madame Rollo's parents to the waiting car.

> *The stepfather, whose breathing was obvious, sat next to her. I was in back, with the pale, dead body propped up, and made efforts the whole way to keep it thus. . . . All along the route . . . [were] numerous checkpoints . . . where gendarmes asked questions, and looked into the car and trunk. I did all the explanations: I was a physician and we were on our way to a hospital to help these obviously very sick and dying old people. Miracle! They let us pass each time.*

When they arrived in Perpignan, Madame Rollo learned that her Egyptian visa had been granted and was faced with a dilemma she found unbearable: she could depart and abandon her parents, or stay by their sides and risk deportation herself. Because they were foreigners, my grandmother wrote,

> *The only hospital available to us was a very miserable one set up on the edge of town for the influx of Republican Spanish refugees during the Spanish Civil War and the debacle which followed Franco's victory. . . . Upon arrival . . . the woman was declared dead and burial permit granted. The man, without regaining consciousness, died the next day.*

My grandmother did not say whether Madame Rollo hesitated and had to be pushed to save her own skin, or whether she abandoned my grandmother and her parents without a backward glance.

Nevertheless, *"I stayed to see both her parents buried in the cemetery reserved for foreigners and Spanish refugees, in a bleak field not far from the hospital. I never saw or heard from the daughter again."* I considered searching for Madame Rollo, but did not know where to even begin; my grandmother could not remember the exact spelling of her sur-name, let alone her given name. But Grandma took the unsatisfying end to this story for granted—what was one more fate among all the ones she had resigned herself to never knowing?

I remembered a taxi ride from Alba during the summer I'd spent there: the driver, a local man, had asked what I was doing in the Ardèche. I gave him a brief explanation, and he inquired, "When did your grandparents go to America?"

"After the war."

"Where were they during the war?"

"Here in France, in hiding. They fled to Switzerland in 'forty-two. My family's Jewish."

"My family hid Jews during the war."

"Where?"

"Here." He gestured outside the taxi. "In the barn, first, then in the attic. I used to bring them food. I remember a family from Lyon with a boy my age. They got out. They moved on, I mean. Don't know what happened to them—always wondered. We never heard from them again." We were silent. Anything could have happened to them, we both knew. "I think about them a lot. I like to imagine them in America." He brightened. "Like you."

"Well, it's because of people like your family that people like my family survived."

Chance encounters like his, or like my grandmother's with Ma-dame Rollo, were incidental, anecdotal, anonymous drops in the rainstorm of history. Among so many raindrops, what was the point of lingering over Armand and Anna? Maybe a half century of silence was incidental, too—even to them, unremarkable in a life full of incompletion. But then I thought of the glance I'd exchanged with the taxi driver, both of us slightly awed at the way unfinished business is sometimes partially laid to rest, a long time later, by other people—two loose threads picked up and tied together, across a hole that nothing could ever fill.

CHAPTER ELEVEN

APRIL CAME AND WARMED THE STREETS OF AVIgnon. In the sun, on certain days, it almost felt like summer, and I decided it was high time to go to Alba. As it happened, a friend of mine from Asheville was teaching English in a high school an hour north of Alba, and he offered to help me open the house. So when Grant's classes let out for spring break, he met me in the train station in Montélimar, and we took the bus to Alba, or rather to the bus stop about a mile and a half away from the village. From afar, the castle and La Roche looked particularly fantastical and imposing in the orange-tinted late-afternoon light, and I felt gleeful and proud to show him the house.

But Shakespeare was right about April's uncertain glory. As soon as we walked under the archway to the rue de la Double, the quiet strangeness of the place struck me. Unlike Avignon, where the sun had melted all but the slightest of chills, La Roche felt as if it had accumulated a winter's worth of dark and cold and was hanging on to them grimly. The contrast from the sunny parking lot we had just crossed was so stark, it felt as if we were dropping down a well. When we got to the house, I scraped the cobwebs off the doorknob and pushed the door open across the uneven stones, breathing in the sweet, slightly mineral scent of the abandoned house.

It was late afternoon, and the daylight was fading fast; we walked down the dim, gray-green hall and tried to get our bearings. I felt a strong wind hit me and heard Grant call out. When I stepped

over the threshold into the back room, I saw that all its windows
had been smashed. So much debris had blown through the jagged,
empty frames that it looked like the back garden had staggered in
and died all over the floor: everything was carpeted in dead leaves
and vines, dirt and stones.

"It must have been kids," Grant speculated, picking up a rock
and turning it over in his hands. He held it out to me, and I took it
and dropped it onto the floor again, kicking it away from me as if I
could punish someone with the action.

We realized there wasn't anything we'd be able to do about it
that night, so we bolted the door and went back to the front room.

"We can do this," I affirmed.

Grant nodded. "It's not that bad."

I regretted my decision not to buy a sleeping bag. We kept ourselves warm by cleaning and reduced the level of filth to the point
that we didn't shudder when we touched things. We sat down to
a cold dinner of cereal, milk, and bananas, which felt even colder
once we realized the gas tank for the kitchen stove wasn't empty.
Then we pulled the curlicued metal bedstead to the center of the
room, as if by doing so we could escape the cool seeping in through
the walls or imagine a fire in the sooty, abandoned fireplace. Grant
climbed into his sleeping bag, and I wrapped my down vest around
my feet and pulled Grant's coat over my shoulders. I was still freezing. It was so cold that the air seemed colored by it, as if the room
were unable to absorb the chill. Unable to sleep, I stared into the
dark and thought about my grandmother, lost in the chaos of the
capitulation, looking for a place to stay.

❧

*I was dumped into the Village Square and handed the paper given
me in Amélie-les-Bains to the Gendarme who met me. Everyone
around viewed me with suspicion. The Gendarme, with a grim*

smile, informed me that nowhere was a room to be had and I better not camp out. What to do?!

I believe it was the village priest, present in the square at the time, who advised me to try the Veuve Flamand. This pertained to a café in a sidestreet whereto I was directed. Below street level, I entered an empty long room, dimly lit, with rows of tables and chairs along the walls. It was cool and I was exhausted. Mme. Flamand met me and I explained my presence. She was short, rotund, wearing dark clothes. Her face was round-squarish, riddled with smallpox scars, her eyes were brown and shrewd. Knowing the history of the disease which scarred her face for life, I recognized a survivor in front of me. She interrogated me tightly while also telling me much about herself. She was a Republican Spaniard who had worked in France . . . and had married old "drunkard" Flamand to get the house with café and some small landholdings. . . . She didn't believe I was a physician. Certainly I didn't look like one in my disheveled, exhausted state. She never mentioned her disbelief, but I knew. Finally after I had a cool refreshing drink, she said she only had an attic room she could let me have, but she didn't think it would be suitable. I asked to see it. Two flights up, the last dusty and dirty beyond belief. At the top a rickety door, poorly closing, giving into a room with a large window closed and shuttered, over the street below. Mme. F. opened window and shutters to reveal a thickness of dust inches deep covering the floor and every other surface. A rusty metal frame bed with mattress and what looked like rags heaped on it. A washstand on a primitive half table, a chair, completed the room's furnishings. Mme. F. with a broad smile questioned me without words. This was it or spending the night where?

I asked if I could get a pail of water, some soap, a broom and rags and maybe a hammer and nails to drive into the wall for hanging up a few of my belongings as there was neither an armoire nor a chest of drawers, after I had cleaned the rooms. Mme. F.

stared at me, collected what was on the bed, saying the mattress wasn't too bad and she'll give me bedding. I don't know if it was then and there, that what I later on called the "university of my life" started. Surely without my war experiences I couldn't have become the person I am today. I followed Mme. F. downstairs and this time into the kitchen with a large open hearth, where cooking was done on tripods supporting the soot-stained pots. A very large table and chairs stood on the dirt floor. A sink with running cold water was placed under large South-oriented windows. I got the pail filled in the sink, was given a large piece of soap (savon de Marseille, the best in France) as well as plenty of clean rags. I can't remember how many trips up and down and how many rags it took to remove the dirt and dust, air the mattress, and organize the room. Mme. F., huffing and puffing up the stairs, brought me coarse, but very white and fragrant sheets and even a bedspread. She admired—with looks, no words—my accomplishment. I asked about the price and with full pension, three meals, it was five francs a day, if I looked otherwise totally after myself. I was determined to stay as at this price my meager savings could last quite a while. I understood that Mme. F. was regarded by the villagers as an outsider and opportunist. She seemed well intentioned toward me, saw me also as an outsider, not being a French citizen.

In the dark, dusty house in La Roche, the green streetlight lit the room just enough to make me feel like a little lost creature shivering at the bottom of a murky sea. I reassured myself by imagining my grandmother in the hot June night, looking around at the temporary home she'd made for herself, the noise and movement in the café ebbing and flowing around her until she dropped off into uncertain sleep. And I pictured Grandma now, lying in her own soft bed in her house in Pearl River, and how proud she would be that I had come all this way, had come to reclaim the house she'd bought so long ago. I felt a little wriggle of belonging, however insecure, and clung to it fiercely.

Just then Grant woke up and pushed open the front room door to go to the bathroom. Seconds later he backed into the room again and shut the door with a bang. "There's a crowd out there."

"A crowd?"

"I mean not people, but a crowd. Of . . ."

"I know," I replied, without thinking. "But they're friendly."

"You know? You can feel them, too?"

I rubbed my eyes and tried to consider this question rationally, then gave up, since it was clearly not a rational question. "Yes, I can. I mean, I know they're there."

"I can feel them looking at me. Looking me over." He shuddered.

"They want us to be here." I pulled Grant's coat around the dissipating warmth at my middle. "They're just checking you out."

"I'm going to pee in a jar. I'm not going out there."

"No, I'll go with you." I got up, clutching the coat around me, and we returned to the hall together. While I waited for Grant, I wondered what it would be like for that sensation to be surprising, to not constantly feel the past crowding around you.

The next morning, over hot coffee in the sunshine on the terrace, we could almost forget the house's ugly, broken-down insides. Grant and I sat soaking up the light and warmth of the day and debated about what we should do next, given that we had no tools, no car, and no money.

At the time I was convinced it was possible for me to reach into the past and feel the contours of my grandmother's experiences, but I now imagine the opposite was true. I see Grandma's spirit reaching forward, across time and space, to help me make a home for myself. On that particular day in April, help came in the form of

Youssef, a handyman I knew from the brief trip to Alba I'd made during the summer I'd spent conducting thesis research in Avignon. Youssef is a man who seems to subsist on nothing at all: no one knows where he is or when he will be there; he is rarely where you expect him to be; and he is always present when you aren't aware you need him. Now that I have actually established a home for myself in Alba, I rarely see him. When I do, he barely stops for a hurried hello. But back then, when I had nothing and knew no one, Youssef appeared out of nowhere and helped. He brought tools to scrape the broken glass out of the window frames, plastic to cover them, and kindling for the fireplace. And most important of all, though I didn't realize it at the time, Youssef invited us over the little footbridge that spanned the Escoutay River to the "Le Camping," Alba's campground, which had an outdoor café and restaurant on a big shady terrace. Things have changed now, but back then it was where people went to grab coffee or a sandwich during the day, or to have a drink after work or on the weekends. Youssef introduced us to everyone he knew, including Yohann, the owner, who offered to let me use the showers when he heard the house in La Roche didn't have hot water.

The plastic on the windows made the house feel less exposed to the elements, but it was still too cold to inhabit. At the end of the week, Grant went back to his teaching job, and I returned to Avignon. Until his departure from France in June, he met me almost every weekend in Alba, usually with one or two friends in tow. When I had visitors from the States, I brought them along, as well. I usually woke up earlier than the others, and cooking breakfast, I'd feel a little like a lady in a mining camp, ladling out porridge and hot coffee to our grimy little crew. Within our limited means, we'd work on making the place more habitable, but also we'd just goof off, walking as far as we could along the dry rocks that littered the bed of the Escoutay River, dancing around the terrace in the late spring rain, playing improvised midnight baseball on the path behind La Roche. The nice thing about rural France, of course, is that you can eat like an empress, even if you are living in a glorified rock pile. We'd cook big dinners, drink wine, and listen to music on a little clock radio Grant had donated to the house, or head across the river to hang out at the campground.

When I tired of jug showers and sleeping in the cold (though I did acquire a sleeping bag after those first awful nights), I'd trek back to Avignon for a nice long bath and a night free of spiders and scorpions. As I began to get to know people in the village, I thought often of my grandmother settling into Caudiès and of the adamant advice she had always given me: "You just have to talk to people. It's how you *sourrwvive*."

❧

At first, my grandmother spoke only with Madame Flamand, sitting with her in the cool, dim kitchen and helping her with the housework and meals: *"To find out if I was a legitimate doctor Mme. F. steered every woman and child with complaints (never men) toward me. She was later on told I must be one, from the way I asked questions and examined them."* In this way, my grandmother made this strange village into something of a home, putting down tiny, tentative roots as she cared for her new neighbors. I wondered what it had felt like to write to her boss with her address so he could ship her possessions to her, whether the pleasure of unpacking her trunks and recovering her bicycle was overshadowed by the pain of losing the position she'd loved so much.

My grandmother had jotted these memories on yellowed scrap paper, in an essay she said was inspired by "the reading of Robert Hughes's *Barcelona*." The clearer-than-usual explanations made me think she must have submitted it to a writing teacher who'd taken the time to edit and ask questions. And for once, I was amazed to see, she not only admitted she had written to my grandfather but even elaborated on how he'd come to visit her in Hauteville after the evacuation of Strasbourg and before reporting for the draft.

This being my grandmother's essay, she segued directly into a story that would have repercussions for her and Armand even after they moved away from Caudiès, about the time she'd been summoned in the middle of the night to care for the local gendarme, who'd been injured in a motorcycle accident. *"He was lying in the middle of the road, crying out loudly with pain. Because of the blackout and faint moon, the assembled crowd appeared in black shadows, as did the vehicles."* I pictured her feeling around in the dark for her stethoscope and listening to his elevated heart rate, placing both hands flat on either side of his chest. When he inhaled, one side of his chest would have fallen under her hand: bad fractures, possibly fatal, if she didn't immobilize them. "It's going to hurt," she would have warned him, working fast, calling out to the crowd for extra clothing to roll up and wedge under him. With no straps or blankets handy, it is likely she had to turn him with his own jacket, placing the bulk of the extra clothing below the broken ribs, then pulling the sleeves of his jacket to keep him pinned still until the ambulance came. *"I explained all this to the gendarme, whose face I never saw, heard only his voice and got to know his chest under my examining hands."* Another man to spark my grandfather's jealousy. *"Much later I found out that my diagnosis was confirmed in the hospital and he was considered lucky that I had been able to be so precise and save him,"* my grandmother concluded. *"He and another gendarme in St. Paul (where I moved subsequently with Armand) kept us off deportation lists."*

The essay's last two sentences, the first irritatingly loopy and long, the second concise and subtly self-critical, made me miss her terribly:

*Myself come from landed Jews—my parents being the first gener-
ation in town; on both sides my grandparents were village people
keeping a general store in their respective hamlets, but their main
interests were in the fields and cattle they owned—I had often
participated in field activities and had listened to lengthy inter-
changes about crops, barnyard residents (hens, ducks, geese, tur-
keys), how to save their offspring when in trouble and such. Thus I
never held back with advice to villagers about such matters.*

Homesick for a bit of that unsolicited advice, which had reassured me in childhood and aggravated me as a teenager, I picked
up the phone and called her. "I just wanted to hear your voice," I
shouted, when she answered.

"Well, here I am, still alive."

"I should hope so!"

"Well, at my age, you never know. It's interesting, in a way, to
watch your body shut down," she observed cheerfully.

I did not feel like shouting about her body shutting down, and
I was sure she didn't either. "I have lots to tell you," I hollered.
"About Alba. I'll write you a letter."

"VAT? Write it in a letter, Mirandali. You know I can't hear
you."

"That's what I said, I'm going to write."

"Very good."

"I just called to say I love you, and I miss you," I went on, but
she had already hung up the phone.

$\sim$

With each visit to Geneva, every few weeks, I cleaned out my grandfather's refrigerator and worried about his decline. I taped index
cards with my phone number on every available surface, so Grandpa
would remember to call me if something happened, and every time

I departed, he took them all down, giving us something to do and discuss before we settled in for tea on the next visit.

Grandpa seemed to be on a fig kick; this time, once again, he put out figs to have with our tea, and just as before, something in the sticky gypsy sweetness at the back of his mouth sparked a story. At first I thought it was the same tale, and I felt disappointed, both for the sake of my curiosity and the sake of his failing memory, but I kept quiet, just in case he added a new detail.

"We ate a lot of figs during the war. I remember walking south to"—he thought better of whatever he was about to say and altered the direction of his sentence—"walking south after I was discharged and picking figs to eat." We chewed our own figs in silence, and he added, "They make you sleepy, you know. But you have to be careful, if you're napping outside."

"Careful of what?"

"Well, for example, you have to pick the right tree. You must never sleep under a walnut tree."

"Why?"

"It gives you a headache."

"Really?"

The look on his face hinted that high umbrage was not far-off. "Why would I tell you so if it weren't true?"

Before, his tone of voice would have stopped me in my tracks. Now I just changed tack. "What did you do during the war?"

"Waited around, mostly, with the *Chasseurs* . . . the fighting was all in the north, you know. I was transferred to the *Tirailleurs marocains* when they found out I was Jewish. And then I was discharged."

"Where did you go afterward?"

"To the Pyrénées-Orientales. I had a job there, picking grapes, and a place to stay." He finished his fig, took a last sip of tea, and picked up the leather pouch that held his pipe.

"With Madame Flamand?"

My grandfather stiffened. "How do you know that name?"

Everything I knew about Madame Flamand I knew from my grandmother, but I wanted to delay Grandpa's rage for as long as possible, so I prevaricated a little. "I—I heard you mention it once."

Grandpa cupped his left hand around the bowl of his pipe, a pinch of tobacco between his right thumb and forefinger. "Of course I knew her. She was a fine woman, a Spanish anarchist. After the war I tried to go visit her, to thank her—I drove down; I wanted to give her some flowers. But she was dead." All was quiet. I worried that he would begin to weep, and we would have to sit in our painful remembering silence, but he went on, in a detached, absent voice: "Her daughter was there. But she didn't seem particularly interested in all of that."

"Did you live with her?"

"With whom?"

"With Madame Flamand?"

"Yes, of course I did." He looked at me as if I were mildly touched, as if to say, *Where else would I have lived?* "She had a sort of an inn, I think, we rented." That rare and fugitive *we*! I waited with bated breath, but Grandpa caught himself. "One could rent a room," he amended. "I worked in the grape harvest." He went back to packing his pipe and made a small uncomfortable motion with his shoulders.

I thought I'd take a little risk. "That's why they didn't send you back to Morocco, right? Because she sent you an exemption saying you were needed for the harvest."

"Who sent me an exemption?"

"Madame Flamand—and my grandmother."

"How could she have sent me anything? I had no address."

"What about a military base?"

"It was the end of the war," he asserted irritably. "Everything was in chaos." He reached for his matches, lit his pipe, and inhaled quietly. A puff of fragrant smoke escaped into the room. "They discharged me with five hundred francs and a certificate saying I'd fulfilled my military service. They'd taken my papers at the beginning of the war—they said I would be a citizen when my military service was over."

"Were you?"

"Of course not." He drew on his pipe. "No, of course not. But they had taken my papers, and when I went to recover them, they were gone."

"Gone?"

"Mislaid, no longer valid—I can't remember exactly." He made the same vague, uncomfortable motion with his shoulders. "All this is in the past." He pushed his empty teacup away from him, put his pipe back in his mouth, and looked out the window at the mountains. The conversation was over.

⁓

As I washed up after tea, I pictured Armand trudging down a long road through the hot summer of 1940, with his feet sweltering inside his boots and socks, his tongue parched in his mouth, thinking of cool water. I imagined in him a dry, expansive longing for my grandmother that exceeded even his great thirst. I imagined him imagining her and feeling a certain tension pressing out from inside of him, a little ache, an always emptiness. One foot in front of the other down the hot dry road with a memory of her dark, soft hair between his fingers. In my mind's eye, sometimes he would pick up speed, lashed along by his passion to have the whole of her. I liked the idea that she hadn't written to him at all, liked to think my grandmother acted upon my grandfather as north spins a compass needle. But probably she was the one who was right, and he simply had her address because she'd sent it to him. Either way, my grandfather would have been hurrying through the middle of a plain hot day that did not yet know what part of history it would become. He was headed to Caudiès because Anna was there, and he was hurrying because he had nowhere else to go.

In my mind, Caudiès was a place the color of cornbread, where the high sun turned the stone buildings into black shadows of themselves. Inside Madame Flamand's café it would have been dim as the inside of a rain barrel, and I imagined Armand ducking his head as he opened the door and walked in, blinking in the light, looking around at this new strange home.

In their first night together at Madame Flamand's, they would have lain in wakeful silence, listening to each other's breathing, acclimating to each other's presence. Looking at the accordion of sky and weatherworn wood made by the shutter, they glimpsed the blacked-out heavens pierced by chinks of light, a multitude of stars clustered as thick as the nerves in their restless, sweaty bodies. In the soft heat, with the silky, dim moon lighting up their skin in little luminous stripes, they would have stared at each other in wonder.

I set the teacups in the drainboard and looked out the window, realizing as I did that shutter slats point down, to keep out the rain, and they wouldn't have been able to see the sky at all. I shook my head, feeling defeated. What other mistakes had I fantasized into their story?

~

By the end of June, it was warm enough to move out of my room in Avignon and live in La Roche full-time, on my own. Grant had finished his teaching job and returned to the United States, and I didn't have any more visitors scheduled for a while. David helped pack my belongings into his car and drove me there. He had donated a mirror, a potted petunia, a teapot, and some mugs to my new home, but when he saw the place, he exclaimed, "My God, I should have given you a cement mixer and a tool belt. Are you sure you'll be all right?"

For a second I saw the place as he must, a dilapidated pile of stones in an anonymous village, and felt a shiver of trepidation. Then I thought of my grandmother and shook that vision off.

"You can always come back to Avignon if you need to," he offered as he left. I thanked him, but I had no regrets about leaving Avignon, no doubt in my mind that La Roche was where I wanted to be.

Once David had departed, I sat for a long time on the terrace wall, watching the sun pass over the orangey lichen, green ivy, and shaggy grasses that covered the basalt crystals of La Roche. If I turned my head, I could see the castle peering down at me from atop Alba's hill, half hidden by trees. The house was scrubbed as clean as it could be, and it was warm enough that having no glass in the windows was no longer a problem, as long as I pushed the furniture out of the way when it rained.

It was a strange responsibility to have taken on, camping out in this wide-open house at more or less constant risk of vandalism. No one ever disturbed the property while I was there, but whenever I left the place for more than a few days, the marauders would return, moving things, upending things, breaking things. The house wasn't mine, but I didn't want to abandon it to its fate. Whatever I had come to France to accomplish, I wanted to accomplish here. La Roche, for better or for worse, was my place. For just a second, I felt gigantically happy, sitting on the terrace wall and watching the wind sift through the leaves on the trees by the Escoutay. With no little awe, I remembered my vision, seven years before, upon seeing the house for the first time. *This is my heart's desire,* I thought, *and I have fulfilled it.* It was an extraordinary feeling.

CHAPTER TWELVE

M
Y EXALTATION LASTED UNTIL THE SUN BEGAN
to dip behind the hamlet. Gradually, the shadows edged
the light and warmth off the terrace, and I put on my
sweater again. Except for the wind, La Roche was utterly silent. If
I shouted, no one would hear me. I thought of the broken windows,
the rotting terrace door, and the leaking roof; I thought of the fact
that the house wasn't mine and might never be; I thought of the fact
that, even if it were, and I did manage to fix any of those things, the
place still wouldn't be comfortable, or even really habitable. The
electricity was faulty; there was no hot water in the bathroom; and
the inside of the house was a warren of unfinished, dingy, imprac-
tical rooms. My happiness deserted me just as abruptly as it had
come, and I felt daunted, even frustrated, by the idea that I had
actually followed through on this strange desire. What had I been
pursuing? What exactly was I expecting to find?

I stood up and hurried out of the house, up the hill to the village,
as if I could elude these questions by moving quickly. At a loss for
anything else to do, I bought myself a newspaper and walked down
to Le Camping.

The terrace was crowded, and Yohann was busy with customers. I ordered a coffee at the bar and took it to an empty table,
where I could see the trees, the river, and the castle beyond. I was
still alone but surrounded, at least, by the hum of people. I was
perusing my paper, feeling nostalgic for afternoons with friends
and family, when I heard a chair scrape across from me and looked

up. It was Julien, whom I had met on one of the Saturday evenings Grant, his friends, and I had spent at the campground. From that first encounter, I had learned that Julien was a stonemason, had lived in America for a year, attended architectural school and quit, and worked with his father restoring old houses. He made puns that worked only if you were bilingual, and he espoused ferocious political, literary, and architectural opinions. He was tall, wore small wire-framed glasses, and had thick sandy-blond hair and blue-gray eyes. From afar he looked a bit fierce, even warriorlike, but up close, he had a deep, infectious laugh and a smile like a delighted little boy. He reminded me of a Greek statue or an archangel missing his wings.

Now he was standing beside my table with his hand on the back of a chair. "Do you mind if I join you?"

"Not at all."

Julien sat down, took off his glasses, and rubbed the bridge of his nose, which was speckled with white flecks of lime plaster. "What a day." He picked up my newspaper and glanced at it. "Am I bothering you? Maybe you wanted to read."

"No, no, I haven't really talked to anyone all day. Nice to have some company." I had wondered, since meeting him, what made him different from the other people I'd met in the village. "Were you born here?" I ventured.

He nodded. "Not far from here—about an hour away, in the high Ardèche. In a commune, actually. My parents are from Paris. Came here in the seventies—back-to-the-land types—you know, Jean Giono and all that."

"Do they still live in the commune?"

"Nope—it didn't really work out the way they wanted it to." He seemed to be considering how much he wanted to tell me. "It's a long story—it ended badly . . . direct action, violence, the SAC, that sort of thing . . ." He trailed off and waved his hand as if to push it all aside. "What about you?"

I told him about the house and my grandparents.

"Yes, but what about you?" he repeated.

"What do you mean?"

"I mean, what are you going to do now you're here? Do you have a job? Are you going to stay?" He had a firm, warm voice that was both humorous and rigorous, and he leaned forward as he asked these questions, fiddling with the spoon that had come with my coffee cup. Then he leaned back and smiled. "You're a bit of a romantic, no?"

"I have a fellowship from my university. For a year. Then I don't know."

"So what are you doing for a year?" He relaxed into the plastic café chair and observed me. He was quite tall, and his legs were stretched along one side of the table. Despite his lounging posture, something about his gaze, or his manner of listening, made me feel as if he could detect the things I wasn't saying, too. "Figuring out what happened to my grandparents and writing about it. They have an extraordinary story—I mean, it's always important to know what happened to your family, don't you think?" I trailed off, worried I sounded defensive.

"Sure," agreed Julien. "But you can't live in the past. Not always, at least."

"You should see my living room. In fact, you should see my whole house."

He laughed. "I'd like to." He stretched. "I've been sitting here for twenty minutes, and I haven't even ordered anything. Can I get you a drink?"

"I don't know—first you call me a romantic, and then you tell me I'm living in the past, and now you want to buy me a drink?"

He waved at Yohann, who started over to our table. "I have nothing against being a romantic," he declared.

When we'd finished our drinks, Julien gave me a ride back to La Roche, and I showed him around the house. When he saw the warped terrace door and the plastic over the windows, his brow furrowed. "What are you going to do about those?" he asked. "When the summer's over, I mean." He squatted down and ran a fingernail over the cement holding the terrace doorframe in place. "This has got to be redone," he told me, brushing his hair away from his glasses. "You see how the water has been running down and rotting the wood? That's why it's warped."

"I know—I mean, I know I'm going to have to replace the door. I actually have a door," I added, brightening. "Youssef said he would help me install it when he had the time."

I led Julien to the tower, where I had stowed the door Grant and I had bought the month before, at Youssef's urging, from a big home construction warehouse. We'd tied it to the roof of Grant's borrowed Renault Super 5 with a ball of twine and driven home with me hanging out the window, clinging to the door so the wind wouldn't push between it and the car and blow us off the road, feeling like *The Clampett Family Visits France.*

Now Julien stared at the door dubiously. "Did you measure your doorframe?"

"I didn't have a tape measure. And the door was on sale . . . Youssef said we should grab it."

Julien didn't say anything right away. Though I didn't recognize it then, I would soon become familiar with the perplexed squint he got on his face when things weren't logical. "Hang on," he instructed, and disappeared through the front door, reappearing moments later with a tape measure, which he unrolled against the frame of the door I'd bought. "Two hundred and four by ninety centimeters. Standard." He walked back out to the terrace and turned to the rotting doorframe. "Eighty-two centimeters. And eighty-three down here." He hooked the tape measure onto the top of the door's stone threshold and stood up again. "One hundred sixty-eight centimeters." He slid the tape measure to the other end of the threshold. "And one hundred seventy point five over here, if you want to split hairs." The tape measure slid back into its case with a clang whose finality passed the judgment Julien was too discreet to voice.

"But Youssef said—" Even as the words came out of my mouth, I laughed at the mental image of trying to get the door to fit. "I don't know what he was thinking."

Julien looked a little aggrieved. "Either Youssef was hallucinating, or he is a far better carpenter than I am." He hooked the tape measure onto his pocket and sat down on the terrace wall. "You're going to have to get a door made, I'm sorry to say. But I'll hang it for you when you do."

I couldn't imagine when that would be or how I would find the money for it.

～

Grandma's words became my creed—you did just have to talk to people. Soon after I moved in, I walked by the hotel where she and I had eaten lunch when we'd visited Alba in 2001 (and where she thought she'd slept back in 1948) to say hello to the owners. Of course they remembered my grandmother. They wanted to hear all about her and about what I was doing in the village, and when they learned I was trying to get together enough money to pay for doors and windows, they offered me a job cleaning rooms and waitressing at banquets. It wasn't regular work, but it was a big help.

"Any honest thing you work hard at you should be proud of," my

grandmother replied when I wrote to tell her about my new job. *"One of my proudest accomplishments was during the war, picking grapes. We picked grapes for fifty-six days straight, without stopping. They said they'd never seen anyone do that, not even the professional pickers."*

I was familiar with this part of Anna and Armand's story. Indeed, it figured prominently in my fairy tale of their life together: an evil power had forced a prince and princess from their rightful stations in life, sent them into hiding, and required them to perform impossible tasks. They'd begun on the shores of the sea, moving through a sweaty haze of sun, dust, and cicada buzzing, the bright green vines wavering over the ochre-colored hills and out of sight. They worked with a ragged horde of people, surely dukes, princes, queens, and ladies like themselves, stripped of their names and their pasts, disguised as migrant workers and gypsies, whole thin families of them lined out between the vines on the big estates, the women clipping bunches of grapes and laying them in the narrow metal containers the men carried on their backs, the older children taking care of the younger ones at the edges of the vineyards.

My grandmother loved to tell of the magic that operated in those times, of how the rocky ground became soft as a feather bed when they lay down at the midday rest. Her favorite part was the abandoned castle in which they slept, to my mind a tacit acknowledgment of her hidden royalty. *A pile of hay in a tenth-century stone tower with the most beautiful view,* Grandma would recount, *unbelievable, how beautiful it was.* And there again, the magic operated: they were wrapped in a mantle of fatigue, so finely woven they barely noticed the pinprick itch of fleabites as they lay in the hay. At the end of the day, with the breeze coming off the sea, they looked out over the land from the dark of the stone tower and did not know when the end of the story would come or what would happen when it did.

"Hard work," my grandmother wrote me now. *"We were so hun-*

gry. We would creep back into the vineyards at the end of the day to pick
the fallen grapes, or the green, hard ones still on the vines, and eat them.
I weighed ninety pounds at the end of that summer."

I put down the letter, feeling ashamed of myself. How could I
have romanticized months of grueling manual labor, no fixed domi-
cile, and near starvation?

They returned to Madame Flamand after the grape harvest of
1940 but didn't stay long with her. By the end of the year, they had
decided it was too dangerous to keep living there and moved to St.
Paul de Fenouillet, a larger market town about ten kilometers to the
east. Though the Vichy government was not yet arresting French
Jews in any systematic manner, by early 1941 they had begun rounding up foreigners, both Jews and non-Jews, and sending them south
to prison camps in the Pyrenees. My grandparents' legal status, or
rather their lack thereof, was more and more of a problem for them,
particularly after the Vichy government passed a law in August
1940 forbidding anyone who was not a French national to practice
medicine. My grandparents may also have moved to protect Madame Flamand, whose citizenship would have come up for review
in 1940, since she was a Spanish refugee and had been naturalized
after 1927, one of the cutoff dates the Vichy government used when
assessing people's nationality. Perhaps they had not wanted to draw
any undue attention to her.

Anna and Armand moved during one of the rainiest seasons on
record in that part of the world, a fact I knew from another of my
grandfather's secret doorways to the past, a small painting he kept
hidden in his apartment, pressed inside a book. I had discovered
the painting during one of the weekends I spent at his house while
attending boarding school. As with all those little symbols, I never
knew why he decided to show it to me. One day he pulled a volume
from a high shelf and took from it a small, many-colored painting

on a piece of thick watercolor paper. It looked like a mosaic, or a window of opaque colored glass, angular forms fitted together in the shape of a shield.

It was a gray day, and the whole of Geneva was filled with a dull, pearly light, which shone into the room where we stood and made the colors in the painting glow as we held it between us.

"Who painted it?" I ventured, finally, when Grandpa didn't say anything.

"Otto Freundlich. Do you know who that is?"

I shook my head. He took out his dictionary of proper names, found the page, and handed it to me, his finger on the entry. I read the first sentence aloud. " '*Freundlich (Otto) Peintre et sculpteur allemand (Stolp, auj. Slupsk, Poméranie 1878—camp de concentration de Lublin-Majdanek, Pologne 1943).*' " Freundlich (Otto) German painter and sculptor (b. Stolp, a.k.a. Slupsk Pomerania, 1878—d. Lublin-Maidanek concentration camp, Poland, 1943). I finished reading about the man whose painting my grandfather kept hidden in his library and handed the dictionary back to him. He put it away without a word. "Did you know him?"

My grandfather had set the painting on his desk to pull out the dictionary. Now he picked it up again; we stood and looked at it.

"I knew him during the war. I'm not sure how he managed to make it down south from Paris, but he did."

"How did you meet him? Did you live in the same town?"

"There had been floods in the south, and they washed away a great many roads and small bridges around Caudiès and St. Paul. So after the harvests were over, I got a job with one of the work crews the government assigned to repair them."

I asked what he'd done on the job.

"I learned to use a shovel. I dug ditches. I mixed mortar." He held out his hands, which were still, even in old age, thick and strong. "I got calluses." We inspected his hands. "But they gave us special titles as compensation: I got to be a *technicien des ponts et chaussées*." He pointed his nose in the air as he said it, and the whole room pulled itself up around us in mock pomposity. "Bridge and roadway technician, if you please.

"And one day I was working on the road," Grandpa made a shoveling motion, "and I saw a very tall man coming toward me, with white hair, very striking. There was something so striking about him that I dropped my shovel and walked up to him, holding my hand out like this." My grandfather reached out and shook my hand, conveying a young man's shy admiration.

"Then what happened?"

"Well, I introduced myself, and he introduced himself. He said his name was Otto Freundlich, and he was a painter. We got to be friends. We—I would go and see them quite often, him and his wife, and sometimes they would reciprocate. He gave me the painting—they had destroyed all his paintings, and he was trying to repaint them all."

"They had destroyed his paintings?"

"They said he was a degenerate artist."

"What happened to him?"

"Someone denounced him. And they sent him to Maidanek."

Silence. We went back to the dining room, away from the silence, away from the book and its hidden memory.

~

"*From Caudiès we went to St. Paul de Fenouillet,*" my grandmother wrote. "*A market town with shops, a doctor, and some nice houses as well as a hotel from where the refugees were lined up for the extermination camps later, and rentals.*" They lived in two locations in St. Paul: first, in the winter of 1940, a small room with an open hearth and an iron tripod for cooking, and then, by spring of 1941, a second-floor apartment in a house with a garden for raising food and rabbits, cold running water, a woodstove for heating and cooking, and two upstairs neighbors: *"Tante Erna [and] an awfully nice and (Polish) excellent seamstress-tailor. Armand worked at the Cooperative, which allotted agronomic and viticultural products . . . for the region."*

Erna, circa 1947.

I knew Erna as my grandmother's best friend and my mother's godmother, whom we used to visit in St. Gallen, Switzerland, before she died of kidney cancer when I was twelve. When my mother and her brother spent time with their father in Geneva as children, Armand would put them on the train to St. Gallen to visit Erna, and then she would put them on the train back to Geneva. That was about all the contact he could bear with Erna, who was too close to my grandmother for his taste. Once Erna had asked him why he refused to speak to my grandmother. "She talks too much," he'd declared, and stormed off.

On my next visit to Geneva, I asked, "What other work did you do during the war, after you were demobilized? Did you spend the whole time working on the roads?"

"No—only that first spring in St. Paul de Fenouillet."

"Grandma—my grandmother—said you worked in an agricultural cooperative," I ventured.

"Did she?" Grandpa's face took on its dangerous look, and I regretted having mentioned her. "I did. I was even the nominal head of the cooperative. But do you know the thing about the agricultural cooperative?"

I shook my head, no.

"I was its only member. Its only employee." His tone had become supercilious, aggressive. "So you see it couldn't last."

This didn't make sense to me, but I was afraid to pursue the subject further. "What else did you do?"

"This and that. Whatever I could. I worked in a workshop that made nuts and bolts. I made brooms, for a traveling broom salesman. He was supposed to bring us the materials, which we paid a small price for, and then come back and collect the brooms, to sell them, and then bring us the money." He smiled ruefully. "But as you can imagine, he didn't. Then for a while I had work as an accountant with a merchant who sold a lot of things on the black market—ham, and chocolate, and so on—which he never shared with us, of course. But times were very hard, you know. He couldn't keep me on. Or so he said."

"Did my grandmother work?"

"No. She didn't have a job. She stayed home," he said dismissively, standing up. "She went looking for food, she worked in the garden, took care of the rabbits, she kept the house. I don't know. I'm going to make some tea. Would you like some?"

"Yes please." My grandmother had described that second apartment to me:

> *Our furniture consisted of a kitchen table, two chairs, and a small chest for the very few cooking utensils, cutlery, and dishes we possessed. Much was kept in boxes. In our bedroom, we had a somewhat larger than a single bed and the second room held our clothes suspended on strings or kept in suitcases. We also stored supplies there of whatever we could get as food shortages grew daily.*

Grandma spent endless hours looking for food, sometimes biking a whole day's journey into the mountains, only to return with a single egg for dinner. Her new place had a garden and room for rabbit cages, which eased their hunger a little. Just as important, it offered companionship in the form of those upstairs neighbors. My grandmother's friendship with Erna ultimately would save my grandparents' lives, but in the spring of 1941 in St. Paul, Grandma already felt it was a godsend. Despite (or perhaps because of) the presence of my grandfather, her loneliness must have been colossal, having fled her position in Hauteville and been stripped of the legal right to practice medicine, her one great calling.

Then their landlord found a wild baby rabbit and brought it home.

> *I sort of fell in love with this tiny creature and proposed to take it in and [see] if it could be tamed. I found a feeding bottle and rubber nipple and fed it first milk, which it sucked well, adding gradually grasses and twigs for its growing teeth. It grew and got fat. We named it Zigomar. I invented the name because the sounds pleased me. . . . Zigomar became tame, following, looking at us, as if he knew who we were and playful. We kept him strictly in the kitchen . . . [which] became too restricted, and he tried to escape*

each time the . . . door was opened. Thus he met a premature and accidental death when he somehow slipped under a moving foot and was crushed. We truly mourned him.

My grandfather called me from the kitchen.

"Would you mind coming in here?"

"Of course not." An acrid smell of burnt plastic hung in the air, and I went to open the window. Grandpa held up his electric tea-kettle. "Something happened to it—it doesn't work anymore." The bottom of the kettle had melted into a ghoulish smile. "See," he put it on the little three-burner gas stovetop in his kitchen, "when I put it on the stove, there's the strangest smell—"

"Grandpa, don't!" I exclaimed. I pulled the kettle off the flame.

"What's wrong?"

"It—it doesn't work anymore. Why don't we go out and get you a new one?" I placed the metal cover on the stovetop and switched off the gas, and then we put on our jackets and took the elevator down to the lobby. "Shall we walk or take the bus?" I queried as we stepped outside.

"I think we should walk, if you feel you're up to it," Grandpa suggested. "Are you in good shape?"

I hid a smile. "I should be asking you that question."

"Why?"

"Well, you're going to be ninety next summer."

"Are you sure? What year is it?"

I told him, and he calculated. "Indeed I am. A regular Methuselah."

At the store, I picked out an electric hot plate and a kettle with a safety shutoff.

"Is this for you?" Grandpa asked in the checkout line.

"In a manner of speaking."

"I see."

When we got home from the store, my grandfather went to sit down while I disconnected the gas and set up his new kitchen appliances. A piece of paper had fallen behind the gas tank, and I reached back to retrieve it, hoping it wasn't anything important. It was the stub of an electricity bill. Grandpa had noted the date he'd paid it, a year before. Beside the date he had scribbled, *"C'est comme si un clapet se fermait sur ma mémoire."* (It's as if a valve were closing over my memory.)

"What's all this?" Grandpa stood in the kitchen doorway and pointed at the hot plate and the kettle.

I slipped the paper in my pocket and smiled at him. "New kitchen appliances."

"What was wrong with the old ones?"

I hesitated, not wanting to make him feel I was infantilizing him. "You know, gas is dangerous in apartment buildings. I think it might be against the rules."

He ran his hand over the sleek white kettle. "I don't know how to use this."

"It's very simple." I showed him the button you pushed to get the water to boil and explained about the automatic shutoff.

"I see you're intent on ushering me into the modern age," he observed. "Well, let me make some tea and see how I like it."

I set the table while he measured tea into the teapot. Beside the box where he usually kept tea biscuits I found another scrap of paper. On it, he had written, *"Ma mémoire = ma passoire."* (My memory = my sieve.)

I decided to show him this piece of paper. He smiled when he saw it. "I can't remember who said that. Ironic, isn't it?"

I nodded, moved by the gentleness this new weakness seemed to engender in my grandfather. Again, I felt a tug of urgency: I had to gather his memories before they disappeared. "Do you remember St. Paul de Fenouillet?"

He nodded. To my surprise, he looked pleased to be talking about the past, as if he were happy to find himself on terrain that didn't involve knowing what was in the refrigerator or operating fancy kettles.

"Do you remember raising rabbits?"

"How do you know all these things, Miranda?"

"I think they're important," I stuttered, not wanting to ruin the moment by mentioning my grandmother but knowing I would have to sooner or later. "You're my grandfather, after all. It's—it's our history."

"Hardly fascinating," he protested, but he was still smiling.

"Do you remember the little wild rabbit that lived inside the house with you and—and my grandmother? She says the villagers thought she was a witch because it followed her around all the time."

The smile snapped off Grandpa's face, and he looked just like old times. I braced myself. "I'll say it followed her around," he sneered. "Do you know how it died?"

"It was crushed to death, wasn't it?"

"Excellent use of the passive voice. Excellent."

"What do you mean?"

"She stepped on it. Didn't see it had hopped up behind her." There was a nasty, metallic clang to his words, as if he were slamming them on the table one by one.

I was horrified.

"She was inconsolable," he conceded, sounding just barely apologetic for his meanness.

I stared at him, speculating about how my grandmother might first have perceived the harshness I'd always known in him, whether it had insinuated itself into their relationship as water infiltrates a stone wall or shot out like a lance when the pressure of the war began to build. I turned my gaze away before he noticed and pulled myself together. I had more questions to ask; I might as well keep going now that I'd started.

"*I had found this summer a wonderful supply of raffia in the most beautiful and varied colors,*" my grandmother had written. "*I made myself a pair of colorful sandals by crocheting tightly the fiber and sewing them together using double layer for the sole and lining the inside with cardboard. These sandals were much admired, light, cool, summery. I was asked if I could do others.*"

With her usual resourcefulness, my grandmother talked the village cobbler into lending her his forms, and she threw herself into shoe production with the same energy she had once spent on patient care and cutting-edge diagnostic techniques.

> *I was a one-person factory, at times Armand helping, and though I remember at the height of production working from very early morning to late at night, I could not produce much, as I also took pride to do it well. Those multicolored sandals were really very pretty.*

In the summer of 1942, as "Free" France grew less and less free and my grandmother searched for a way out, everything, even a few strands of raffia, began to look like a lifeline. "*I was told that an American Jewish Agency [in Marseille] tried to get out Jews and also supported those stranded. . . . They could do nothing for me, and they could not give support either anymore.*" She couldn't remember if she'd sent them a sample pair of sandals or simply asked for advice, but someone in Marseille had found a retail outlet for her sandals. For a time, she wrote, "*I could have had a real factory with many workers to fill the orders I got subsequently.*" But not for long: the raffia ran out, and there was no more to be found anywhere. Since there was, to my knowledge, no organization called the American Jewish Agency operating in Marseille in 1942, I surmised that she had written to the American Relief Center, run by Varian Fry, whose memoirs I was reading at the time.

"Have you—did you ever hear of Varian Fry?" I asked my grandfather.

"Of course I have."

"Did you ever try to contact his agency?"

"Why would I do that? It was all hopeless by then." He pressed his lips shut, as if to crush the memory of those myriad disappointments, and gazed away from my face. "Besides, he helped artists and writers and such. Who was I? Do you know the Yiddish word *chutzpah*?" Although he meant the word in its traditional sense of shameless effrontery, I privately thought my grandmother had shown it in the American sense of self-confident audacity. I wondered whether they'd argued about her writing that letter, and although loath to mention my grandmother again, I saw no way around it. "My grandmother says that she made raffia sandals and you helped her, that summer, and that she—"

"*She* made them?" he interrupted. "*We* made them." He sniffed. "She wouldn't have been able to do it without me. It was hard work. Crocheting the raffia tightly was difficult enough, but she wasn't strong enough to sew the soles together, once she'd made them. We spent all day together, working on those shoes."

All day together. I saw them sitting at that kitchen table, bent over the same task, united. All the things that must have bound them to each other: waiting to hear from the American Relief Center in the hope it had found some way to get them out of France, waiting to hear from the shop in Marseille, waiting to hear from the woman who'd sold them the raffia. And beyond that, all the little ingenuities their everyday life demanded of them—not to mention missing their old life, craving things they could not have—and, threading through it all, fear. They must have loved each other, I thought, even if it was only the causal consequence of eating together, working together, sleeping together. Surviving together. *Sourrwviving.*

"Did you . . ." *Did you love her?* I wanted to ask. I hesitated; my courage failed. "Did you like it?" I finished, lamely. "That is, I mean, did you find it satisfying, working together? Selling something you had made?"

He looked thoughtful, almost dreamy. "When I look back . . ."

I waited.

"When I look back, it's as if . . . it's as if I were blowing on leaves. Like a layer of leaves spread out" . . . he held his palms together, facing up, "and I blow on them" . . . he blew a puff of air over his hands, "and they lift for just a second" . . . he made a fluttery, upward motion, "and fall" . . . he fluttered them down again, "before I can really see what's under them."

～

Julien had told me to call him if I wanted a ride from the station in Montélimar when I returned from my grandfather's, and so I conquered my shyness and did. When I stepped out of the train, I saw him waiting for me in his old gray Citroën. He got out of the car as I approached, and we kissed three times, left cheek, right cheek, left cheek, as people do in the Ardèche. He put my bag in the backseat. "How was it?" he asked. "How's your grandfather?"

"It's hard to tell." I recounted our adventure with the kettle.

"Have you thought about what you're going to do when he can't live on his own anymore?"

We left Montélimar and drove over the Rhône River. "I have thought about it. And I don't know. He has no plans, and he doesn't seem to believe it's ever going to happen. And it's not like I can force him to move."

"What about your mom and your uncle?"

"They're so far away . . . what can they do? At least I can keep an eye on him."

"But then who keeps an eye on you?"

I shrugged. I had felt excited, excited in a purely youthful, non-grandparent-obsessed way, upon seeing Julien. His questions made my heart swerve back to all my worries, and I felt a bit like crying, which in turn made me feel embarrassed. It felt strange, talking to someone who seemed to tap into my feelings so directly.

"You and your questions." I mustered a smile. "I don't have any answers today. Tell me what's happening with you."

"Same old, same old," he said. "It was a pretty good week. Minus is getting big. Minette is going to reject her soon. I need to find her a home." Minus was the kitten of Julien's cat, Minette.

"I'd like a kitten."

"You live too close." He looked at me out of the corner of his eyes and grinned.

"Why is that a problem?"

"The kitten will find its way back to my house, and you'll follow it, and my house will be even more crowded than before. You've seen my place. It's small enough as it is."

"Minus would stay with me," I insisted. "I'd take good care of her. I'd shower her with affection."

He laughed. "Seriously, I can't give you a kitten. What would you do with it when you go back to America?"

"Maybe I don't want to go back to America," I countered. "Maybe I'd rather have a kitten."

"Oh, really?"

"Who knows? I like it here."

"Well, if I give you a kitten, does that mean you'll stay?"

I smiled and shrugged. "We'll see."

Julien dropped me off in La Roche. "There's a little music festival this weekend. You should come. Maybe I'll see you there?"

When Saturday night arrived, I made myself go. I stayed out late, listening to music and chatting with people. I was pleased to discover how many familiar faces there now were in Alba. Toward the end of the evening, I ran into Julien, and he invited me back to his house for coffee. It was two o'clock in the morning, and neither of us is the kind of person who drinks coffee at two o'clock in the morning, but we're both people who like to do what we say, so we sat at Julien's table and drank our coffee, talking about this and that, Minus the kitten playing at our feet. When we had finished, there was a shy silence. "I should be going home," I said, getting up. Julien rose, too, and walked me out onto his terrace, which was overgrown with honeysuckle. The stars were out. The air smelled sweet. It was chilly, and Julien wrapped his sweatshirt around my shoulders. He kissed me on the forehead. *"Je vais m'occuper de toi,"* he promised. "I'm going to look out for you."

CHAPTER THIRTEEN

THE NEXT DAY, A SUNDAY, I WALKED UP THE HILL to Alba to buy groceries for the week, my new market basket swinging on my arm. The first person I ran into was the innkeepers' daughter, who winked and said, "Julien, huh?"

I blushed and smiled, and she laughed. "Good for you. He's a good guy." And that was how I learned there are no secrets in a village the size of Alba.

This realization made me think differently about my grandparents' time in Caudiès and St. Paul. I had always used the words *hiding out* to describe their time in the Pyrenees, had always, in my childhood nightmares, searched for a place to hide. But now it occurred to me how extremely visible and exposed they—and particularly my grandmother, with her cures for the sick and her unsolicited advice—had been. Now I understood: my grandparents had not survived because they were hidden. They had survived— miraculously—because they were known.

In St. Paul de Fenouillet . . . I knew the doctor and had made friends with some of the upper-crust citizens. One of them—an elderly lady living in a substantial house on a square surrounded by the important shops; i.e., the center and not too far from the side street where we lived—held sort of a "salon" in her very large front room. . . . Whoever came for anything to the center [of town] stopped by and in to dispense news, comments, sit down, had a drink, tea or else. I was there almost daily and apparently popular—I believe . . . her name was a typical one for the region, "Peyralade." She was important, respected, valuable for advice and help. . . . It was she who ordered a pair of wool gloves for the gendarme, gave me the wool, afterward said they fitted and were appreciated. When Erna and her roommate at four a.m. were woken up and me to interpret, one new gendarme (apparently) asked about me. I froze, when the other gendarme—I thought later had the gloves I knitted—turned to the questioner and asked: "Is she on the list?" whereupon I was asked my name, not being on the list he was told that they had yet to get elsewhere, and they left with Tante Erna and her roommate.

I had been in Alba just a few weeks, and already the baker knew what kind of bread I bought, the grocer knew the brand of dish soap I preferred, and the man at the newspaper shop knew I read *Le Monde* and the *International Herald Tribune*. There were no house numbers in the village, but the postman delivered my letters to me all the same, from the very first day. People in villages are masters of discreet prying. Several times a week I found myself explaining who I was to a total stranger—only to realize halfway through the telling that they knew already and were just seeking confirmation. "Jacoubovitch," they'd muse, when I mentioned my grandfather's family name. "Ah, yes, that house by the river. I remember."

I thought of my own arrival in Alba: Youssef bringing plastic sheeting for my windows; the innkeepers offering me work when they learned I needed money to fix up the house; my neighbors bringing me vegetables from their garden. Perhaps Grandma had wanted a house in a village in the South of France as a kind of insurance policy. If she was capable of sending a jug of kerosene to my mother through the U.S. Postal Service "just in case," then why not hang on to the house in La Roche for the same reason? Maybe this was the place she'd always intended me to be, so that I, too, could learn to *sourrwvive.*

> *It was the summer of 1942. . . . Under the Vichy Government [the] foreigners [had been] assigned to "forced residencies" under surveillance of the gendarmerie. In [St. Paul,] this small town of 2,000 inhabitants, the largest group resided in its only hotel. Many were old, feeble, and sick.*
>
> *After the roundup, all were taken to the gendarmerie to await a truck, which would transport them to a destination unknown to the locals. Clever tactic! as many French, though looking benevolently on German rules, nevertheless would shy away from a "final solution," meaning pure and simple, unadulterated murder. Only the victims knew.*
>
> *By eight a.m. the collected group was still crowded in the narrow entrance hall of the gendarmerie, sitting on benches, on the floor, or their scanty luggage containing the few essentials they were allowed to take with them. They hadn't eaten since the day before and were full of apprehension and foreboding. So was I. To allay anxiety and fear I started going from shop to shop begging for food. Most, so approached, gave, some generously. Guilt, pity, powerlessness, shame? Who knows? Some food items we hadn't seen in ages, traded on the black market and not given out, even when we had rare coupons for them.*
>
> *To convince a French inhabitant to bring food to the gendarmerie was hopeless, and their warnings that I risked to be equally retained and shipped off if I went were not encouraging. But I did go, ashamed of my fear and heart beating into my throat. The gendarmes, when I arrived, ignored me, looked away, some scanning the road for the expected truck. The misery I saw was difficult to bear, and what could one say? Some women weak and sickish had collapsed or fallen asleep wherever they were, and the air was*

*filled with gloom. At noon the truck had still not arrived. I made
a second trip. The atmosphere had become more unbearable.*

*I learned later that the truck hadn't come but close to five p.m.,
when I was on my way for a third visit and had been retained by a
gossipy neighbor, which might have saved me. The memory of this
day never faded. For a long time during and after the war, I had
to deal with "survivor guilt," and this brief, evanescent, modest
act did not count.*

On that day in 1942, when the gendarmes arrested Erna and her
Polish roommate, they were sent south toward the sea, to the camps
France had originally set up to house refugees from the Spanish
Civil War. Now they were overcrowded with luckless people for
whom both visibility and invisibility had failed: refugees from the
north and the east, Jews, Communists, political dissidents, gypsies,
homosexuals, and foreigners. The camps had harsh names: Gurs,
Argelès, Rivesaltes, Le Barcarès.

When my grandmother delivered food to those awaiting deportation, Erna's roommate gave her a pale pink damask napkin
as thanks, to remember her. At five p.m. she was taken away, most
likely to Rivesaltes, where she would have waited no more than a
week before being deported to Drancy. Two or three days at most
in Drancy, and then to Auschwitz. Of the 41,951 people France deported to Auschwitz in 1942, 784 men survived to the end of the
war. And only 21 women.

My mother used the damask napkin every Passover as our matzo
cover, doing her sad best to adopt its owner into our family and
our memories. I have spent many an hour searching for traces or
hints, a way to dredge Erna's roommate out of the silence, but the
French were not assiduous record-keepers. Someday perhaps I will
come across a table or a list. In the meantime, she and I will have to

make do with this ghost of an echo and the unsatisfactory mantra *I remember.*

Erna fared better than her roommate, the Polish seamstress. She was not Jewish; she was an Austrian ex-baroness, and a Catholic, and she was not deported as quickly as the other inmates. She was sent to a camp by the sea. Its big rolls of barbed wire looped all the way down to the beach, and conditions were so disorganized that it was easy enough to slip away for a walk. One day Erna was walking near the water when she saw someone on the other side of the fence. He beckoned to her.

When Erna approached, he asked, "Would you like to leave?"

"Yes," she replied.

"Come on." He pointed to a place where the big loops of barbed wire grew wider and higher and helped her push them aside until a gap appeared. When she'd made it through and stood up, he rearranged the fence behind her, and they walked away.

The man was a priest, and he escorted Erna to a safe house. There she learned the address of a convent in Lyon, where the sisters might help her escape to Switzerland. Erna could have gone straight to Lyon. But she didn't. Instead, she traveled back to St. Paul de Fenouillet, back to her friends Anna and Armand, and saved them.

❧

"A miracle." How many times had I heard Grandma use that word? *That you even exist is a miracle; a miracle that you're here; a miracle we're alive; a miracle that we survived.* As a child, I'd thought miracles were good. But Jewish tradition teaches that miracles are ambiguous. After all, if the universe really was created in the image of the Divine Spirit, there should be no need for miracles. A miracle happens when we humans rip holes in the universe's perfection, and the Divine Spirit bleeds through the holes. Thus a miracle cannot prevent or undo the damage humans inflict; it can only alleviate some of the suffering caused by that damage. The question that follows a miracle is the same as the question provoked by tragedy: *Why me?* In those days, the only answer I could summon was, *To remember.* And I would look around the bleak living room in La Roche and feel afraid, as if I had faded entirely out of the present and transmogrified into some kind of remembering hermit crab, holed up in a bunker for unbearable memories.

~

Each time I visited my grandfather, I found that the mess of papers and books had encroached on the apartment a little further, despite my regular efforts to tidy up. He did seem to be managing with his new hot plate and kettle. I noticed he had kept the instructions I'd pasted to them, as well as the notes I had left on the fridge and on the door to remind him to check his supplies and bring a list when he went shopping.

I'd try to find ways to test his memory, to gauge the extent of the loss and how far back in time it had seeped. "Did you buy *Le Monde* yesterday?"

"Why wouldn't I have bought *Le Monde* yesterday?"

"Do you remember where that Indian restaurant you like is?"

"I haven't been there since I gave up my car. But don't you re-call? The waiter was quite impertinent the last time we were there."

Like my grandmother, he seemed more and more tired. Often he retired right after dinner, before I could work up the courage to ask him any questions about the past. And even when he didn't, I'd find myself at a loss for what to ask: the subjects about which I felt most curious sparked so much anger and chagrin in him that I didn't usually have the heart to broach them. Once asking questions had felt dangerous to me, like provoking a spider or driving on the wrong side of the road. Now it felt dangerous for him, to set off so much emotion in someone who was becoming so frail. Once he was in bed, I'd sit with my memories in that high-up, quiet apartment. I'd call Julien or distract myself with a book. One night, after he'd bidden me goodnight and closed his bedroom door, I wandered into the kitchen. At the table, which had once been his favorite sitting spot, a pile of papers had engulfed the radio, the teapot, his crystal ashtray, his silver cup of pencils and pens. Idly, I began sorting them into piles. If he got mad the next morning, I reasoned, he'd forget it before lunchtime. Mostly, it was just old copies of *Le Monde* and newsletters from the various charitable organizations he supported, which I piled on the floor to be recycled. But not very far down I noticed a single photocopied sheet of paper, looking battered and worn, as if a storm had tossed it up from somewhere deeper than those newspapers. I pulled it out and saw a poem:

> *It is late last night the dog was speaking of you;*
> *the snipe was speaking of you in her deep marsh.*
> *It is you are the lonely bird through the woods;*
> *and that you may be without a mate until you find me.*

I shivered. It was *that* poem, his explanation for why he couldn't come to my bat mitzvah, why he couldn't bear the thought of facing my grandmother. What was it doing there? What had I stirred up inside him?

⌒

Slowly, almost without realizing it, I made a life for myself in La Roche. As the summer went on, friends visited me in the house and lent a hand: we stripped the blackberry cane out from among the tiles on the terrace, painted the shutters, weeded the garden. I saved my pennies and ordered glass for the windows and a door for the terrace. Julien and I went to parties and cookouts and on excursions together. He drove my friends back and forth to the bus stop and the train station. I met his friends, his mother, his father, his stepmother, his brothers. And we laughed a lot. One afternoon in particular, I remember sitting on the couch with him. The front door was open, the sunshine was pouring in, tinted green from the honeysuckle vine on the terrace, and we just sat in the soft end of the day and laughed and laughed. We laughed so long we forgot what started us laughing, and then we laughed some more. And I remember looking at him and thinking, *This is what falling in love is like.*

Through all of it, I wrote to my grandmother. It was the best habit I ever acquired. Grandma was a firm believer in the adage that actions speak louder than words, but since letters combine the two, she liked them better than almost anything. That year in France I learned she was right. Our letters to each other brought back the closeness we had shared when I was a small child, and though she is gone now, when I open her letters, she is almost there again.

Not that she answered any questions in the way I wanted. She still zipped off on a tangent from whatever subject I raised. She was far more interested in what I was making of my life on the other side of the ocean than she was in digging up the past. "Write about your life now," she urged me. "Tell me your plans." But what was interesting about the now? What were my stories worth compared to my grandmother's memory of November 11, 1942, the day Nazi Germany invaded France's Free Zone, where she and my grandfather were living?

Your question brought back to memory another "miracle" I never recorded, not even "en passant." When I returned from Lyon and by "miracle" wasn't apprehended in the junction waiting room (which later on saved three, Armand, Erna, and I), I arrived late in Perpignan, no more buses for St. Paul—the Nazi organization

*frighteningly efficient!!! Every major street already bearing signs
in German to the "état-major," the hotels, different military services. I was told that there was not a room to be had anywhere,
all occupied by the Nazi Army. Besides, I was afraid to go to one;
everything seemed dangerous.*

Anna had been to Lyon to bring food to Armand's sister Rosie,
who had just given birth to twins. Even before she learned that
France had fallen, she had bad news to bring back to St. Paul. Although Armand's brother's wife, Rose, already had been deported
from Tours, Armand's parents, Leon and Gitla, had refused to travel
from Tours to Lyon to shelter with their daughter Rosie, saying that
no fate could be worse than disturbing her new family. Now I pictured Anna alone in the cold streets of Perpignan, sick with fear.

*After eating in a "better" restaurant surrounded by German offi-
cers who eyed me strangely, I got even more scared, how to survive
the night till a bus to St. Paul. Through the St. P. village doctor,
well inclined toward me but unable to help or use my knowledge,
I got to know an ophthalmic surgeon (friend of his) in Perpignan
who occupied in a fancy quarter, in a beautiful apartment building, a whole floor, part practice part living quarters. I had twice
done anesthesia for him and assisted in his operations, so—it was
already dark, late fall—I went there carrying my suitcase through
the unlit streets. A "miracle" itself to find the house and climbed
one? two? three? floors to the apartment. A dark and unfriendly
woman opened, standing in a way not to let anyone enter. I stated
who I was and my plight. She regretted [to say] the doctor was
away (I believe it was a weekend) on his country estate. While I
pleaded and envisioned myself at least being hidden in the building, under the stairs maybe, three German officers, one older, two
younger, noisily climbed up, startling us both in front of the door*

to silence. One of the officers in grammatically correct but strongly accented French said to the woman, they must see the apartment and requisition any available rooms for their officers. She stared, looked frightened; I repeated what had been said, and the officers were ready to shovel her aside, so she entered the hall, me after her, and the officers following. She showed them first (smart) the practice room, then, their big bedroom and others definitely not bedrooms, coming to a small—back-looking-out—bedroom, where, tired, I deposited my suitcase, and she said I was her daughter who had just arrived and that would be the only room otherwise available. The officers left, she and I were saved. I was too tired, scared, agitated. Still don't know if she was the doctor's wife or housekeeper? I had to ask for a glass of water, I remember, and left very early for my bus to St. Paul the next day, through empty streets patrolled by Nazi soldiers. A miracle!!! Upon return to St. Paul, we planned our escape out of occupied France. This was a labor of love for you. I am not too well and can hardly write anymore. Can you read it?

I pictured my grandfather waiting for my grandmother all through that long night she spent in Perpignan. I pictured him pacing the floor, then seated by the stove with his head in his hands, certain she was lost. I pictured him filled with guilt and regret—it was his sister she was visiting, after all. I pictured their mute relief when she walked through the door and how quickly it must have been replaced by more fear.

If this were a novel, I would say their love shone like a searchlight against this backdrop of heroism and terror and survival. But it is not. I have no evidence there was much light of any kind. All I see now is the tarnished gleam of a little silver dish with AUBETTE stamped in the bottom, which one of them packed in a pocket or bag when it got too dangerous to stay in St. Paul de Fenouillet and they left for Lyon.

One night in late summer, it was insufferably hot. The heat was keeping us from sleep, or maybe it was after a party, or maybe we were on our way back from Le Camping. Whatever we'd been doing, when the heat didn't dissipate, Julien and I made our way down the footpath and into the darkness cast by the trees over the river. The nighttime in the woods and vineyards and fields was unusually still. We crossed the little wooden footbridge over the Escoutay, clambered up the bank on the other side, and checked for cars. Ahead of us, a glimmer or two escaped from the surface of the municipal pool. We climbed the fence and dropped onto the concrete surrounding the pool, which had been warmed all day by the sun and the slap of children's feet and still smelled of hot terry cloth and sunbathers. We stripped off our clothes and jumped into the water. It whispered over our heat-cranky skin. I paddled around for a while, and then I flipped over and drifted on my back. Above my head was the awesome hulk of Alba's castle, where a single light gleamed from a tower window. Beyond that La Roche looked like an old man drowsing in a battered nightcap. The lights of the village and the hamlet gleamed green and gold in the dark sky, where the Milky Way was just barely visible, a silver fuzz of stars stretching through the firmament. The water lapped around my back, my kneecaps, my ears. It was so quiet you could hear the figs growing. I felt something inside me begin to shift, fingers letting loose. Lying in the water, I thought, *Maybe despite all my efforts, my grandparents' story will slip away from me. Maybe I'll never know all the things I want to know.* And for a sliver of a second, I thought, *Maybe it doesn't matter. Right here, and right now, I am happy.*

Chapter Fourteen

In early September, the glass panes I had ordered for the windows arrived, and Julien installed them. The figs had ripened and were beginning to fall off the trees; the grapes in the vineyards had turned dark purple, and tractors towed vats of them through the village to the vintners' cooperative. The sun was beginning to slide through the day sideways, filling the air with a yellow as rich as lemon bars, and the nights were growing cold. For a week or so, the house felt blessedly quiet and protected, with the plastic gone and the new glass sparkling in the window frames. But the north wind blew hard against the walls, and soon the stones lost all the heat they'd stored up over the summer. Just as I had when I'd first arrived in April, I wore more clothes inside than I did outside. I knew I was going to have to give up.

"Move in with me," Julien said. "There's no point in your freezing down there by yourself."

So I swept the house, covered the furniture, and turned off the electricity and the water at the mains. Then I shut the door, wondering if I'd ever come back to live there again. I picked up my bags and called for Minus the cat, whom I had adopted, and, just as Julien had predicted several months before, was moving back in with him.

The house wasn't entirely secure yet. I was still waiting for a new terrace door to replace the one that had rotted away. So every couple of days I'd walk down to La Roche to check that everything was all right. Every time, I'd stare up at the dark walls and feel a strange mix of guilt, surprise, and defeat. Why hadn't I managed to stay? Why had I ever wanted to? Now that I had left it, the house would retreat right back into bleakness.

∼

I watched my grandparents slip away from me, my grandfather before my very eyes and my grandmother on paper. *"I am too tired to write more than a few lines,"* she'd tell me. *"My hands are shaky—can you read this?"* I should have felt a greater sense of urgency. But it was still too much a fairy tale to me, a blend of truth and magic, and though I'd given up on the house in La Roche, I kept sifting through the information I had, convinced that if I brought their stories to life in writing, I would be able to locate the secret password, the magic formula, the right question to unlock their silence.

∼

In my grandmother's account, the days in December 1942, between her, Armand, and Erna's departure from St. Paul de Fenouillet and their arrival in Switzerland, were like the *dayenus* our family said at the Passover seder every year: "It would have been enough for us." Just like the miracles of the Exodus from Egypt, my grandmother recounted each of the miracles that had enabled them to cross the border as amazing in its own right: the miracle in which my grandmother was helping an old peasant lady in a train station and was passed over during an identity check because the gendarme thought she was the old lady's daughter; the miracle in which my grandmother recognized the same gendarme checking papers as she was leaving St. Paul with Armand and Erna and got them to run away in time; the miracle in which she and Erna dressed up as prostitutes to get to the convent in Lyon where the nuns were giving out the address of a group of *passeurs* on the Swiss border; the miracle in which they weren't arrested in the train because they were sharing a compartment with a Catholic priest; the miracle in which they weren't arrested on the bus because the police chief was moving that day and had corralled all his men to help him—on and on, over the mountain.

Now I wanted specifics, as if pinpointing their geographical co-ordinates would help me decipher their feelings.

"I'm afraid I couldn't say," my grandfather responded when I asked how exactly he had traveled from St. Paul de Fenouillet to the place where they had crossed into Switzerland.

"You took the train from Lyon."

"Yes, I believe so."

"And Gran—weren't you riding in a train compartment with a priest, so the *milice* man didn't check your papers, because he thought you were together?"

He smiled. "Who told you that?"

"My grandmother."

"Well, we did ride with a priest, yes. But I don't know whether it did us any good."

"And where did you take the train to?"

"I couldn't be certain."

"And then where did you go?"

He looked vague. "I'm afraid it has escaped my memory."

"Near the Col de Coux?" I asked hopefully. That was all my grandmother could remember. *"The name of the village escapes me now,"* she had written me, *"but it was near the Col de Coux."*

"Perhaps." He looked thoughtful. "It's in a book. I told it to a woman who was writing a book." He pulled a slim red paperback off the shelf in the dining room and held it up for me to see. It was called *Passer en Suisse: Les passages clandestins entre la Haute-Savoie et la Suisse, 1940-44* and featured a pencil drawing of a round-faced and ragged refugee tramping through a barbed-wire fence. Grandpa opened to a chapter called *"Les points de passage,"* skimmed through it, and then handed the book to me.

The journey, though long, was relatively safe. But it was reserved for the hardy. . . . Most of the time [refugees], having resorted to taking this route, . . . found a passeur or "safe" person whose address they knew, without really realizing how difficult the trip would be, or perhaps convinced they'd be able to make it through anyway. Once they had started out, when fatigue began turning to discouragement, they repeated to themselves that it would be foolish to stop now, that the goal was in sight, that their life depended on it. Armand Jacoubovitch told me of his journey. Father Philippe of Les Gets, whose address he had been given in Lyon, took him, his companion, and an Austrian refugee into his care. With the help of two young men from Morzine, they started off toward the Col de Coux:

"We left very early, around six in the morning. The young men hiked an hour or two with us. They explained that we had to hike in a big curve—instead of walking due north, we had to make a big detour to the east, to avoid the patrols. After we had doubled back, we would arrive at the passage. This was in December 1942."

My grandfather had underlined in pencil the words *"young men from Morzine"* and put an asterisk beside them. At the bottom of the page, he'd added a footnote of his own: *"Constant and Albert BAUD, woodworkers from Morzine."*

I knew this part of the story from my grandmother. That morning they slipped their warmest socks onto their feet and laced up their thin shoes. They ate a little, sitting quietly and looking into the precrepuscular dark, and packed the rations of food the innkeeper and his wife had given them. They crept down the stairs and out the door and walked to the meeting place the village priest had assigned them the previous day. With their guides, they began the ascent through the thinning woods. The ground was the color of breadcrumbs, covered in places with patches of snow, which lent some brightness to the leaden sky and the dirty-cobweb smudge of the bare deciduous trees, but as they moved upward, the pine trees sucked all the light into the depths of their dark green needles. Occasionally, they crossed a pasture, where the only cover was the tenuous protection of the dim dawn. It was steep going, breathless, an immense effort to lift one foot and plant it in front of the other, push with all their might, repeat. They looked up once, from a narrow glen, to see the reedy figures of German soldiers walking far above them, with mushroom-helmets and twig-like rifles, and the little group pressed down behind the rocks and held their breaths.

By the time they reached the tree line, the weak daylight was leaching out of the sky. Tiny snowflakes landed on their clothes. The guides pointed out the Col de Coux and went over the little map they had drawn, enumerating the things the travelers should remember: customhouse, barn, the smugglers supposedly waiting near the border to accompany adventurous refugees—for a fee—into Switzerland. Not much farther to go, the guides assured them. And while the bareness of the mountaintop made them more visible, there would be nightfall and snowfall to cover them. The walking would be a little easier. There was a round of hurried well-wishing, thank-yous, and clasped hands, and then Anna, Erna, and Armand were alone.

The snow, which had begun to fall with a rapid hush, blew around them like a cape as they trudged to the pass. Before long, they were pushing through waist-high drifts that slowly soaked through their shoes. The wet and cold crept through everything,

through gaps in their clothing they hadn't known existed. It softened the tops of Anna's shoes so that they scarcely clung to their
thin wood soles. Erna, an experienced mountaineer, kept them on
the path. It was slow going, leg after leg, hard-pushing steps up,
careful stumbles. Erna first, then Anna and Armand behind, sometimes one before the other, sometimes the other way around, the
three of them groping their way with cold-blinded feet. The pass
was not very far away for longer and longer, first fifteen minutes,
then half an hour, an hour, another hour after that.

Suddenly, Anna fell. She landed sideways, in a snow-filled
hollow in the ground. Like a nest. She peered up at the landscape,
and it seemed to bend down all around her, like a mother toward a
child. The snowflakes, if chilly, were soft on her face; all told, she
thought to herself, she felt quite comfortable. The back of her mind
asked the front of her mind how it was possible for everything to
feel so agreeable, with her pack poking at her back through her wet
clothes, and her arms and legs twisted around in a funny way. How
was it, the back of the mind persisted, that she didn't feel cold? She
was reminding herself that damp wool was a very good insulator,
thinking of sheep, and watching Armand and Erna standing over
her, shouting at her. She struggled to listen. They were telling her
to get up. In a minute, in a minute. She would get up. Soon. Not
quite yet. I need a rest, she thought. It's so restful, with the snow
all around.

Anna's face looked like a hasty assemblage of shadows to Armand as he bent over, tugged at her, watched her, shouted, thinking
she looked so dark in all that white, so lost. The snow had already
begun to accumulate on her body. Far off in his mind, questions
began to ring, would they have to leave her, how would she die,
would she suffer, tucked into the snow like a sleepy child. He stood
over the little hummock and called to her. He tugged at her.

"She has to get up on her own," Erna insisted. Gently, she pulled him away and then leaned her face down to her friend. "Anna," she barked, like a cop talking to a loiterer, "get up."

Anna looked up at her with a soft, silly smile.

"Don't be an idiot," Erna snapped. "You know you'll die if you keep lying here."

Armand twisted his hands. How long could this last? Still, he hung back. Erna's sudden transformation was unsettling. Her normally clear, pleasant voice had been replaced by a raucous snarl.

Anna shook her head, still smiling. Erna leaned closer to Anna's face. "Son of a bitch!" she bawled. She pulled back, then leaned in again. "Get out of that goddamn hole, you feebleminded cunt!" The smile disappeared from Anna's lips. She whimpered.

Armand came closer to Erna and touched her arm. She brushed his hand away as a horse gets rid of a fly. Leaning as close as she could to her friend without losing her balance, she roared, "Motherfucker! You listen to me, Münster." Anna lifted her head. "You lazy piss-ant! Good-for-nothing piece of shit! You whore—"

"Erna!" Anna pushed herself up on one arm, offended that her repose was being disturbed by this sudden change in ambience. What had gotten into her friend?

"I could give a sheep's asshole," her friend interrupted her. "Right now it is colder than a witch's tit, and we have a motherfucking mountain to climb, and I will shit on my own parents' graves if I'm going to watch you lie there in the snow like some old drunk."

"Erna, stop it," Anna murmured, struggling to sit. She had to make Erna stop. What was wrong with her?

Erna ignored her. "I will spit on my own grandmother. I would spit on your grandmother, if she weren't too busy—" Clumsily, suddenly shivering, Anna got to her feet, and Erna grabbed her arm.

Armand choked up with relief. He rushed over to her.

"Let me go," Anna said to Erna. "What's gotten into you?"

"Get moving," Erna urged.

Anna obeyed. It was hard. She couldn't go very fast. She felt aged and tired.

"Keep moving," Erna commanded, walking with her, pushing a little, brushing the snow off her briskly.

Anna stopped and looked around her, disoriented. "What happened?"

"You fell. You had to get up on your own. Now keep moving."

"It was so comfortable," Anna reflected, brushing a snowflake off her cheek. "I couldn't imagine how it could be so comfortable, lying in that position."

"Keep moving," Erna repeated. "Don't stop. Stomp your feet, and rub your hands together. You could have died."

Anna looked back at where she had been lying and down at her bag in the snow. The awful realization flooded into her faster and heavier than the cold. She was overcome with remorse. "I'm sorry." She felt two sharp stings on her cheek.

"Don't cry. It'll leave marks on your face." Erna reached out and gave Anna's arms a last rub. "Let's just keep moving. It's almost dark."

Armand moved closer to the two women. He brushed snowflakes from Anna's hair. "I'll take your bag," he offered. They started moving again.

"Where did you learn to curse like that?" Anna asked.

"Taxis. Viennese taxi drivers have the foulest mouths in the world."

They walked in silence, five minutes, ten, twenty. The snow accumulated under the darkening trees, their feet speaking to themselves in the silent language of snow steps.

"Look!" The two women followed Armand's finger to a low oblong shape. "That must be the customhouse."

They pushed through the snow faster, with Erna in the lead. They had nearly reached the low building when Erna pulled up short. She nodded her head, indicating something ahead of them to the right. It was a man. He was waving at them. He waved harder. Cautiously, they stepped closer, a footfall, then another, until he gestured at them to stop. With no words, he pointed toward the customhouse. He pantomimed guards on patrol, then shook his finger, no. He motioned them to come back tomorrow. They nodded big exaggerated nods to show they had understood. He turned away and melted off into the rapidly dimming afternoon.

"What do we do now?"

"We go to that barn, I guess." Erna pulled out the scrap of paper their guides had used to sketch a map. "It should be down behind those rocks." They followed it, but there was nothing there.

"Are you sure you went the right way?" Anna questioned.

"Positive. Besides, there's a clearing here. It's the logical place for a barn to be."

They walked around the clearing, kicking away the snow, as if the barn might somehow be hidden under it. Erna walked over to what looked like a dead tree trunk and examined it. She kicked at it gently with her foot. Pieces crumbled away: black charcoal. "Looks like someone burned it down."

A little bird of fear fluttered in them. The silence dilated; the night began to open its eyes; the mountain, hard and high, gathered snow. *What do we do?* None of them wanted to say that question aloud so they listened to the snow instead.

"We'll have to go back to the customhouse," Erna decided.

After an hour's stumbling through the waning daylight, the three of them made it back. It was shut tight. They each felt their way around it, checking doors and windows, hoping against hope. The light was nearly gone when Armand felt a handle different from all the other ones he had tried. It moved. He wiggled it and pushed down, and it gave. His heart beat faster. It was open. It had to open. He pushed down again, and the door opened. A stench, like an unfriendly animal, slunk out and filled his nose. He reached into the inside pocket of his coat and found his matches, struck one, and peered in. He called out for Anna and Erna.

"Well," he said, when they'd made their way to him. "It looks like they left the outhouse open." He lit another match. "There's even a cover on the latrine."

"Will we all fit?" Anna asked.

"We have to." Erna took off her bag and carried it inside. She set her bag down.

"If we stack them," Armand pointed out, "we can keep them in here with us." They all squeezed in, Armand last. He rested his bag on top of the others, fumbled it open, and pulled out a candle, which he lit.

"Anna, can you give me your watch?"

Anna pulled it off her wrist and handed it to him.

Armand held his thumb up to the candle, sliding it down the candle's length and moving his lips as he counted thumb measurements. They all watched the flame, as if observation might encourage it to burn all night, as if its burning all night could keep them warmer.

Anna bunched up her toes in her shoes. She knew her shoes were wet; logically they were wet. She thought she was curling her toes. She couldn't really feel them. They had hurt a lot, then nothing really, a low burning sort of hum—frostbite symptoms. She knew from her medical textbooks that if she took off her shoes, her toes would be white. Not that she would take off her shoes. She concentrated on the candle.

~

I considered that candle, too. The night in the outhouse was the first story my grandmother ever told me about her experiences during the war. And now that I thought about it, my grandfather had featured prominently, with his calculations of how long they could burn the candle each time they lit it, so it would last through the night. "Smart man," I remembered Grandma saying.

The next morning, at first light, Erna found what looked like a path, and they struck out again. As they scrambled and lurched their way down the mountain, the snow turned to sleet, and finally to a steady, heavy rain.

Just as the sleet was turning liquid, and hitting their skin a little less sharply, Anna felt a change in the air. Someone. She looked up—at least in her telling of the story—and spotted a man in a dark, heavy coat walking toward them. Though my grandfather always had claimed that he was the one who spotted the *passeur,* I liked to think of Anna jabbing Erna, tugging at Armand's sleeve, stopping them in their tracks with a barely audible "Look."

No one ever told me whether they hesitated before making their way toward the man, advancing with their feet turned sideways so they wouldn't slip in the mud, whether they fully considered that he might hold their fate in his hands.

When they got near enough to speak, they gave the code words they would have learned from the village priest, and the man nodded. "Where did you sleep? You can't have hiked all night."

When they explained, he whistled softly. "Lucky—you must have gotten there a few minutes after the border patrol knocked off. They closed the road through the pass yesterday afternoon. I saw the guards head home at sunset." He led them to a primitive cabin used by herders when they grazed their cattle in the summer, which lay abandoned the rest of the year. When he lifted the latch they saw a number of other refugees huddled in near-darkness, including a mother holding a sleeping toddler in her lap. "I'll be back around nightfall," he announced to the group. "Everyone be ready."

"There was a kitchen in the cabin with hard bread, hard cheese, and tea," my grandmother recalled in an essay.

It seemed heaven. We were soaked to the skin, having marched under heavy rain. We were also dehydrated and starved. After drinking much tea and eating something, we stripped and Armand placed our clothes near the cast iron wood stove, which steamed outwardly while drying the wet clothes. We were assigned a big bed covered with a duvet, into which Erna and I crawled, to fall promptly asleep.

The rain swished and muttered and drummed around the cabin all through the day, and the other refugees slept or spoke in low voices among themselves; the mother occupied the toddler as best she could. Anna drifted in and out of sleep, dreaming that her feet belonged to someone else, that she had put them on backward, that she had left them in the bottom of a well.

Darkness crept into the cabin. Anna opened her eyes and saw the others moving around. It must be time to leave, she thought. She didn't want to move from the warm spot she had created in the bed.

Everyone started when the smuggler opened the door to the cabin.

He looked from the assembled company to Erna and Anna in the bed. "Time to go," he called out.

"I'm not leaving," Erna asserted, calm and put together as always.

The smuggler looked perplexed. "I said, it's time to go."

Erna shook her head. "It's pouring outside. Our clothes aren't dry, and I think I hurt my ankle on the hike. I'm not ready to move it. I'm staying put. I'll walk down later."

The smuggler stared at her.

Anna made up her mind and chimed in. "We're too weak. I'm not moving either."

I wonder what went through my grandfather's head as he watched this exchange. *"Armand reluctantly followed our lead,"* Grandma recalled, *"resisting the curses and threats of the smuggler, who finally left, leaving us three in the cabin."*

Their plans would have been set by then: they were to go to Erna's cousin's apartment in Lausanne, then split up. Armand would travel to Zurich, in the hope that his birthplace would be willing to take him back, while Anna and Erna would stay with Erna's cousin Ria, whose uncle was the mayor of a nearby village. Theoretically, then, Armand could have departed with the smuggler and gone straight to Zurich. But perhaps he balked at the idea of a sudden change in plans and at the thought of the smuggler coming back—or not—for two solitary women. He couldn't very well leave them now. Besides, how would he have paid the smuggler?

Alone in the cabin, *"in heavenly peace . . . we had a good night, a peaceful, restful day,"* with a kerosene lamp throwing eerie shadows on the walls, the sound of the slowing rain lulling them to sleep. The following afternoon, as they were preparing to depart, the door opened, and an unknown person stepped inside, looking as spooked as the three of them felt. "I thought the whole lot of them had been arrested," he exclaimed. It was another smuggler, come to inspect the cabin after his colleague had been detained with the previous day's group of refugees (who would subsequently have been deported), or perhaps to close up the shelter until the Swiss border police turned their suspicions elsewhere. Their separation from the group was another terrible miracle to take in stride as they helped this stranger hide the signs of life in the cabin, closed all the shutters, and started down the mountain. The air was chilly and damp, but at least it had stopped raining, which made trudging along the muddy paths and picking their way across icy, swollen mountain streams a little bit easier.

Before they got on the train, they had to pay the smuggler: *"We had almost no money, and Erna left a silver* tabatière *to be recovered when we could pay cash for the smuggler's services."* My grandmother never forgot the fear of discovery she felt upon reaching that first town. Someone had put her coat too close to the woodstove on their first night in the cabin and singed a large burn into the back. *"It made me look like a refugee,"* she deplored. *"It was so noticeable."* She was careful to stand against walls and sit down whenever she could. In the train, she leaned back and sat still, praying she looked insouciant, natural. *"We shared a . . . compartment with [a group of demobilized border guards], who, in Swiss dialect, told each other that we were Jewish refugees but they were off duty. . . . In Lausanne, Ria Berger, Erna's cousin, was at the train station. Another few days of recuperation with food we hadn't seen for ages in a fine apartment and loving concern. We were in Switzerland, no doubt, and another chapter of my life began."*

I stopped reading. *"Another chapter of my life began."* Not *our* life. *My* life. My heart beating rapidly, I flipped through their refugee dossiers. I had always thought my grandparents separated more or less against their will upon their arrival in Switzerland. Now I wondered if they'd still been together. I picked up the phone. "Grandma," I shouted when she answered, "I have an important question for you."

"Speak up."

"What happened with you and Grandpa when you crossed the border?"

"What?"

"When you crossed the border into Switzerland," I repeated, "what did you do?"

"Ria had an uncle, Uncle Sprenger, who was the mayor of a small village. They spent summers at his house when Erna was a girl. And we couldn't stay with Ria more than a day in Lausanne; it would have looked suspicious, her taking food for three people and using all that water and such. So we went to the uncle, and then he went with us, and we turned ourselves in to the police, and we spent a couple of nights in jail, but he pulled some strings so we weren't sent back over the border and could be in the same camp together."

"Who?"

"Ria's uncle."

"No, so who could be in the same camp together?"

"Erna and me, of course. It was very damp in that jail, but they had the BBC. I remember we got to listen to the BBC. The first time in the whole war."

"What about Grandpa?"

"What do you mean?"

"Where was he?"

"He went to Zurich. He was born there."

"That was it?"

"What?"

"You just left each other?"

"Mirandali, I can't hear you. You know the phone makes me tired. Write it down. Write it in a letter."

⌒

The next time I visited my grandfather, I took Julien to meet him. We drove to Geneva across the Rhône valley and past the Massif de la Chartreuse, where my grandmother had had her first residency, under and around the edges of the Alps. When we arrived at my grandfather's apartment, we drank tea and chatted about literature and politics. "He's a nice young man," my grandfather pronounced, when Julien was out of earshot.

"I think so, too."

I remembered my question. "Grandpa, what did you do when you got over the Swiss border? Where did you go?"

"Zurich. I thought I might get some kind of special treatment there because I was born there."

"Did you?"

"No. They took all my possessions and threw me in jail."

"In jail?"

He smiled. "It was all right. I was in there with a—how do you say it, a *maquereau*—"

"A pimp."

"Yes, a pimp, wearing a fancy suit, who kept conducting his business very loudly from the window of the jail. And a florist. He was very kind. A pacifist—they threw him in jail every year because he wouldn't perform his military service. We played chess together. And there were some German deserters, too, I remember. I steered clear of them."

"Then what happened?"

"They sent me to a labor camp."

"What was that like?"

Grandpa looked sad and dreamy. "It was on the floor of some sort of abandoned factory. Iron beds with straw mattresses. And I remember they would call us in the morning, and we had to assemble in the stairs and wash up outside. In the winter you had to break the ice in the washbasins."

"Where was my grandmother? Do you know where my grandmother was? Did you write to her?"

"Of course not. How could I know where she was?"

~

"Maybe there was nothing," I said to Julien on the way back from Geneva. "Maybe they were never in love. Maybe they ended up together for no good reason at all and then stayed together because they felt bad about leaving each other."

"What do you mean?"

"You know, maybe they just happened to be sort of dating, and then the war broke out, and they just happened to continue to be together, and then they were stuck." I fidgeted in the passenger's seat, feeling melancholy and out of sorts, ashamed I had ever blown their story into anything more than it was, ashamed to have romanticized anything about that horrible time. "I mean, why should they have a special reason to be together? Or apart? Why does anyone get together or break apart? Does anyone ever know?"

"I know why I'm with you."

"Why?"

"What does your dad like to say? 'Cause you look so cute when you get riled up,' " he said in English, putting on a silly American cowboy voice.

"Thank you, Rock Hudson."

Julien took a hand off the wheel and stroked my hair. "Really, since when is this about reason? You think they had a reason? We're talking about *feelings* here. Did you have a rational reason to take up with me?"

"Sure. Indoor plumbing." I opened the window all the way and pushed my hand against the air. "I think war makes you crazy. I think that's it. They're just another casualty of a goddamn genocide."

I put away all the letters, papers, and notes. It was early November, and my grant money was almost gone. In less than a month, I would no longer have any legal residency status in France, and I'd have to return to the United States. I decided to spend my last weeks in France enjoying my time with Julien.

So we shopped for groceries, fed the cats, read the paper, watched movies, argued, made up, listened to the news, caught colds and recovered from them, went for walks, ate dinner by ourselves, ate dinner with friends. As the weather got colder, we cooked soup, built fires in the fireplace, and added blankets to the bed. The cats crept inside at night. And despite my unfinished story and unanswered questions, I felt the same uncurling motion in my heart that

I'd felt in the pool that summer. Through all of it, I kept thinking, *I am happy.*

⁓

Finally, one day, I received word that the terrace door, custom-made to Julien's specifications, was ready. We borrowed a truck to pick it up, and I paid everything I had saved to make sure the house in La Roche could be shut securely around its emptiness.

That weekend it froze for the first time. It was so cold on the north side of La Roche that Julien was worried his mortar wouldn't set. My grandmother would have said that the sun was shining through clenched teeth, a Romanian expression she loved. We drove the door down to La Roche and carried it to the house. When we opened the door and felt an exhalation of cool air from the dark interior, it was difficult to imagine I had been living there just a couple of months before.

In the living room, we rested the door against the wall while Julien pulled the broken door off its hinges and pried the rotting wood of the doorframe away from the house's stone wall. He drove nails into the soft mortar on the inside of the now empty opening, and then we brought the door outside and leaned it against the blackberry cane already growing up again through the terrace tiles. He drove more nails into the new doorframe, then set the door and frame into the stone opening, using thick steel wire to twine together the nails on the doorframe and the nails in the wall's opening, checking with his level after every twist to make sure he was setting it straight. I brought him buckets of water, and he mixed a wheelbarrow full of mortar, which he used to fill the space around the doorframe, throwing it off the back of his trowel with easy, precise motions. Then he smoothed it all out, and we stood back to admire his handiwork.

It was beautiful. Looking at the honey-colored wood and the clear glass panes set into the speckled stones, I saw for the first time what the house might be like if I did manage to rescue it. For a moment, I forgot the cold, the dust, and my grandparents' bad blood and felt the same longing that had made me swear to myself all those years ago that I would make this place my home. And then, just as it had in June, the first time I'd sat by myself on the terrace wall, the enormous contrast between my fantasy and the house's reality clamped down on me, and I wondered how I could ever have believed that getting doors and windows on the place would make it less of a ruin or teach me anything about my family history.

Julien turned away from the door and began assembling his tools. Wistfully, I admired his work for a moment longer and then went to help him.

"Thanks for doing this. I'm a bit of a busman's holiday for you, aren't I?"

"Here." He handed me an empty bucket and his level. "We can take everything to my mom's house and rinse it off in her garden." He straightened up and winked. "Not a problem, by the way. It's never a bad idea to make a pretty girl feel obligated to you."

I took the tools from him. "Very chivalrous."

"At your service, milady," Julien said, packing his leftover mortar around a loose stone in the terrace wall.

I set the tools in the wheelbarrow, feeling like an arctic explorer who'd just discovered that the north pole was a figment of her imagination—that the house could be my home, that my grandparents' relationship had ever contained so much as a spark of tenderness. From far off, Anna and Armand's love had shone like a blaze of starlight. Closer study had revealed the glow of a single bedraggled candle and two people thrown together by a terrible set of circumstances, who, through some strange lapse of judgment, ended up marrying and purchasing a rotting house.

As I looked at the dark ruins, it occurred to me that I'd gotten the nature of my grandparents' fairy tale all wrong, or rather had failed to recognize its true meaning and message. After all, there is no love in most fairy tales; they are better characterized as sad and cruel. All but one of Bluebeard's wives are killed; Cinderella turns into a princess, but her stepsisters' eyes are pecked out by pigeons; Little Red Riding Hood gets eaten by the wolf—and those are the nicer ones. I'd been exposed to too many Disney movies, I decided, feeling abashed. Real fairy tales are about calamity. Julien had been right, that day at Le Camping: I was a romantic, trying to pretty up affliction, to streamline and simplify the grotesque, to make a love story where there was none, out of a little silver dish and some painful twists of fate. I looked around me. La Roche certainly seemed like the perfect setting for a fairy tale, with its crazy wrecked castle perched on an elderly plug of hardened magma, its cicadas, and its lazy river running over ancient stones.

"You okay?" Julien interrupted my musings.

"I guess. I was thinking about fairy tales."

"I told you that first day at Le Camping. You're a romantic."

"That's what I was thinking about. It made me mad at the time."

Julien grinned. "You know I love it when you get mad."

"Actually, what I was going to say is I think you might be right."

"I like it even better when I'm right," Julien teased. "Now, if you will just help me load all these tools into the wheelbarrow, I will take you home and show you what a real Prince Charming can do." He winked.

"What, now I'm some sort of damsel in distress?"

He waved his trowel in a curlicue motion and bowed, then tossed his trowel into the wheelbarrow, retrieved his tape measure and level, and picked up the old door. "Grab that wheelbarrow," he instructed.

"I thought I was a damsel in distress."

"Well, studies show that shoving a wheelbarrow around is the first step to recovery."

We locked the house and loaded the tools into his car. The sun had begun warming the day. The frost made the vines and the grass sparkle like an illustration in a children's book. A bird called out from somewhere on La Roche. Behind that new terrace door, the house was gray and cold, settled in for another long slumber. And up the hill in Alba, there was a fire in the fireplace, soup for dinner, cats on the sofa—a home. Julien is my home now, I realized. And then sadness crept over me again, because in a few days, I would have to leave him, too.

Part III

*A photo of my grandparents found in
my grandfather's papers after this book's manuscript
was completed, dated July 12, 1944—their wedding day.*

CHAPTER FIFTEEN

IN DECEMBER 2004 I RETURNED TO ASHEVILLE FOR three months in order to apply for a visa at the French consulate in Atlanta, hoping to spend another year in France. I still clung to the idea that an additional twelve months would represent nothing more than an extension of this parenthetical period of my life. I believed I would return to America soon enough, pick up the thread I'd dropped when I graduated from college. I hadn't measured—or even fully acknowledged—how potent that feeling of homecoming had been the first time I set foot in Alba. I didn't realize how far I'd proceeded along the path Grandma had laid for me. A second year to finish my book and spend more time with Julien didn't seem like much of a commitment, no more than the first year had.

In those three months, I needed to find a job in France that provided me with a visa—either that or prove to the French that I already was a citizen. By all rights, I should have been one: both my grandparents and my mother had held French passports for significant portions of their lives. I set about assembling the papers to prove it.

Since searching for work abroad and negotiating with French bureaucrats does not keep a girl in fans and feathers, I found a job reading fortunes at a local New Age bookstore—which made my grandmother crow when I called to tell her I was making use of my fallback skill: "See, I told you it would come in handy!" When it wasn't my shift to read cards, I stocked the store, helped customers, wrestled with the intricacies of shelving New Age books—with channeled materials, do you alphabetize by the name of the channeler or the name of the spirit being channeled?—and considered such thorny questions as whether the store needed a special permit to carry ritual daggers for pagan ceremonies and which stones worked best in pendulums. Then I'd drive home to my papers and notes with Utah Phillips and Ani DiFranco on my car stereo: "No matter how New Age you get, old age gonna kick your ass."

I arrived overprepared and half an hour early for my visa appointment at the French consulate, armed with a giant stack of birth certificates, death certificates, marriage and divorce certificates, naturalization papers, and more. I included pictures of the house in La Roche and writing samples from my book. My parents temporarily transferred money into my bank account to make it look like I was independently wealthy or at least had enough to live on for a year. I brought proof of insurance, proof of robust physical and mental health, and a letter from Julien stating that he would house and support me, all in triplicate.

The man at the consulate tossed everything aside but the letter from Julien. He held it out to me as if he were presenting evidence to a guilty party. "If you're going to live together, why don't you just get married?"

"Well . . . um . . . ," I stammered, "I mean, we've only—"

He cut me off. "You're already living together."

I nodded.

He gave me an accusing glare, and an image of the Monty Python sketch about the Spanish Inquisition popped into my head.

"Yes," I suppressed a smile, "but we've only been together six months."

"What do I care?" he said crossly, indicating my file. "This is just an inconvenience to everyone."

"But I don't want to get married."

He looked me in the eye. "You are already living together," he repeated, enunciating like a cop talking to an unruly drunk.

I pulled myself up in my seat, the Spanish Inquisition forgotten. "Sir, you're not advocating I marry for papers, are you? Isn't that illegal?"

"YOU. ARE. ALREADY. LIVING. TOGETHER. It's up to you. I'm just saying, if you get married, you can go back now. Otherwise you may be stuck here indefinitely."

"But maybe we don't want to get married!"

"Then why are you living together?"

"But I fulfill all the requirements," I argued. "I have all my papers in order."

"That remains to be seen. There's no guarantee you'll be granted a visa." He stood up, impassive now. "We'll contact you in six weeks or so."

"What about going back?"

He shrugged. "You can always go back on a six-month tourist visa next year."

"But I need a job. I need a real visa."

"That's not my problem."

⌒

I stormed out of the consulate in tears, convinced I would be stuck in America forever. On reflection, I see that I was what the French would call *allumée*—inspired and blinded and a little bit crazy from a light that colored everything I saw. Luckily, Julien was home when I called, sobbing, from the parking lot.

"Sweetheart, pull yourself together," he consoled me. "This is not 1942. You're fine. We'll see each other again."

I could not help noticing the great difference in our reactions, and it occurred to me it might be worthwhile to make an effort not to live in the strange looking glass of memory. On the drive back from Atlanta, I tried to estimate how much of my life I'd spent, as Julien put it, thinking it was 1942, waking up bathed in the terror of my nightmares or clenched with panic, keeping my shoes by the door, comparing every moment I could to an analogous instance in my grandparents' lives, as if by tracing my experiences over their own, I could make up for something that had been lost. I stopped for a coffee and drank it outside, seated on my car hood and looking around at the winter landscape. I pulled out the big refugee file, which I'd brought with me in the vain hope that I could guilt-trip the French consulate into giving me a visa, and flipped it open to one of the many pages I'd marked, a sheet of finicky administrative questions my grandfather had answered in handwriting I recognized as if it had been scrawled yesterday.

What is your native language? *French (or Yiddish?)*

Beyond the profession for which you were trained, what type of work could you learn the most easily? *Multiple skills: translator, teacher, accountant, laborer, interpreter, assistant land surveyor, proofreader, etc., etc.*

Why did you leave your country of origin and why are you unable to return to it? *Because I am a Jew and I risk deportation.*

Of course I realized it wasn't 1942. Any self-respecting historian knows—intellectually, at least—to beware the all-too-human tendency to identify with her subjects. At the same time, although my encounter at the consulate could not actually teach me what my grandparents had felt as they filled out forms for hostile bureaucracies, it did make me think about being placed at the mercy of stacks of paper and bored civil servants, struggling against the hard, blind edges of the law. Even if my anger was a privilege of my station and my grandparents had not reacted similarly, the comparison pushed me to think about reduction, about what it was like to be pared down to a series of answers on a piece of paper. My grandparents had been categorized so many times, as Jews, as immigrants, as survivors. I thought of Anne, the daughter of friends of my grandmother, and her crusade to record and preserve survivors' memories of the time *before* the war, before that generation had been reduced to remembering the Shoah for the benefit of history. I shuddered, thinking of the endless punishment it must be to live with both the personal and the cultural aftereffects of a trauma: while other people their age had been granted a quiet lifetime of ordinary memories that would evaporate peacefully into the hereafter when they expired, my grandparents were hounded not only by the memory of what they'd lived through in the war, not only by the loss of all that had been destroyed in those six years, but also by the exhausting injunction, "never forget."

I got back into the car. Now I am certain that the poetry of my grandparents' silence and the hidden time bomb of the house in La Roche were both the lure with which they drew me in to remember and record their stories and their last-ditch attempt to blast themselves out of that series of reductions. But back then I was too busy trying to see my way to the center of their story to notice what it might look like in its broader arc.

As I drove, I tried again to picture Anna and Armand during their last night together, in Erna's cousin's apartment. I strained to listen: Were they whispering plans to each other? I squinted my eyes against the highway to see if I couldn't conjure up two young, tired bodies, thin and trembling with emotion, unable to fathom all they'd just survived. I wanted them to hold hands. I wanted Armand to get up, rummage through a bag, and then slip that silver dish with AUBETTE printed in the bottom to Anna, as a sign, a coded promise.

But perhaps the little silver dish meant something else entirely. Perhaps it was a memento, a brave acknowledgment that they were not right for each other and should part ways. And of course, given my grandfather's penchant for cutting people off to avoid the complications of saying goodbye, maybe they weren't even speaking when they left each other, and the AUBETTE dish lay forgotten at the bottom of a bag.

The next day I went back to my job at the New Age bookstore, telling total strangers what to expect from their lives and shelving books on delving into past incarnations—the irony of which was entirely lost on me at the time.

~

Soon afterward I drove to New York to pick up my grandmother and bring her down to her house in Asheville, which she visited more rarely now that she didn't fly.

From Pearl River to the northern tip of Virginia, I looked for a way to raise the questions I wanted to ask. At lunch I watched her comment on American consumerism and Bush's imperialism to the couple in line ahead of us at the Cracker Barrel. She was having so much fun I didn't want to interrupt. Once seated, we ate our cornbread and gossiped about the customers at the other tables. I listened while she explained how she'd toilet-trained all the babies over six months old in her refugee camps so they could save the few precious diapers they had for the infants. *Let it go,* I thought. She should remember what she feels like remembering. That's enough. But not for nothing did Grandma have a reputation for witchiness. As soon as we got back into the car, she asked about my book.

"I'm writing *a* story, but is it even your story? I don't know. I've learned so many disconnected things about you—it's hard to put them into a narrative."

"What are you talking about? You have all my papers. Like I

always say, when I'm gone, you can just publish them and be very rich, like the others."

"They would need some editing," I said lightly, thinking of the jumble of writing she'd sent me and the hours I'd spent figuring out what exactly had happened when.

"Sure, sure." Her voice wasn't exactly wistful, and it wasn't exactly bitter. It must be very strange indeed, I thought, to see others rising to fame and supposed fortune just because they had managed to recount their memories in a cogent way. Bearing witness must be the worst kind of celebrity there is. Grandma, of course, had no time to waste on such thoughts. "Don't you talk to your grandfather?" she pursued.

"Well, yes, but you never have the same stories."

"Like what? What did he tell you?"

I tried to think of all the questions on my list. "Well, for example, do you remember losing your watch when you were picking grapes in the Pyrenees?"

"What?"

I repeated the story my grandfather had told me once, of a day in September when the sun had started to slant and the foreman had called them in from the vineyard where he and Anna were harvesting grapes. One by one the pickers came to the ends of their rows and returned to the truck, pitched their grapes in gently, and stood waiting for the daily liter of wine that came with their pay. They talked tiredly to each other, compared rows picked, sore shoulders, suntans. Suddenly, Anna looked at Armand in dismay. "My watch," she exclaimed.

"What's wrong?"

"My watch. My watch is gone. The watch my father gave me." The watch had been a graduation gift from Josef to Anna on the day she graduated from *gymnasium*. (He hadn't come to the ceremony, and she believed he had forgotten all about her; it turned out he had been held up helping someone in need. He told her that the watch should remind her that she was always on his mind, but that she in turn should remember others who were less fortunate than she.)

The pickers stood there silently. This wasn't a time to be losing things. "Where did you lose it?" one of them asked.

What a stupid question, Armand thought. *If she knew, it wouldn't be lost.*

Anna didn't seem to notice. "I don't know, I had it on this morning. I had it on at the break, too, because I looked at it when it was time to go back."

Another picker said, "Good luck finding it. How much ground did you cover today?"

Anna shook her head. A tear escaped from the corner of her eye. Another tear escaped. She kept shaking her head. Another. She bit her lip. They kept coming, tears and tears blurring the endless identical rows of vines. She couldn't stop. Armand had hardly ever seen her cry.

"I'll find it." He touched her arm. "You'll see." He set off along one of the rows, looking down at the pale earth, the dust and rocks and the gray trunks of the vines. He stopped. He pressed his hands to his temples. He pictured the rows they'd walked slowly all day, his entire body tense with the effort of visualizing their path. He had to find it. He began to move, his eyes narrowed, fixed on the ground at the gnarled feet of the grapevines. The cicadas' creaky roaring seemed to shut him into his looking. At first he chose his rows randomly, then with more and more purpose. Within a few minutes, he saw the watch glinting on the ground. He stooped to pick it up and felt a lightness wash over him, a sense of freedom like the first time he had seen the sea. He was so happy. He stood, squared his shoulders, and walked back to Anna, who was still standing, small and bleak-faced, by the truck. "Here." He extended it shyly. "I found it." Anna reached her hand forward, and he took her left wrist and fixed the watch back onto it.

In my imagination, Anna would have stepped forward, and they would have embraced, she with her head buried in his shoulder, their feet planted on the ground, with the smell of the dry wind about them and the comfort of arms clasped, long familiarity, blind love. But I didn't say that part to my grandmother.

As I talked, I waited for Grandma to jump in and correct me, or at least to cut me off and change the subject. But she said nothing.

I waited. The car was silent, so silent that for a moment I wondered if she had stopped listening and fallen asleep.

"He told you that?" she asked finally.

"Yes, he did."

I took my eyes off the road and stole a glance at her. Sure enough, I saw the sad, surprised expression that settled over her face whenever we spoke about my grandfather. "I can't remember that at all."

"Really?"

"Not at all, no."

Silence filled the car again. My mind raced, thinking of what and how I could ask about their separation after crossing the Swiss border, their subsequent marriage.

"It's a romantic story," I ventured. "It seems surprising when you know what happened later—"

Now Grandma did cut me off. "Romantic?"

"Sure—you lose your watch, you're brokenhearted, he finds it for you against all odds. By sheer force of will. Out of love for you."

"Ach . . . no . . ." She trailed off and sighed. "He never really loved me."

"Why do you say that?"

"Well, you know that saying."

"The saying?"

"The opposite of love is not hate—"

"Oh, right." It was my turn to interrupt. I finished the sentence for her. "The opposite of love is indifference." Grandma liked that one. She said it to me often.

"Right. Exactly." Grandma went on. "The opposite of love is not hate. It's indifference."

"So? What does that mean?"

"So, I'm indifferent. Once I loved him, now not." She held up her hands, weighing the two ends of the story in her palms; they balanced out. "But he hates me. He hates me."

I didn't know what to say to that. It was true, of course, and it had done a great deal to ruin my family's mental health, but it still seemed too awful and mean to acknowledge it baldly.

But Grandma wasn't waiting for me to say anything. "It's logic, simple logic. You can only conclude he never loved me."

"No, Grandma!" I exclaimed. "That's a fallacy. If the opposite of A is B, that doesn't say anything about C."

"You sound like your mother teaching one of her classes. Talk sense."

"I mean, logically, you can't conclude he didn't love you."

"Why not?"

"Well, if we take what you said about the opposite of love, then if he hates you, the only thing you can actually conclude by logic is that he *doesn't* feel the opposite of love for you. I mean, I'm not exactly sure if this fits into a logical formula—"

"So?" Grandma cut me off.

"Look, I'm saying the fact that he hates you now doesn't mean he never loved you. It means that he never felt the opposite of love for you. Maybe it means he never actually *stopped* loving you."

"You think so?"

"I do." I'd said it to comfort her, but as I reasoned it out, I realized it must be true.

"Hmph," was Grandma's dubious response. She turned away from me to look out the window at the mountains. Then she turned back. "Well, it's good you're there to take care of him. Don't talk to me. I'm going to sleep."

⌐

My grandmother and I didn't speak about my grandfather again during the rest of her visit to Asheville. "You can put them in a letter," she said, when I tried to ask her questions. "I can't—it makes me too tired. To think I used to believe being blind was worse than being deaf," she added, the closest she ever got to complaining about herself. Between my shifts at the New Age bookstore, we sat in her living room, with the flowered, fringed tablecloth and the Russian flag in the hand-thrown vase, and played Rummikub, which she called "The Game," since it was the only one she knew, other than solitaire. I'd play as slowly as I could, as if to stall time by doing so. "Don't do me any favors," she'd remonstrate whenever she saw I might be letting her win. So I'd pull myself together and beat her every time, contesting, for old time's sake, all the rules and exceptions she'd woven into her game. "Got time for another?" she'd ask at the end of each round, sweeping the Rummikub tiles into the plastic ice cream tub she kept them in. And I'd shake my head in admiration at the zest and adventure my grandmother managed to inject into everything, even a game she'd played a million times, and we'd play again.

One time she told my fortune, and one time I told hers. I don't remember what we said to each other, except that we agreed on one thing: people get their fortunes told for one reason only—they want you to tell them that everything will be all right.

"And of course you can, or of course you can't. It all depends on how you look at it. Take your grandfather. Nothing was ever all right with him."

I nodded. "And you—"

"As I say, whatever comes, comes for the best. Gratitude is the most important human emotion."

She put the cards back in their pile and gave her little birdlike cackle that reminded me of things pleasant and prickly and salty, like cocktail crackers or pickled beets. And then she looked at me, just as she had once or twice before in my life, and said, "You're like me, Mirandali. You'll *sourrwvive.*"

Now I understood it was a command, not a prediction. And I looked at her indomitable smile, the coal-black streaks in her silver hair, and the turquoise and gold earrings quivering in her ears and wished for a lifetime more with her to figure out exactly what *sourrwviving* entailed.

But there wouldn't be a lifetime more of years, I knew. Anyway, Grandma had planted the seeds of my *sourrwvival* long ago. Sooner than I expected, and despite the grouchy man at the consulate, I got a job in Le Teil as an English teaching assistant, which came with a work visa from September to April. September was six months away, just the length of the tourist visa for which I was eligible after my three months in the United States. I gave my notice at the bookstore and bought a ticket back to France. "Good," Grandma declared when it was time to say goodbye. "Good for you. Don't come back," she reminded me, pushing away the hug I'd attempted to give her.

⤙

Julien came straight from work, dressed in plaster-spattered clothes, to pick me up at the train station. He'd bashed his lip with a hammer the day before. I'd been traveling for the past thirty hours and was wearing an oversize hand-me-down coat that made me look like a homeless highland shepherd. I needed a shower, and I probably also needed a haircut. Certainly, if you had seen us from afar, or even up close, that morning in early March 2005, we wouldn't have looked particularly romantic. But in my memory, our reunion was a soaring, violin-tinged affair, filled with the peculiar yellow-gray light that suffuses the winter sky in the Dauphiné. We stood and hugged amid the noises of the trains and the echoing footsteps of other travelers, and just as I had that summer in the pool and that autumn in Julien's wood-paneled house, I felt the full weight and force of my own life, lived for myself and not for the past or my grandparents. Our hands and faces were the only parts of us uncovered in the cold air. We touched them together almost shyly. Then, arm in arm, we walked out to the parking lot and got into the car, headed for Alba, headed for home.

Chapter Sixteen

WHILE CONVINCED THIS ADDITIONAL YEAR IN France was simply a brief pause in my real life, I also shipped over a throw pillow, a couple of coffee mugs, a challah plate, and a handmade quilt, the items I'd been saving ever since my obsession with homes had evolved from building little dioramas to collecting actual objects. Julien's coming-home present to me was even less temporary-seeming: he surprised me with an antique writing desk restored by a friend of his. An outside observer, or perhaps my grandmother, would have thought we at least sensed the meaning of these gestures, but one of the things that made our relationship work so well was our shared faith in the impermanence of all things.

So for a few months, I continued to believe I was on a kind of warm-weather hiatus, writing a fairy tale—calamitous as it might be—in a fairy-tale setting. Three or four days a week I waitressed at my friend Françoise's restaurant in La Roche, serving *boeuf aux mille épices* and lavender *crème caramel* to happy tourists and friendly regulars. Julien and I would wake up together and have coffee and croissants, and once he left for work, I'd sit and write until it was time to leave for the restaurant. From time to time, we went to see my grandfather, whose condition, to my great relief, seemed stable enough.

During my stay in Asheville, my mother had given me the AUBETTE dish, a tiny shred of evidence that my grandparents' love had, at some point, truly existed. Why else would they have carried it so long and so far? I looked at it a great deal but held it sparingly, as if I might rub off the last remains of their past. It smelled like my grandmother in reverse, mostly metal and a tiny whiff of roses. I reasoned and insisted it into a symbol of all they couldn't say to each other, or to me.

Armand in an internment camp in Wald, Switzerland, March 1943. *Anna in 1942, a head shot most likely taken by the Swiss border police.*

I returned to their refugee files, which I had largely neglected the year before, trying to trace their steps in the months following their separation in Switzerland, searching for hints of what had come after.

Each of their files contained a badly photocopied picture of them, looking shadowy and lost. As logical as it was to find their photographs there, I still felt startled and moved when I stumbled upon them, as we all must be when we come across little flashes of the people we love preserved as anonymous figures by hands who never knew them. Mostly, I gleaned useless tidbits, half-personal details, like how much soap my grandparents were allowed each month or that their meal rations didn't include chocolate. In the hundreds of pages that documented their sojourn to Switzerland, Anna and Armand appeared never to have been in the same place at the same time. I briefly reconsidered my twelve-year-old fancy that they'd never actually met.

The bulk of the pages consisted of entry and exit notices with dates and the innocuous-sounding names—Victoria, Bristol, Régina—of the empty resort hotels that had been converted into refugee lodgings for the duration of the war. Any list on which my grandparents had appeared was included in their dossiers. As a result, there were pages and pages of names: names of those to be sent from one camp to another, names of those given leave for a day, names of those released to attend school, to work in the fields, to participate in classes and conferences. I imagined the galaxy of memories that accompanied each name, and I hoped each one had a person like me attached to it, scrambling to remember, to stitch together a story before it was too late. I began to feel dizzy with all the remembering.

⁓

In Geneva, I tried sounding out my grandfather about life in the refugee camps.

"What is there to say? Mine was hardly an interesting case."

When I prodded him, he admitted, "It was prison. There was hard labor. Slave labor, almost. In the fields all day . . ." He trailed off, shook his head.

"But you weren't there very long, were you? Wasn't there a program that helped you go back to school?"

"Of course, yes, there *were* good people," Grandpa amended. "I remember one woman, a social worker in one of my camps, telling me that if I asked to go to church, they had to let me out."

"Did you?"

"I'll never forget the sermon the priest gave."

"You actually went to church? Why didn't—" I wanted to ask why he didn't spend his free time elsewhere, but Grandpa cut me off.

"Of course, what else would I have done? We were prisoners.

They were monitoring us." He looked around him as if that were still the case. "But the priest—he had white hair and very big blue eyes, and he leaned over his pulpit and shook his finger at the congregation and said, 'If you imagine that you are worth more than the others because the war has spared you, *you are wrong.*' "

My grandfather stopped. I saw he was weeping and reached across the table for his hand, something I never would have dared to do before his fading memory softened him.

"Did you ever get out to do anything else?" I persisted, when he had put away his handkerchief.

"To do what? You couldn't just leave, you know."

"Did you write to anyone? Did you have contact with anyone?"

He shook his head. "I had no one in Switzerland. Some very distant cousins in Zurich, but they had never been in contact with us, so I gave up on the idea of going to see them."

For my part, I gave up on being circumspect and took the plunge. "Did you ever see my grandmother? Did you write to her?"

Instantly, my grandfather's face darkened. "How could I?" he asked, incensed. "Where would I have gotten a pen or paper?" He stood up, and briefly I thought he was going to storm out of the room. "All of this has been written about before. I've already answered these questions. Just a moment." He walked into his sitting room and returned with a stack of books about Swiss refugee policy, Swiss economic policy during the war, and Swiss collaborationism.

"Is there anything about you in these books?"

Silently, Grandpa pointed to one of them, and I opened it to a page he'd marked:

In Arisdorf, corruption reigned in the camp: the refugees realized the milk was being skimmed and that very little meat reached them. M. Ja. was charged by his comrades with protesting these dishonest acts.

"Monsieur Ja. is you?"

He nodded. This was the first indication I'd seen that my grand-father had had any kind of status or engaged in any positive action in the refugee camps; he'd only ever spoken of his experiences in vague, pessimistic terms. "So you were a rabble-rouser," I teased, smiling.

He smiled, too. "I'm not sure you could say that. I was just bet-ter at putting things into words than the other chaps were."

"So you did have access to pen and paper?"

He shrugged. "I suppose so, yes."

"So did you write to my grandmother?"

The offended look returned. "How could I have? How could I possibly have known where she was?" I let it go, wondering whether he was rebuffing me because he didn't want to talk about it or be-cause he actually couldn't remember.

～

My grandmother was as voluble as my grandfather was taciturn about her experiences in refugee camps. She'd written pages and pages about her life during that time, pages I'd once set aside be-cause my grandfather was not mentioned in them. Returning to those essays now, I had to admit to myself that I'd also discarded them because they described something I thought of as "after," a time she was already "safe." I felt ashamed of how conditioned I'd been by all the Holocaust literature I'd read, slightly horrified to realize that I had, unwittingly, neglected this period of her life for the spectacular and semiapocalyptic moments closest to oblivion, memories she barely could bring herself to recall.

Despite what they now claimed, my grandparents would have been able to keep in touch through Ria's family, who could have forwarded their letters. Reading my grandmother's vivid essays, I wondered if she'd sent similar accounts to my grandfather. I wondered if he'd felt jealous of her status as a camp physician, or jealous of her camps, which were, on the whole, more comfortable than his.

She'd first been put to work as a physician in a camp in Wesen, caring for ninety-six children and eighty-six women, under the direction of an authoritarian pro-Nazi who forced his charges to go on "health marches" around the freezing grounds of the camp. She had arrived at night, after a train ride with a young military escort who gave her dark chocolate to eat—the first she'd tasted in years—and perhaps listened to her reminisce about taking the very same train during her years in medical school. *"When, as a student, we came along this lake,"* she wrote me,

> *the train-rails ran so close to the shore that one could hear the murmuring water . . . the hills and mountains on the opposite shore were clearly visible. The lake's look was mysterious . . . over-hanging mountains threw strange shadows which blackened the water . . . with the play of the sun it created iridescent hues of numerous shades. . . . In my fantasy I [would] stop . . . one day to explore its mysteries. . . . [My] fantasy was to be fulfilled, but not in the circumstances of my choice. I was to live along its shore, but hardly be able to enjoy its beauty.*

Upon her arrival, my grandmother was led through the cold, blacked-out streets to an uninviting hotel, which had been transformed by the Swiss military into refugee lodgings. She followed her escort through a lobby filled with women chatting in a mixture of German, French, and Yiddish. Their conversation died down as she walked past and resumed again as she climbed the stairs to a tiny, unheated attic room. Her new quarters, which must once have housed the hotel's servants, contained a single bed, a rickety wardrobe, and a washstand. Even dead tired, Anna was careful to dwell on the positive: *"My relief and thanks for having a single room were immense."* Left alone, she undressed and lay down, noticing as she did the extreme cold seeping in from the single, drafty window. She shivered miserably beneath the covers, unable to warm up. A bare fifteen-watt bulb hanging above her new domain only added to the gloom.

Her battle against self-pity was interrupted by the sudden appearance of the village doctor and the camp director. She spent several tense minutes listening to them discuss her future. Dr. Gygax, who had been caring for the inmate population in addition to his normal roster of patients, had requested a pediatrician to relieve him; now he learned that Anna was a chest physician. The central administration, assuming that any woman doctor was necessarily an obstetrician or a pediatrician, had failed to ask her about her specialization. The two men argued back and forth until Gygax thought to ask Anna whether she had worked with Dr. Paul Rohmer, a renowned professor of pediatrics at the Strasbourg medical school. *"My answer (I had done two instead of only one [rotation] in his hospital . . .) seemed to please him."* Dr. Gygax announced he would bring her a pediatrics textbook and let her figure things out for herself. *"True to his word, he returned the same evening with the pediatric textbook. Did I start going through the book, which I finished in two days, the same evening and read through the night[?]"* I wondered if she had written to Armand about that awkward meeting and whether imagining her receiving two men from her bed had sent him into a lather of jealousy that prevented him from empathizing with her lonely, chilly predicament.

Since the hotel in Wesen was only a transit camp, it slowly emptied as the women and children were transferred to homes or other specialized camps. After a time, Anna was assigned to a new internment home, this time with Erna, who worked as the assistant to the director.

This camp was being prepared for pregnant women, some very close to delivery, mothers with infants and/or toddlers up to age four. [. . .] After arrival of the refugees, I only slept fitfully, a few hours, during the night. Frequently summoned by anxious mothers about their child who had awoken them or women with false or real labor pain, I had long days and insufficient rest at night. The women who had to be examined by an obstetrician, other than myself, or were ready for delivery, accompanied by me, had to be brought to the hospital in Sierre.

I knew from the refugee files that my grandfather had been interned for a time in Sierre, and I considered the possibility that my grandparents saw each other there. I checked the dates; naturally, they did not coincide.

It appeared as if their luck had diverged when they separated. While my grandfather slept in a filthy straw bed in a makeshift dormitory in an unused factory, my grandmother had her own room in the maids' quarters of a vacant hotel. Then again, if my grandfather had dwelt upon the speed with which he was released from the camps to return to his studies, or upon the fact that he was often exempted from manual labor to help with secretarial tasks in his camps' administrative offices, or the fact that his position as group leader afforded him a larger allowance than the other refugee laborers, and if my grandmother had dwelt upon her festering chilblain, frostbitten toes, hours of overwork, and unpleasant role as middleman between the inmates and the camp administrators, perhaps I would think of their luck in exactly the opposite terms. If their fortunes differed, it was likely because my grandmother had taken her stubborn high spirits with her when they parted ways.

"My luck always held," Grandma wrote, recalling the precious minutes she'd lose negotiating with the camp director for a taxi to

the local hospital every time a new mother went into labor at night. By the time the director conceded and the taxi arrived, *"I often feared the event would occur in the car. The driver, hearing the labor wails, became nervous and had to be reassured."* Anna would sit in the back, enjoining her chauffeur to keep his eyes on the road, and then make the taxi wait while she checked the patient into the hospital. Afterward she'd rush back to the camp to update every baby's nutritional chart so that the milk kitchen could prepare the correct formulas for the following day. Each baby was fed a carefully tailored combination of barley, oats, corn, rice, and wheat, whose ratios my grandmother would adjust over time. Her staff was given only two cans of Nestlé condensed milk per month, which was barely sufficient to supplement the formulas of the weakest babies and which explains why, ever after, my grandmother refused to purchase anything marked "Nestlé." To reassure the mothers and give herself some measure of peace, she also posted her young charges' growth charts on her office door, another task that ate into her already short nights.

No matter how she slaved over their babies, the mothers questioned Anna's every decision: *"My skinny self way below one hundred pounds, due to starvation in France, and inability to gain weight on camp food, made me look much younger than my age, and invited mothers to point out my unmarried state and lack of children."* Her response to their objections echoed a warning I'd heard more than once during my teenage years: *"What do you have to do to make a baby? Open your legs twice in nine months, that's what. But to raise a child—that requires experience and wisdom."* In her essay, she'd concluded: *"I advised that, having done the former, they should leave it to me to help them with the latter."*

As ever, my grandmother's heroism entranced me, much as she hated it when I used that word: *"The wish of the young to make heroes of individuals who have experienced events—by chance or imposed by circumstances—can be explained by the affection they have for them."* But how else could I describe her losing sleep so new mothers would fear less for their newborns, standing up for her fellow inmates when they went on a hunger strike to protest their insufficient rations, saving a baby's life by cobbling together an intubation system out of a length of glass tubing and a kerosene stove, or preventing a scarlet fever outbreak in a badly equipped camp by adapting a remedy she remembered from a book about medieval medicine?

Now, though, my need to inhabit my grandmother's skin, to project myself into her younger self and imagine when she would have had the time to think about my grandfather, to reach out to him, to return to him, made me understand her objections to my calling her a hero. The war had not vaulted her into some special state of being; it had not banished her quotidian self. Her headaches were headaches; her fatigue was fatigue. The cold she felt during the war was not any more—or less—cold than the cold she'd felt during any other period in her life. The beauty of the mountains around her was neither enhanced nor diminished by her current circumstances. She wanted that to be true, in any case. History had robbed her of her right to be ordinary, and she was protesting that injustice.

Maybe that's why they couldn't let go of each other: they each held within themselves the memory of who the other person was before the war made them remarkable in ways they had not chosen.

⌒

Though I was beginning to lose hope that I ever would find anything to illuminate the mystery of their love and estrangement, I kept combing through the refugee files for any indication that my grandparents had at least crossed paths. With my shaky grasp of German, it was hard to be sure, but as far as I could tell, there was only one recorded instance of my grandparents being in the same place during their time in Switzerland. In May 1944 the chief of police in Bern had written to the Bureau of Civil Internees in Geneva:

Sirs,

We hereby confirm our telephone conversation of earlier today and ask that you grant permission to the following persons to go to "Mösli," near Zurich, on May 27, 28, and 29, 1944, to participate in a conference of the Oeuvre Suisse d'Entraide Ouvrière:

No. 7808 Mr. Armand Jacoubovitch, born June 13, 1915
c/o Berchtold, 14, Cours de Rive
No. 7130, Miss Anna Münster, born August 8, 1913
c/o Berchtold, 14, Cours de Rive

That was something. As of May 26, 1944, my grandparents lived at the same address. In my faltering German (and with some outside help), I puzzled through the letters that had been written around that date. This time, my patience was rewarded.

July 23, 1944

To: the Swiss Federal Police Offices, Bern
Re: Deposit at the Schweizer Volksbank

In payment for my work at the Sanatorium Sursum in Davos a deposit of 95 Swiss francs was made in my account at the Schweizer Volksbank. Please release this entire amount to me. I make this request because I was married in Geneva last July 12th. Leave to do so was granted so suddenly that I had no time to apply to you to release the necessary funds. My friends placed the necessary funds at my disposal for immediate expenses such as a dress, shoes, and

some undergarments, and I must now reimburse them. The receipts
for these purchases are available for your inspection at any time.

Please consider that I am in these circumstances because I have
been in Switzerland for some 20 months with nothing more than
the clothes I had on my back when I crossed the border, and that I
badly need to purchase further undergarments, stockings, etc.; so I
ask you to disburse me the entire amount I have on deposit.

I thank you in advance for your help and remain
respectfully yours,
Dr. Anna Jacoubovitch-Münster

In their entire refugee dossier—hundreds of pages—this letter
was the only mention of my grandparents' marriage. But whether
they wed for love, loyalty, or my grandmother's beautiful black hair,
at least now I knew the date: July 12, 1944.

Chapter Seventeen

IT WAS JANUARY 2006, AND ALMOST A YEAR HAD passed since my return to France and the triumphant discovery of that wedding date. I'd waitressed a full season at the Petite Chaumière and taught a semester at the high school in Le Teil. My teaching contract would end in a few months, and when it did, my visa would expire again. Julien and I were sitting in bed in his house on the rue du Code in Alba. We'd done a lot of work on it that year, opening up an office area for me at the top of the stairs, building storage shelves and a countertop, adding a couple of closets, replacing the stove, and planting roses and geraniums alongside the forsythia, honeysuckle, lilac, and oleander. To me, the little house felt like a cozy storybook home, tall and narrow and paneled with wood, like the inside of a tree or a Beatrix Potter illustration inhabited by friendly hedgehogs or chatty field mice. It made me sad to think about leaving again. "What are our options?" Julien asked.

"Well," I proposed, "I could go back to the States and do this all over again—find another job, or reapply for the teaching program and wait another three months."

"Or?"

I stared at my hands. "Well, if I start looking now, there's always the chance I could find a job from here that comes with a visa."

"But you'd still have to go back and apply for the visa from there, wouldn't you?"

I nodded. "Yeah, I think so."

Julien poked me and smiled. "Isn't there another option?"

In spite of myself, I smiled, too. "Yes."

"Which is?"

"Which is . . . we could get married."

"We could."

"We could," I confirmed. "Just like the consulate guy told us to."

⁓

In mid-April 2005, after I learned that my work visa had been approved, I flew back to the States to pick it up, in time to celebrate my stepfather's seventy-first birthday, on May 23. My stepfather was what the French would call *mon papa de coeur*, my "heart-father." I called him "Abah," which means "Daddy" in Hebrew. In my later childhood, he had been the most present of my parents, the one who cooked me breakfast, shuttled me to and from school, and waited up for me at night. He was the rock in my life, my very definition of stability. The week I bought my ticket to Asheville, Abah had lost function in his left arm and went to see a neurologist for a battery of tests. By May 23 we knew he had a deadly brain tumor. That trip was the last time I saw him upright.

I returned to Alba for six weeks, during which Julien and I worked so much we barely saw each other, I as a waitress on lunch and dinner shifts and he on a project that required him to be at work before six in the morning. By the time I got home at night, he was asleep, and he left for his job long before I woke up.

The Internet had recently come to Alba, and one day, on a break between shifts, I thought to look up the Central Database of Shoah Victims' Names on the Yad Vashem website.

I entered my grandfather's family name, and more than a thousand records appeared. I went back and entered my great-grandmother's first name as well, which narrowed the search results to 167. Feeling a familiar chill, I searched through the list until I came to a woman from Strasbourg. I clicked the name and saw a dim image of my great-grandmother on a page of testimony submitted by my grandfather's eldest brother. I followed a link to the other pages he had submitted. There were my great-grandparents, my grandfather's sister-in-law, Rose, and Paul, her son. Rose had been deported in Convoy Number 8, on July 20, 1942, when she was twenty-eight. Gitla and Leon had been deported in Convoy Number 45, on November 11, 1942, the very day Anna had returned from her visit with Rosie and spent the night in Perpignan with her accidental savior, the very day the Germans invaded the French Free Zone.

I typed "Convoy No. 45, November 11, 1942, Auschwitz" into the search engine, which brought me to Serge and Beate Klarsfeld's memorial, "Chronological Table of Deportation Convoys." Convoy Number 45 was sent from Drancy to Auschwitz carrying 745 people, 634 adults and 111 children. Five hundred and ninety-nine were gassed on arrival, and two were alive when the camp was liberated in 1945. I sat back from the computer screen, as if the numbers might reach out and pull me into one of the nightmares I so feared.

If this was a fairy tale, then I was Little Red Riding Hood, crossing into the dark wood at whose edges I had grown up, whose shadows had tinged my grandmother's stories and ringed the light cast by the Shabbat candles at my grandfather's table. Perhaps my grandparents' strange silence and byzantine story were merely an effort to prevent me from going down that path, straight into the mouth of the wolf. I felt ashamed of my illusions about love affairs and ruined houses. Tables, lines, numbers; Convoy 45, November 11, 1942: this was the weight I was supposed to carry.

～

Abah's tumor symptoms worsened, and Julien and I took time off from our jobs to return to Asheville and help my family care for him. The Sunday before we were supposed to leave, Julien's mater-

nal grandmother died. We booked a train to Paris for the next day,
so we could be at the funeral, where I met most of Julien's family
for the first time. We mourned his grandmother, then boarded the
plane to Asheville, where we spent the rest of the summer with
Abah as the tumor laid waste to him. He died on August 21, 2005.

After the funeral, I surrendered to my grief. I hacked off all my
hair. I wept a lot. I shut down. I couldn't bear to be touched. And
I whirled dangerously close to a Charybdis of guilt over leaving my
mother, who had been chronically ill since my early teenage years.
Somehow she had pulled herself together to care for Abah, with astonishing force and energy, but now she was all alone, and I was terrified that if I left her, she would wilt like a vine without a stake to
cling to. By some strange miracle of synchronicity, my return flight
to France with Julien had been booked for the day following Abah's
memorial service, and as it approached, I was overcome with self-
reproach. Wondering whether I should stay, I caused an explosion in
my relationship with Julien, one of the few we've ever had.

"You can't take care of everyone forever," he exclaimed. "Your
grandfather, your father, your mother—who's next? Who will be
after that? When is it your turn?"

"But they need me."

"I need you, too," Julien objected. The two of us were sitting in
the car, on our way to pick up some MRI scans that had been taken
too late to be of any use or interest. "And more important, *you* need
you. What's it going to be? At some point, you're going to have to
live your own life."

Unbidden, a memory of a moment a week or two before Abah's
death floated into my head, when Abah could no longer move or
speak and Julien and I were sitting by him as he lay in a hospital
bed in my parents' room. Julien had brought Abah roses from the
garden, twining them onto his oxygen tube so he could smell a little
bit of summer. The roses looked like a boutonniere, and I couldn't

help thinking of all the times Abah and I had talked about what my wedding would be like, idly, with no special person in mind, just because we liked celebrations. Once he'd asked me whether I would make him wear a tux for the ceremony, and I'd told him he could wear whatever he wanted. "Maybe I'll wear one," he'd said. "Maybe it'll be hot pink." We'd laughed because we'd both have gotten exactly the same kick out of a hot pink tuxedo. Now, holding his hand as he lay in bed with a posy of roses fading over the pocket of his T-shirt, which also happened to be hot pink, I saw with brutal finality that he would never be at my wedding. And then I looked across the bed at Julien, steadfast and caring as he gripped my father's other hand, and I thought, *Maybe this is stronger than walking down the aisle. There are other consecrations than a wedding. Maybe this is one of them.*

So I got on that flight with Julien. We went back to Alba and continued the process of braiding our lives together. I worked my jobs. I waited to surface from my grief. I didn't write anymore. I sat next to our new woodstove and read novels or stared into space. I corresponded with my grandmother about the minutiae of our daily lives. On my trips to Geneva, I watched over my grandfather's worsening forgetfulness, wondering when I was going to have to intervene and what exactly I would do when the time came.

~

Now, sitting in bed with Julien on that January night in 2006, I thought over the whole sad, hard year, the bad storms our relationship had withstood. And I remembered the night when we held my father's hand and watched the roses move up and down on his chest. *Life has already married us,* I thought. *Our happiness has been weatherproofed.*

We turned to face each other, smiling big, uncontrollable smiles.

"I know this is serious," Julien said.

"It is," I agreed, still smiling.

"What do you think?"

"I'm not sure there's anything to think about. If you see what I mean. What do *you* think?"

"Well," reasoned Julien, "if I'm going to spend the rest of my life with someone, and I'm going to have children with them—then that person is clearly you."

"I feel the same way."

"Well, there you go."

"All right."

So that was that. We turned out the lights, snuggled down against each other, and went to sleep.

～

Julien and I were married on March 25, 2006, seventy years after my grandparents met, almost sixty years after they bought the house in La Roche, some fifty years after they ceased speaking to each other forever, and nine years after my grandfather first brought me to Alba. *"To think that house I bought so long ago brought you to the love of your life,"* Grandma wrote.

> *Wonders never cease. . . . You have my blessings and prayers for a good outcome! . . . I continue to wonder what I am still doing here, the <u>only</u> highlights being your mother's and your existence, as well as the wonder of a purchase, made on a dreary November day, that led to an alliance. . . . Strange and miraculous at the same time, which brings up questions of destination and predestination and such.*

By then Julien and I had made a lot of decisions about our future, notably that it was time to leave Alba for Paris. I found a job as a translator. Julien, once he had finished his projects in the Ardèche, would begin work at a company in Versailles that restored historical monuments. Our wedding crowned and concluded our time in the village, marking the beginning of a whole new life.

We got married at the Alba town hall, the same town hall I'd once sat in front of while my grandfather voted. Now it was filled with people we loved. Julien's mother sang, and everyone joined in:

> Dodi li
> *My beloved is mine*
> Va'ani lo
> *And I am his.*
> Haro'eh, bashoshanim.
> *Who pastures among the lilies.*

When she had finished, the mayor cleared his throat several times and blew his nose loudly. "I've watched Julien grow up, you might say, with particular interest. He's a fine young man, with a fine set of parents, a fine future ahead of him. And I remember Miranda's grandfather from when I was just a teenager—when I saw her here for the first time, I thought, I know she's coming home. Young people are the life of our village, and when I look at these two, I feel confident in our future. It seems only right," he concluded, "to be marrying them—two of the village's children—and I couldn't be more pleased."

He read aloud the French civil ceremony, and Julien and I exchanged rings and signed the paper that made us husband and wife.

"Now for the best part," the mayor announced. Julien and I kissed, and the room filled with whoops, hollers, and claps; a musician friend began to play, and everyone spilled out onto the town hall steps in a melodic springtime hubbub.

We ate, drank, and danced all night, and the music seeped out of the stone walls, into the streets, across the vineyards, down to

La Roche, to hide in the chinks of the darkened house among the shadows. I imagined another generation of dreams and intentions coming to rest in that abandoned place, abandoned to time and unknown to all but those who'd left them there. If Grandma was willing to accept that life unfolds slowly and mysteriously, across many decades, then I would, too. The house was not for me. My grandparents' secret was not mine. And maybe that was all right.

CHAPTER EIGHTEEN

A WEEK AFTER OUR WEDDING MY GRANDFATHER'S neighbor called me. "I think you need to come quickly. I ran into your grandfather in the elevator, and he told me he's being evicted."

I arrived in Geneva the next day to find Grandpa sitting at his dining room table in a snowdrift of papers.

"They keep saying I haven't paid the rent. They say they're going to throw me out of the apartment if I don't pay. *Those dogs.* I know I paid, I know I did." He gestured in mute frustration at the papers on the table, then looked up at me. "Can you do something?"

In the silence that followed his question, I understood he had been pretending for a long time, and I'd wanted so much for him to be all right that I'd let him. He'd done nothing with the carefully ordered piles and to-do lists I'd made him—nothing but hide them away. I took a week off from my job and set to work, locating old bills, late rent notices, letters from collection agencies, and empty tax forms. I dragged loads of papers—newspapers, discarded mail, circulars, magazines, newsletters—to the recycling bins, fascinated by the flotsam that churned up as I sorted: a letter I'd written him when I was eleven (corrected, of course); wedding invitations, obituaries, pictures of the babies of unknown friends; ancient birthday cards. And everywhere, battered photocopies of that poem he'd sent me all those years ago.

It is late last night the dog was speaking of you;
the snipe was speaking of you in her deep marsh.
It is you are the lonely bird through the woods;
and that you may be without a mate until you find me.

Sometimes my grandfather hovered and watched me work; at other times, he retired to his sitting room and leafed through a book of poetry or read the newspaper. Whenever I told him what I was about to do—file his papers, engage an accountant, settle a bill with a collection agency—I cringed, expecting him to lash out at me. But he said nothing. I waited until the end of the week to tell him that I was arranging for meals to be delivered to his apartment twice a day, for someone to stay to heat the meal and remind him to eat, for a nurse to come check on him daily, for weekly house calls from a doctor and a social worker. I stood back when I had finished, afraid he'd never speak to me again. Instead, he touched my cheek. "You're like a fairy. I don't know what I would have done without you."

That night I made dinner for the two of us, and in the silence as we ate, I almost could believe that everything was normal, that my grandfather was still an elaborately defended fortress of grudges, rules, and resentments. But then he would look up, and I would see the shy, unassuming smile of a little boy, reminding me that his intimidating presence and inflexible will were all but gone. When he smiled, he left off eating, the fork and knife forgotten in his hands. "Eat your dinner before it gets cold," I urged gently, and he obeyed. After dinner I washed the dishes, and he dried them. I made us an infusion of verbena, and as I poured the hot water from the kettle, I thought of the way verbena tea was once special and absolute, like everything else in his life, and how its aesthetic perfection had once seemed like a reprieve from the eggshells I tiptoed over all day. He served it in a pottery pitcher he reserved for herbal infusions. Its matching cups were precisely the right width and thickness, so that the infusion cooled quickly enough but not too quickly.

"Where are your verbena cups?" I asked.

"I'm sorry?"

"The green and yellow bowls we used to have our verbena tea in."

"Oh, yes. Thank you for reminding me." He stood to look for them, then sat down. "I'm afraid I don't know what I did with them."

"It's all right." I poured the tea into his ordinary tea bowls, and when we had finished drinking it, we wished each other good night. My grandfather went to brush his teeth, and I shut the door to the sitting room and sat down on my bed, the little daybed full of memories that were only mine now. I had thought after Abah's death that I never would cry again, but of course we all have room in our hearts for infinite measures of love and loss. I put my face in my hands and wept. When I saw my grandfather's light go out, I called Julien and told him everything. "I'm going to have to find him a nursing home." I felt far away, frightened, homeless.

"It's going to be all right," Julien reassured me, just as he had when my father had gotten sick. "We'll do it together. It will be okay."

～

As it turned out, my grandfather got along quite well with the system of nurses, social workers, and health aides I'd set up, at least until Julien and I were settled in Paris. My job in the translation firm started before Julien had wrapped up his commitments in Alba, so for the first eight months I lived in a nearly empty studio in Belleville. I had a futon bed, two camp chairs, a pot, a bowl, two coffee mugs, and a single set of silverware. My neighbors included my neurotic landlady who was terrified of the floor buffer machine the super used to clean the front hall, and a woman in the garden apartment below my balcony who drank whiskey outdoors on warm nights and intoned *"Plus jamais, plus jamais"* into the darkness in a gravelly, throaty voice. On weeknights, I'd walk through the city or write to my grandmother; on weekends, I took the train home to Julien, or he visited Paris.

Eventually, I tired of my solitary and wildly expensive apartment and rented a room in my friend Eve's house in Fontenay-sous-Bois, just outside the city. Eve, aware that I was supposed to be writing a book, set up an office for me, but I just sat looking at my notes or rifling through my grandmother's letters, without making any progress. Maybe I felt lost and displaced without a real home and without Julien; maybe I was sick of all the sadness and the space it had occupied in my life; maybe taking care of my grandfather left me too depleted to bring him to life on the page. Maybe all those things, but most of all, I had realized that I was now the keeper of whatever memories I'd gathered from my grandfather. The rest were disappearing or already gone. And what do you do when a silence vanishes into a different, vaster kind of oblivion? I'd spent a good part of my life searching for the words of the tragic, angry poem of Anna and Armand. And now it was evaporating, along with legions of other words I now recognized it was my job to remember and record. The task was too daunting. It was a long eight months.

It seemed to me I'd cut myself off and drifted away, from the United States, from my book, from my plans to become a historian, all for that unprecedented feeling of happiness that unfurled inside me when I was with Julien. And now I was alone in Paris, translating the minutes of shareholders' annual meetings and copy for perfume advertisements, with none of the things I'd abandoned along the way to Julien—and no Julien, either.

At my new job, I exercised my genetic predisposition for translation and interpreting—was this, too, a gift to fall back on, to help us *sourrwvive*? There was my grandmother: *When Erna and her roommate at four a.m. were woken up and me to interpret . . .* And my grandfather, of course, had studied German literature in Strasbourg and then attended interpreting school in Geneva during the war. Translation is writing without the commitment; interpreting is an invisible and evanescent form of brilliance performed on someone else's words. They are ghostly occupations, best suited to those who, for one reason or another, do not have a place they call home.

My office was in the Fifth Arrondissement, right across from the Île de la Cité. The bathroom, on the top floor, overlooked the Cathedral of Notre-Dame, and though it was cold and drafty up there, I loved to sit and stare at the view. I'd been inspired to study history on my first visit to the cathedral; I remembered touching the stone pillars in the nave and feeling a kind of electric ripple as I imagined the hands that had carved them. I knew my own hands were lingering in places those long-gone fingers had been. That, I thought, was history. Now I realized that the electric ripple that had so entranced me was not history but rather the gulf that separates the past from the present. I felt the same ripple, and the same gulf, when I touched the AUBETTE dish. History, I had learned, was easy enough to write. But not emptiness. What can you do but stare when confronted with an ever-widening gulf?

The worst part was watching the gulf swallow my grandparents. My grandmother's letters grew shorter and shorter. She rarely complained, but she had no illusions about the future:

> *My health—as expected at my age—is deteriorating, not as fast as I wish, as lingering I find very painful and unsatisfactory.*

❧

That summer, during a heat wave in Geneva, the nurse who visited my grandfather every day called to tell me he had been admitted to the hospital. When I reached the attending physician, she explained that he'd gotten the flu and become dehydrated. When the emergency room doctors tried to insert an IV, he'd panicked and become aggressive, then suffered a minor heart attack. He was recovering nicely, she assured me, and he'd be able to speak to me the next day, when he was out of intensive care.

"I was with him last week," I said. "He seemed fine. What happened?"

"Dehydration occurs very quickly in older patients, and it often aggravates senility."

"Irreversibly?"

"I'm afraid so," she admitted, and then added, "I take it he's a Holocaust survivor."

"How did you know?"

"I gathered from a few of the names he called me."

"I'm sorry. That must be pretty hard to take when you're caring for someone."

"We get used to it. It's pretty common, actually."

"What, for your patients to accuse you of being a Nazi?"

She laughed. "In a geriatric ward? You'd be surprised. But I meant the memory loss. It's pretty common for people with painful war trauma to lose their memory. That, and marriages gone bad."

❧

The next day, when I called my grandfather's room, he sounded relieved and incredulous. "Thank goodness you reached me. They were keeping me in some sort of prison."

"You're in the hospital." I tried to sound soothing and reassuring. The attending nurse had told me he'd barricaded himself in his room all night, pushing all the furniture against the door and screaming bloody murder when they tried to enter.

"Yes, they moved me. They let me out. I'm still under arrest, but now I'm in some sort of hotel."

Your heart really does ache for people, I thought. The expression is true. I could hear all the old fears chattering around inside him. "It's not a hotel," I explained. "And you're not under arrest. I promise. They're taking care of you. It's a care facility—a kind of hospital."

"No, no, it's a hotel."

"It's a place called the Hôpital de Loëx, in Bernex."

"No, no, Bernex is hundreds of kilometers away."

"No, Bernex is near Geneva, and you're in Bernex."

"I have no way of verifying that."

"Grandpa, you're all right." I was at a loss for what to tell him. "You're going to be all right. I promise."

"I would have called before, but I don't have any money. Not a cent."

"You do, Grandpa. It's fine. Everything's fine. Your money is all in the bank, and you can get at it."

"They took everything from me when I came here." His outrage was palpable. "They stripped me and searched me. Even my coin purse—my billfold, my knife, my watch, my pen—I can't even find my glasses."

I'd been trying to cure myself of the habit of linking everything to my grandparents' past, but in this moment, the connection was unavoidable. I could see, in my mind's eye, the page from my grandfather's police deposition:

Mr. Jacoubovitch presented himself voluntarily at the Zurich Central Police Station as a political refugee today. He declared that he had traveled here from France, and [believed he had] crossed the Swiss border on the night of December 10–11, 1942, near Champéry/Wallis.

> *1 Billfold with misc. papers.*
> *1 Pair spectacles with case.*
> *1 Knife.*
> *1 Coin purse.*
> *1 Watch.*
> *1 Fountain pen.*
> *1 Mechanical pencil.*

～

"He has to go to a nursing home," the attending physician declared the following week. "I can't release him in his own charge. I'll put in for a transfer to a long-stay geriatric unit until you find a place."

"It's good you're there to take care of him," Grandma wrote again, when I told her of the latest development in Grandpa's life. *"He'd be lost without you."* For the first time, it occurred to me that her interest in his welfare was rather extraordinary after all those years of bad blood.

I cannot let their story go, I thought, as I began looking for a nursing home. *I cannot let them disappear like this. I have to figure out what happened.*

～

By then Julien had begun his new job restoring historical monuments in Versailles, and we finally had moved into an apartment together, in the Fifteenth Arrondissement in Paris. He left for work at 6:30 a.m., so I spent the mornings before I departed for the office paging through the refugee files, buoyed by the wild hope that I had missed something, that my grandparents might have been interned in the same camp, or at least the same town, so that I could explain their reunion by a stunning coincidence. I decided to plot a map of all the places that appeared on their entry and exit passes, and in this way I traced them through camps and villages across Switzerland—Wald, Arisdorf, Olsberg, Wesen, Montana, Bienenberg, Finhaut, Territet. My hope deflated—carefully rereading their files merely confirmed that they had never been interned in the same place—then rebounded when I noticed that Arisdorf and Bienenberg were neighboring villages, less than five miles apart.

With a new sense of urgency, I wrote to my grandmother about the two moments I knew they'd spent near each other—their time in Arisdorf and Bienenberg and their residence at the mysterious "chez Berchtold."

In her replies, I noticed my grandmother stumbling over her English—another sign of the widening gulf between now and then, between remembering in silence and the oblivion of forgetting. *"Only once was I able to meet Armand in Basel for lunch with the Koppelmans. The last letter before end of war received from my mother had the latters' address in Switzerland."* What fear and tension were concealed in my grandmother's dense, newly shaky handwriting, a lifetime of emotion concealed in those two words: "last letter." Of course Grandma did not dwell on this final, frantic gesture from mother to child, a wave in the direction of a relative Mina hoped could help. Grandma had stayed with Mr. Koppelman and his wife in Basel during a weeklong course on refugee care in which she'd been enrolled by the Swiss refugee camp administration. *"The K's lived in a huge apartment on the outskirts of town in new apartment building complete with fancy beautifully uniformed maid and impressive valuable art."*

The book on Swiss refugee camps that included interviews with my grandfather describes the living conditions in the camp in Arisdorf, from which he would have traveled to lunch with my grandmother that day:

Lodged in barracks, the refugees slept in dormitories in groups
of about forty, on straw mattresses stacked on bunk beds. . . .
To wash in the morning, one had to go outside and use cold
water, when it wasn't frozen, in which case the refugees rubbed
snow on their faces.

Grandpa's great antipathy toward the very rich, which I always
had ascribed to a mix of ideology and jealousy, suddenly seemed
human and inevitable when I pictured his arrival at the Koppelmans' luxurious apartment and his bewildered recollection that he,
Anna, and Erna owed these prosperous people a *"dette d'honneur,"*
three hundred Swiss francs loaned for train travel when the three
had arrived in Switzerland.

Alone at my desk in our apartment in Paris, I listened to the city
come awake and tried to will myself into the recesses of my grandmother's memory, into the mind of a gaunt, black-haired young
woman perched on the edge of a costly sofa, wearing someone's
cast-off clothing, drinking an apéritif, and waiting for her lover
to arrive. I thought of *Dora Bruder,* in which Patrick Modiano describes his own attempt to write about the silent past:

I believe . . . at times, in a gift of clairvoyance in [writers.] . . .
It is simply part of the job: the efforts of imagination necessary
to this work, the need to fix one's mind on points of detail—and
this in an obsessive manner . . . all this tension, these cerebral
gymnastics, might possibly provoke, over time, brief intuitions
"concerning past or future events."

Anna and Armand were starved—for food, for affection, for
comfort, for beauty. And now they had a single afternoon to fill up
on all those things. Fixing my mind on the details of that lunch, I

felt a kind of hyperawareness in the two of them, a sensation of observing and being observed. Perhaps my grandparents worried their hunger and poverty would make them seem like savages; perhaps, to the contrary, they saw a kind of brutishness in the plush affluence of their hosts. Either way, they must have felt the Koppelmans' eyes on them as they lifted their glasses to their mouths, sliced their meat, and wiped their fingers on the soft cloth of the napkins. And at the same time, Anna and Armand must have noted every word the other said, every glance across the table, every motion the other did or didn't make. It was August 1943, and they had not seen each other for eight months.

My grandmother summed up the afternoon in a single sentence: *"They liked your charming, well-read grandfather."* The strange economy of her hurried writing again both masked and highlighted the way she cohabited with tragedy: *"K's only sister and child were not saved early enough by him bringing them to Switzerland, and she died, having become mad from starvation and running naked through the Transnistrian concentration camp, where my mother's brother and family also died."*

My grandmother's entry and exit passes confirmed that she had been released from Bienenberg for a weeklong training program, but I couldn't tell when or how my grandfather had obtained leave from his camp in Arisdorf. Thinking back to his story about going to church, I wondered whether he had hidden a part of what happened that Sunday.

There was no clue as to whether they spent even a moment alone together that day, whether Armand had time to murmur a few words to Anna that patched up or palliated their separation, everything they had endured or inflicted in their struggle to survive. What breathless shock must have bolted through the air when they first saw each other: I imagined my grandfather trying to gather his thoughts, turbulent as snowflakes, my grandmother flashing that search-lamp smile. An afternoon would not have been enough time for their idealized memories of each other to chafe against the reality of being together; it only would have been sufficient to rekindle a ghost of the spark that had flown across the table in the Café Aubette so many years before. There is a faint reason to believe he proposed to her then, in the hurried privacy of a hello or a good-bye, for my grandmother's letter went on to say, *"They approved of my marriage to Armand."* I imagined everything they had forgotten, given up, left behind, floating between them like a curl of smoke. Anna had spent the previous months cradling and examining other people's babies, but to Armand, Anna's hair and skin likely would have been his first tender contact with another body since they'd parted ways, the softest, most sweetly scented thing he had touched in months. I remembered my grandfather's broken voice the one time I'd had the courage to ask why he'd married her. "What else could I do?" he had cried.

Seen in that light, it was only inevitable that he would have said those three words: "Anna, marry me."

But if I had hoped for some romantic detail, a hint of the dizzy lurch they must have felt leaning toward each other, some shred of evidence that Armand had reached into his pocket and placed a small silver dish in Anna's hand to pledge their troth, all I received was another tightly compressed line with which my grandmother occluded still more pathos. *"[The Koppelmans] greeted my pregnancy with your mother as irresponsible on my part, which ended my contact with them."* I was appalled at this well-to-do Swiss couple weighing in on the probity of my grandparents' life choices. *"But your grandfather repaid our 300 S.F. debt when he worked for the French Ministry of Justice who hired him for Nuremberg,"* Grandma added, and for once, my grandfather's stupendous acts of subtle hostility seemed jubilantly, ferociously fitting. My grandmother moved on to my second question:

Berchtold was the middle age French woman widowed by her Swiss husband, where [your grandfather] found lodging when liberated from camp to study in Geneva at the École d'Interprètes at the University. Forgot her first name, could be Irma. (Your grdf should remember she was very fond of him, not so me, but let me stay at her lovely apt. with elevator to 4th floor with balcony over the street). There I got pregnant when living with him and attending the 6 month course "pour réfugiés d'après guerre." I saw her regularly when I visited from America and after my separation from your grandf. She was employed during WWII by the International Red Cross to research the whereabouts of French prisoners of war and you all had three names because she explained to me that someone . . . could only safely be traced by a second or third different name.

I marveled at everything she had packed into that paragraph: her nagging insecurity that my grandfather's refined allure was more potent than her guileless, tactless charm; her faithful visits to her onetime landlady long after etiquette would have allowed her to stop; the odd formulation she used to account for the conception of their child; and tacked on at the end, an explanation for our all having three given names, which I always had chalked up to my family's eccentricity. Not a word, though, about what it had been like to live with Armand.

～

In the geriatric ward, the doctor encouraged me to speak with my grandfather about his past. This, of course, I was eager to do. I mentioned the Koppelmans, and his face darkened. "Terrible people," he sniffed. "They don't merit any discussion."

I tried Mrs. Berchtold. This time, he looked dreamy. "Yes, she was very kind to me at one time. Very kind. I stopped speaking to her, after the war, though. She appeared to have taken sides with your grandmother." As always, he uttered those words as if they carried dangerous, ominous overtones, "and so you see I had to stop all contact with her."

"Do you remember living in Rive, during the war?"

"Rive. That's in Geneva. I used to live there."

"You still do."

"No, no," Grandpa shook his head.

"Where do you live, then?"

He looked at me haughtily. "I'm afraid I've not been provided with the information necessary to answer that question."

~

I learned from the refugee records that Anna and Armand spent four months in Madame Berchtold's apartment on the Cours de Rive. They were required to report to the Geneva central police station every Monday to prove they weren't violating any rules, hiding any illegal refugees, holding any unauthorized jobs, engaging in any political activities, or working as spies. For four months they slept in a bed of their own, cooked meals, went shopping, followed the news. Would they have heard that French troops had pushed through to the Rhine and captured Strasbourg?

I knew from my grandmother how much the two of them wanted a baby. At the end of the summer, a doctor—a colleague perhaps, or someone treating her for the pellagra she'd contracted in the camps—told my grandmother that years of starvation had shrunk her uterus to the size of a walnut. He said there was no hope. My grandmother went to another doctor and another. By December, the Battle of the Bulge had begun, and hopes flagged. A million men fighting in the woods, in the snow. The Allies registered huge losses.

My grandmother found a doctor who was researching the benefits of high doses of vitamins. He gave her regular vitamin K injections and told her not to worry. The Nazi forces withdrew from the Ardennes. The Soviets captured Warsaw; they liberated Auschwitz. Churchill, Roosevelt, and Stalin met at Yalta. By January, my grandmother was pregnant.

When I finished assembling this chronology of events, I read it to Julien.

"Can I see that?" He took the paper from me and scanned it. "Do you really associate your mother's conception with the Battle of the Bulge?"

"I'm being symbolic."

"Come on," he objected. "They must have known better than to pin their lives on the ups and downs of the war. Did they even know what was going on?" Julien flipped through the stack of travel permits I'd assembled. "It doesn't look like they saw much of each other."

"No!" I exclaimed. "That's why I'm reduced to the damn Battle of the Bulge. Even afterward—if you look here, they lived together from November 14, 1944, till"—I shuffled through the pages— "1944 . . . November, December, January, February, 1945 . . . till March 6, 1945."

"That's it?" Julien picked up my grandmother's letter again. "Where did she go on March 6?"

"To a professional course of some sort." I found a letter from her refugee file and read aloud:

Major de Rham, who greatly appreciated Mme. Dr. Jacoubovitch's services during her time in Leysin, has asked her to run a course being organized in les Diablerets. Given that Mme. Dr. Jacoubovitch is pregnant, this will allow her to continue her excellent work under less physically tiring conditions than in her current post in the sanatorium. Mme. Dr. Jacoubovitch has enthusiastically

accepted the proposal. She will, naturally, be performing this work
as a volunteer.

I flipped forward a few pages. "And here it says her permit was
extended to July 31, 1945. Do you think they were avoiding each
other?"

"How much choice could they have had?" Julien asked.
"Wouldn't they have had to take whatever jobs were being offered?
Where was your grandfather?"

"In Geneva." I handed him another of my grandmother's letters
from the file, this one in my grandmother's handwriting:

Since my letters of July 9 and 25 went unanswered, I am tak-
ing the liberty of confirming the information I gave therein, and I
ask again that you notify me of your continued approval. As my
contract with the Military Hospital ended on July 31, I advised
the Commandant at Leysin that I would be traveling to Geneva,
where I would like to remain until my husband, who will be repa-
triated to France around August 25, 1945, leaves the city. Please
allow me to go to Sierre after his departure. My delivery date has
been estimated for mid-September, and I would like to be certain
that I can prepare for the event at the La Providence maternity
hospital, whose director is a friend of mine.

"I guess they spent a few weeks together right before she gave
birth," I said. "And then my grandfather left the country, to start
preparing for the Nuremberg Trials."

"So once they were married, they lived with each other for"—
Julien counted—"November, December . . . four months—and then
maybe three weeks before your grandfather left."

"Plus the five-day leaves she talked about in her letter," I pointed
out. "That would make . . . two leaves—ten more days."

"What do you think those months were like?"

I recalled the picture in my mother's album of my grandmother leaning against the railing on Madame Berchtold's balcony and gazing at my grandfather.

"Maybe that was their problem," Julien suggested. "Maybe they'd spent so much time apart, they'd started to idealize each other, and it was a disappointment to live with the real thing."

I was still thinking of the photo and the erotic tension it seemed to betray. "Or maybe they spent just enough time together to keep idealizing each other, and the disappointment set in later."

"When the war was over," my grandmother wrote on a page in her notebook titled "Free Associations,"

for me it was strange, to feel so little, not to say nothing. All the—over four years—of hoping, waiting, imagining what it would be like, what I am going to do, flew away, when the moment of realization that it had really happened arrived. And then suddenly, doubt, fear, what now? Put together a life, different because the world was different, was it possible? Could one do it? Another memory was the sadness for what had been lost, the carnage, cruelty, and inhumanity, never dreamt of it could exist, became a burden to be part of one's life from now on, not to be forgotten or repressed because it would be an insult to the victims, and only our memory could serve their heroism or cowardice. I remember becoming busy, with what? as if to rush into what would be real life, as if the other one during the war years, wasn't or hadn't been real.

Indeed, everything seemed to accelerate in 1945. My grandmother returned to her work as a physician; my grandfather completed his training as an interpreter and was recruited to work at the Nuremberg Trials. On August 22, 1945, my grandfather left Geneva for Paris, with a *laissez-passer* that read:

> It has been Switzerland's privilege to offer you shelter in your time of need. It was not always possible for us to give everything we might have wished to the numerous refugees to whom we offered asylum. We hope nevertheless that your stay in Switzerland was of service to you and we wish you all the best for the future and the future of your country.

All those years of tension and waiting culminated in a few polite lines printed on a flimsy piece of paper. Suddenly, it occurred to me to ask what had followed the war's end. The kaleidoscopic fragments of their lives shook out into a new pattern to decipher, and I began to wonder whether the fissures in my grandparents' relationship might have come after, not during, the war.

CHAPTER NINETEEN

IN THE GERIATRIC HOSPITAL, MY GRANDFATHER HAD to be sedated most days. Otherwise he'd run away, or become hysterical and barricade himself in his room, or scream for help long into the night.

During one of my phone calls to the hospital, a nurse inquired, "Was your grandfather a lawyer of some sort?"

"No, why do you ask?"

"Sometimes he recites things . . . it sounds like legal language. Like a trial. I just wondered. I wouldn't bother you with it, only sometimes it's rather gruesome."

When I was younger, the Nuremberg Trials had been one of the few parts of his past about which my grandfather would talk freely—or so I thought. He showed me the pictures of him in General Telford Taylor's memoir of the Trials. He made me laugh with his description of Henri Donnedieu de Vabres's giant mustache, which the French judge used for cover as he whispered commentary on courtroom proceedings to my grandfather, who had been selected to facilitate the judges' deliberations partway through Trial One. He told me about being inducted into the U.S. Army and receiving a uniform and better pay. He explained the system of lights the interpreters used: yellow to slow down the speakers, red to signal a technical breakdown or a problem at the interpreters' desk. He took pride in the fact that he never leaked anything to the press. He recalled French prosecutor François de Menthon's kindness in helping to arrange his French citizenship—the first time in his life

My grandfather (second from the right) in the interpreters' section at the Nuremberg Trials, probably taken during the shooting of a publicity film that explained the innovative translation system and technologies the Trials employed.

my grandfather had ever been a citizen of any country. He described how hard it was to interpret for Göring and how he grew to see Speer as *"le moins pire"*—the least worst. He remembered some of the female interpreters refusing to translate obscenities. He told me about the tensions in the judges' secret meetings; about their endless debates and disagreements; and about the Russians' insistence that the Nazis had committed the Katyn Forest massacres, prompting Judge Donnedieu de Vabres—again under cover of his mustache—to lean toward him and breathe, "They're liars."

So I thought I knew quite a bit about my grandfather's first experiences as a professional interpreter. I had filed his role at the Trials under "proud accomplishment" and forgotten it in my quest to trace the story of my grandparents' relationship, overlooking its impor-

Armand on his first visit to meet his new daughter, Angèle, during leave from the Nuremberg Trials in December 1945.

A photograph from a series of Anna with Angèle taken in 1946 and sent to Armand while he was working in Nuremberg.

tance because my grandmother hadn't been there. All over again, I was awed by their ability to camouflage the very existence of their continued relationship: until now, it had never crossed my mind that they had been married at that time. Married but far apart from each other. What effects did this separation have on their lives?

I remembered a photo of my grandfather holding my mother as a baby, looking pleased and slightly surprised, as if she'd landed in his arms out of nowhere. Now I realized that the photograph must have been taken during one of his leaves from Trial One and that it documented meeting his daughter for the first time. Similar pictures of my grandmother, in which she observes her new baby with intense, almost ferocious, love, had been taken in Armand's absence, as he worked in a corner of the courtroom in Nuremberg.

My grandfather's refugee file ended with his departure for France, but my grandmother's continued through 1949. I noticed my grandfather's handwriting on one of its pages:

Armand Jacoubovitch
c/o Tribunal militaire international
20, place Vendôme—Paris

Nuremberg, 2 January 1946
Federal Department of Justice and Police
Police Division
Reference: refugee no. 7130 Vö

Dear Sirs,
I thank you for renewing the refugee permit of my wife, Madame Anna Jacoubovitch-Münster, until 1 May 1946. I am particularly grateful for your efforts given the peculiar situation in which I currently find myself: my parents were deported in 1942, our property was pillaged in 1940 when the Germans entered Strasbourg, and, finally, our house was destroyed by bombing. I am therefore obliged to start over from nothing, and, since I am currently working in Nuremberg as an interpreter at the International Military Tribunal, I am unable to bring my wife and baby to France, as I possess neither furniture nor household linens, and you are certainly aware of how difficult it is to find housing in Paris at this time.

I therefore propose to bring my wife and my child to Paris upon my own return to the city; that is to say, once the Nuremberg trial is over, no doubt sometime in April.

Under the circumstances, I would be most obliged to you if you would kindly ask the Geneva Police to renew my wife and child's residency permit, which currently runs only to 31 January.

If you could extend the permit to 1 May 1946, my wife would be able to avoid taking the steps that would otherwise be required for its renewal, steps that are rather difficult for her given that she is all alone and still nursing her baby.

Sincere regards,

A. Jacoubovitch

Until April! Poor Grandpa—that main trial had lasted until October 1946. Transcripts of the Nuremberg Trials are available online through the Lillian Goldman Law Library at Yale Law School, but I'd never taken the time to look at them. I clicked through until I came to January 2, curious to learn what my grandfather's work had been like that day. I scanned the page, and the enormity of what I'd been missing hit me.

Car after car was filled, and the screaming of women and children and the cracking of whips and rifle shots resounded unceasingly. Since several families or groups had barricaded themselves in especially strong buildings and the doors could not be forced with crowbars or beams, the doors were now blown open with hand grenades. Since the ghetto was near the railroad tracks in Rovno, the younger people tried to get across the tracks and over a small river to get away from the ghetto area. As this stretch of country was beyond the range of the electric lights, it was illuminated by small rockets. All through the night these beaten, hounded, and wounded people moved along the lighted streets. Women carried their dead children in their arms, children pulled and dragged their dead parents by their arms and legs down the road toward the train. Again and again the cries, "Open the door! Open the door!" echoed through the ghetto.

I began shaking. That familiar, gruesome sorrow gripped me. I shut my computer and tried to breathe. All those words had come out of my grandfather's mouth as he worked. How foolish I'd been. I'd never considered what impact this experience might have had on him.

~

When I next visited my grandfather, he seemed more at ease, despite the nurse's reports. "This mission is quite dull, really," he informed me in a low voice. "I'm hardly in the booth at all. I'll be going home soon."

"I see," I replied, not quite sure how to tell him that wasn't true. "Do you think about the Nuremberg Trials? Do you remember them?"

"Of course."

"It must have been very difficult for you."

"Well, interpreting is quite a difficult job," he said, as if I had suggested he was mentally impaired. "Not everyone can do it."

I wondered if this might be a personal jab, since I myself was working as an interpreter by then, but I doubted he remembered that. "I meant the content of the Trial," I elaborated. "The things you were interpreting. Do you remember any of that? The nurse said . . ." I groped around for the right way to describe it ". . . she said you were having nightmares, and I wondered if it was about that."

My grandfather was silent. "It's like a black box. I carry it . . . I have it with me, but when I open it, there's nothing inside."

~

I began researching the Trials and my grandfather's role in them. I learned from an interview my grandfather had given to the *Berliner Zeitung* in the mid-nineties that he broke down in the interpreters' booth during Göring's testimony. In another account, I read that Göring had criticized the interpreters directly; at one point, he supposedly barked, "You are shortening my life by several years." I could find no record of his comment in the trial transcripts, but I wondered whether my grandfather had been the unlucky recipient of one of his barbs and whether it had contributed to his crumbling under the strain. Certainly, interpreters' breakdowns were common during the trial, so common that they kept a team of substitutes waiting at all times. Armand and the other Jewish interpreter had been furloughed to the translators' section when what they were hearing got to be too much for them.

Historians and eyewitnesses of the Trials agree that of all the defendants, Göring was the most daunting: he spoke in long, tricky sentences and deliberately obfuscated, baiting the prosecutors, derailing direct examinations, and tearing through cross-examinations at a speed that often tripped up the interpreters or the cross-examiners themselves. I remembered my grandfather telling me stories to that effect, though at the time I'd thought they were amusing anecdotes: in German, verbs are conjugated partly at the end of sentences, and by the time Göring arrived at the end of his sentences, he'd often forgotten how they'd begun. "Sometimes he didn't make any sense," I remembered my grandfather recounting, "and I had to tell the judges that the sentence was of no importance." In his memoir of the trials, Richard Sonnenfeldt recalls, "At Nuremberg, as I anticipated meeting Göring, I felt the Jewish refugee I had once been tugging at my sleeve," and I thought, *Grandpa still was a Jewish refugee at the time.* What must it have been like for him, speaking for Hitler's second-in-command?

I contacted Tomas Fitzel, the author of the article in the *Berliner Zeitung*, to see if he could give me any more information; he replied,

> *Unfortunately he broke off contact because I wrote that he had a breakdown when he had to translate for Goering. A colleague told me this information about him, not he himself. Perhaps he felt ashamed, but my intention was to talk about this extremely hard and sometime inhuman job he and his colleagues had to do.*
>
> *In our interview, he wanted to say that because you had to be so concentrated on your work of translating, afterward you could not remember; it passed through you. But instead he used a wrong—or better—the right metaphor: the work had been like a filter. So the knowledge of the horrible testimonies was to a certain extent kept out. But in reality the filter was he himself, without being conscious that what he translated became something he kept in him.*
>
> *I remember that I never thought before our interview of who he might be: a Jew, a victim, has his family been killed? The moment I rang the bell of his apartment in Geneva, I looked at his name and felt like I was reading it for the first time; I thought oh my God, how stupid I am.*

If indeed my grandfather had a breakdown, he never mentioned it to anyone, and he went back to interpreting quite rapidly. But the content of the trial altered the rest of his life.

My grandfather was present when the films shot by the U.S. Army upon liberation of Nazi concentration camps were projected on November 29, 1945. The court was shown affidavits signed by the filmmakers attesting that the films had not been tampered with or altered in any way. That's how unbelievable they were.

No one knew what to expect when the American prosecutor Thomas Dodd said, "This is by no means the entire proof which the prosecution will offer with respect to the subject of concentration camps, but this film which we offer represents in a brief and unforgettable form an explanation of what the words 'concentration camp' imply."

It's said even some of the defendants wept openly in the courtroom. Supposedly, one of the judges took to his bed for three days.

And my grandfather, alone in a wrecked city in former enemy territory, new to his job, shy around his colleagues, sitting awkwardly near the projection screen in his corner seat in the interpreters' section? My grandfather can only have thought:

Those are my parents.

He was one of the first to see the human skins tanned for lampshades and paperweights, the scars, the tattoos, the piles of clothes and shoes and gold fillings, and worse. Much worse. He saw all these things before they became common knowledge. He saw them before there were words like *Shoah* or *Holocaust*, before six million became a meaning-laden number, before the documentaries and museums and archives and memorials and school lessons gave us some sort of awkward carrying device for that terrible darkness.

My grandfather was thirty years old when the trial began. In trial footage, he looks younger but haggard, as if the testimony he was hearing were taking years off his life and causing him to relive the war, this time knowing all that would happen. He moves restlessly as he works, hunching over and then leaning back, fidgeting with pencil and paper, unsure where to put his hands, twisting in his seat. Seeing him for the first time in video clips preserved by the Steven Spielberg Film and Video Archive at the U.S. Holocaust Memorial Museum, I had the creepy sensation of watching myself: I moved in the exact same way when I worked in the interpreting booth—another strange imbrication of my life and my grandparents'.

I knew from experience that the intense focus required by the job would have meant that as long as he kept working, every sentence he said would be replaced by another and another; he didn't have time to remember or think about any particular one. But inevitably, every day he worked in Nuremberg became a day of knowledge he possessed and my grandmother did not. What happened when he returned to her? He would have arrived carrying all those words, packed away somewhere in his mind. Did he know the damage this was inflicting on him? Regardless, he must have seen that the fault line separating their personalities was becoming unbridgeable.

In the very days and weeks when my grandmother was returning to the world of the living, nuzzling their new baby and nursing sick refugees back to health, my grandfather was sitting in a dim, smoke-filled courtroom, helping invent a vocabulary for a universe more frightening and hellish than anything he ever could have imagined. As one witness, Dr. Franz Blaha, said when he asked to testify in German instead of his native Czech: "A large number of special and technical expressions relating to life in and about the concentration camps are purely German inventions, and no appropriate equivalent for them in any other language can be found." Imagine being one of the people who had to bring to life concepts and acts so inconceivable that the vocabulary for them did not exist in other languages.

No amount of loyalty and optimism on my grandmother's part could pull him out of that abyss; no amount of sorrow could match the horror he had felt; no amount of pride in his intelligence and accomplishment could palliate the pain of participating in the world's attempt to bring some measure of justice to the unpardonable—especially as atrocities such as the Katyn Forest massacre came to light and undermined his confidence in those who claimed to be among the just. They broke apart because of what he knew and my grandmother did not.

They broke apart, but how could they let go of each other? How could they let go after all they had been through?

～

In November 2006 my grandfather was transferred to the extended stay unit of a new hospital, too quickly for me to come and accompany him for the move. For a while, his nightmares and anxiety worsened. When Julien and I visited him for the first time, we checked in at the nurses' station before going to his room, and the nurse on duty said, "I need to warn you, he's looking very unkempt."

"Why?"

"He won't let us near him to cut his hair. We've tried clippers and scissors, but he completely panics and calls us the ugliest things. I take it he's a Holocaust survivor."

I nodded.

"Poor thing. They're always the hardest with grooming and personal care. They like being handled even less than the other patients. Maybe it'll be different for you, though," she suggested. "Would you mind trying?"

She handed me a sheet and a pair of scissors. "Don't worry about the hair on the floor. We'll come sweep it up when you're finished."

My grandfather's face lit up when he saw us. "Hello!" he called joyfully. "How on earth did you find me here?"

"I always know where you are," I assured him. "I talk to your doctors and nurses and make sure everything's all right—even when I can't come visit." I braced myself for an outburst, but my grandfather smiled.

"That's a comfort."

"You could use a haircut," I ventured.

He reached up to touch his hair. "I know," he acknowledged ruefully. "But I don't have any money to pay a hairdresser."

"Well, it's your lucky day." I showed him the scissors and sheet and bowed. "Miranda the hairdresser, at your service." Once again I expected a tirade, but my grandfather sat down and looked up at me expectantly, with the same meek, trusting smile I'd noticed that spring. So Julien sat on the bed and chatted with him while I snipped. Grandpa relaxed visibly under my fingers. The room was spare and quiet and looked out over a tree-filled park. The window was open, and we could hear birds singing. Grandpa stopped talking and bowed his head slightly. He looked peaceful, more peaceful than I'd ever seen him. I wondered if the memory loss might actually be something of a boon to him.

When I'd finished his haircut, we walked to the hospital cafeteria for coffee.

"Do you think about anything in particular?" Julien asked him.

Grandpa shook his head. "Not really—I watch the trees in the park . . . and the birds . . ." He pointed to the gardens through the window and trailed off. We waited for something more, but it didn't come.

"When you think about your life, is there anything in particular that comes back to you?" Julien pressed, gently.

"Not particularly—the war. The war, I guess."

"Which part of it?" I asked. "Your time in the army?"

"No, not really—that was quite dull."

"About the Pyrenees?" I suggested.

"Yes." He picked up a packet of sugar and hesitated, trying to recall whether he'd already put some in his coffee.

"You put in one sugar," I pointed out.

"What? Oh, thank you."

"That's a difficult time to remember," Julien said. "A sad time."

My grandfather nodded, squinting out the window into the sun as if he were looking for something hidden over the horizon. "No doubt . . . ," he drew the words out slowly, picking each one with care, "no doubt the woman with whom I was living . . . she was very practical . . . no doubt she contributed greatly to our survival."

The hair stood up on the back of my neck. "You mean my grandmother?"

Grandpa looked blank.

"You mean . . . you mean Anna Munster?" I suppressed an urge to look around and make sure the building was still standing. It was the first time in my life I had uttered her name in his presence.

He nodded slowly. "Yes, that's her. That's the name. She's the one."

CHAPTER TWENTY

THANKS TO THE GOOD OFFICES OF MY GRAND-father's niece and her husband (with whom Armand had been close and then, as was typical of him, stopped speaking to years ago for a mysterious set of reasons he kept recorded in a special binder he would brandish at me from time to time), Grandpa was placed on the emergency list of Geneva's one Jewish nursing home. In the spring of 2007, his social worker called to let me know there was a room available for him. I traveled to Geneva to prepare for the move, and Julien joined me that weekend to help get him settled.

When we opened the door to my grandfather's apartment, the familiar scent of bergamot, rosemary, paper and pencil, and pipe tobacco bowled me over. I stopped on the threshold, and Julien squeezed my hand. "Think of how much better off he'll be," he reminded me. This was undeniably true. I squared my shoulders, and we stepped inside.

I took out the list the nursing home had given me: trousers, shirts, underwear, socks . . . "All his clothes are in there." I gestured at the blue lacquered doors of his bedroom wardrobe, lowering my voice as if we might disturb someone. "I guess I'll take care of his toiletries and the personal things." We began making neat piles on the bed.

Still shy of invading Grandpa's privacy, I waited until everything else had been packed before I emptied the drawer of his bedside table. While Julien organized bags to be brought down to the car, I gingerly tugged it open. Inside was an unmarked, unsealed manila envelope. Out of it, I pulled a photocopied booklet folded in half over a single sheet of paper, a letter. *"Dear Monsieur Jacoubovitch,"* it read,

> *The French State wishes to extend its deepest regrets over its part in the deportation and subsequent death of your parents, Leon and Augustine Jacoubovitch.*

There was the deportation date, their arrival date in Auschwitz, and nothing more. Nothing about the state's great guilt, nothing about the suffering it had inflicted, no real apology, nothing. Just that terrible withering down to numbers, place names, and dates. I lifted the letter and saw the title of the booklet beneath it: *Suicide, mode d'emploi. Suicide: A Manual.*

Julien was outside, loading the car. I was alone in the apartment.

Not knowing what else to do, I folded the papers and put them back into the envelope. I sat on the bed for a moment, holding my grandfather's terrible secret. It occurred to me again that his dementia might be a reprieve, granting him the freedom to live a few years with those unspeakable memories effaced, to be relieved of the task of remembering.

I directed my attention once more to the drawer, wondering what red thread he'd clung to all those years, what had kept him from following through with the instructions in that manual. The drawer was empty, save for a travel alarm clock and an old wallet. I opened the wallet. It looked empty, too, but I looked through the pockets anyway. In one of them I found a white rectangle marked with a date. I took it out and turned it over. It was a photograph of my grandmother. She was young and beautiful, smiling for the camera, her black hair curled around her face and a polka-dotted scarf knotted around her neck. I looked at the date again: July 12, 1944—my grandparents' wedding day.

Chapter Twenty-one

Later, much later, my grandmother finally told me about her married life, what little she had of it. In an essay titled "Marriage," she confirmed what I already had observed in my grandparents' refugee files:

Married life consisted of being together during my leaves from camp, every 6 weeks for five days until I was recognized to have pellagra . . . which liberated me from camp and allowed me to participate in a 6 months course (on scholarship) preparing a group of individuals for after-war assistance in the East when camps, prisons, and populations were freed from Nazi occupation.

I wondered if either of my grandparents thought to comment on the irony of being brought together twice by the same nutritional deficiency, first in the dissertation Armand had helped Anna to edit and then in its physical manifestation in my grandmother. Pellagra causes skin lesions, hair loss, and edema, as well as disorientation and confusion. In my experience, my grandfather's penchant for venom disappeared in the face of others' weakness or suffering, and I hoped he had been kind to my grandmother in the first weeks of their life together in the room they rented from Madame Berchtold. In another letter, Grandma wrote:

We were so busy, that except for meals or evenings we hardly saw each other, or weekends. But there, I became probably more aware

*of the opinion he had of me as, yes, a well educated, but unsophis-
ticated Romanian peasant, one of his favorite insults among many
others. I had a strong and well-established ego from home and
always knew that his insults revealed more about himself than me.
At work, in studies, I was usually well appreciated and regarded;
preventing a total break, though often during our relationship, I
thought I had come close to it.*

*What really ended the marriage was my discovery that af-
fective and cognitive development can be totally divorced from
each other. By that I mean that intellectual understanding and
brilliance in abstract notions had little or nothing to do with affection, empathic feelings, and consequently the need to respect
others' aspirations and meet them. The shock of this discovery
revealed also, in great part, my naïveté, having been dazzled by
the brilliance, but also the underlying hardness (like a diamond),
never guessed.*

So that's what Grandma had to say, sixty years later, about her
husband, their relationship, the fault lines in her marriage: Grandpa
was brilliant, but he was cruel, and he didn't—he couldn't—love
her. Her letter ended, *"Don't forget my memories from so long ago had
been most likely modified by time and events. . . . I keep thinking much
about you and wishing, that whatever happens, together you'll make it as
you have each other to sustain you."*

Untangling the thread of my grandmother's memory, I saw
there must have been a kind of honeymoon period in the four
months she and my grandfather spent at Madame Berchtold's. My
grandmother's illness, the newness of their being together, the
fact that they "hardly saw each other," all would have limited my
grandfather's inborn peevishness; what's more, given the level of
irritability common in both their families, my grandmother likely

would have taken an occasional volley of cranky, nasty insults in stride. I knew my grandfather dealt with stress and pain by being mean. The closer he was to you, the freer he became with his hypercritical nastiness. If he had loved her, if he was intimate with her, I only can imagine how horridly he must have treated her—but in a way to which she sadly must have been accustomed, and which would have been mitigated by the good news of the end of the war, my grandmother's pregnancy, and my grand-father's new job.

The more I considered it, the more certain I became that the rupture must have happened later. I recalled my grandmother telling me that in 1948, when she took her parents on the train to Marseille and bought the house in Alba on the way back, she broke down and confessed to her mother how bad things were. Between my grandfather's departure from Geneva in 1945 and that train ride in 1948, one major event had occurred: Nuremberg.

After the Trials, the hardness set in. For how could Armand possibly have described to her the chemical tinge of the lights, the rustle and thud of papers and binders being distributed, the high-pitched clatter of the steno typists re-turning to their machines, sounds that seemed to suck all possibility of the outside world from the big brown room? How could he have told

Probably Armand's first passport photos, taken in Paris in 1946 after the French legal team at the Nuremberg Trials helped him obtain French citizenship.

her of the cold sweat that must have gripped him when Fritzsche or Speer nodded hello to the interpreters as they filed in? How could he have conveyed how he fidgeted off his drowsiness when it was not his turn to work, turned his attention to the people in one corner of the courtroom and then another, stared at the men sitting and listening to the charges against them, fought off waves of boredom, anger, hostility, grief, exhaustion, disbelief, then coiled himself awake, into the tensest, densest kind of listening, when it was his turn to work? The interpreters had little recall of the words they rattled off all day long, but nearly all of them complained of nightmares.

And every so often, like a diver surfacing for air, Armand would notice the words he and his colleagues were saying and feel a wave of understanding splash over him. And then the torrent of words would rush forward again, and he would forget the phrase and lose track of the meaning. The words seemed to roll off him. As they came out of his mouth, he learned the crimes committed against his family. And then his mind closed back around them, and nothing ever looked the same again. Who could wear a wedding band after learning of the stacks of them stripped off perished fingers? Who could read by the light cast through a lampshade? Coats, hats, children's toys—everything had been marked, stained, destroyed. My grandfather's personality could not withstand it. He hardened around that knowledge, and his hardness cut my grandmother to the quick.

The enormity of my grandfather's silence, I realized, was commensurate with the enormity of the knowledge he carried away from Nuremberg. He did not know how to live in a world where love and *that* existed. And my grandmother, whose zest and ingenuity had carried them both so far—my grandmother did. And because she was able to continue loving, she left. I thought of the courage it must have taken to break her bond with that terrible weight of sadness and bitterness, a weight the whole world believed she ought to bear with Armand, and go live her life. She could love a man with whom she had been through so much, but she could not let him drag her down into an existence devoted to remembering. Anna was brave enough to move forward, even if it meant leaving the one person who connected her to her past.

But she'd never fully abandoned him. All the ways she nudged me back to him over the years, starting with sending me to boarding school in Geneva when I was a teenager, were, I believe, her final attempts to save him, to show him how to love again. And in the process, she saved me. She'd refused to let the weight of our sad past pull me under; recognizing my childhood fears, my frequent illness, my sense of displacement, she had pushed me away, pushed me to the house in La Roche, pushed me to be alive. Unlike her, I was lucky enough to be young in a time where I could live and love as I wished. While I was trying to remember, Grandma was urging me to forget, to put it down on paper and get on with the labor of living.

⌒

By the time I finished reconstructing and recording my grandparents' story, my grandfather was too senile to read it, but I had grown up enough not to regret that: I'm sure it would have taken him about a paragraph to fly into a rage and never speak to me again.

But as I had dreamed, my grandmother did read it, all the way through, at the age of ninety-seven. I was nearly five months pregnant, and I had flown back to the States to visit her for what we both knew would be the last time. "I loved it," she told me. "I'm glad you got it all written down."

"But did I get it right?" I asked. "I can't have. It must be full of mistakes. What should I change?"

She sighed and leaned back on her pillows. "Mirandali, it's so long ago now. Who can remember?"

I stretched out next to her in the bed, and she scooted over to make room for me. We lay there spooned up against each other, and I tried to soak up all I could of her, so that the little baby I was carrying could get a whiff of that indomitable zest for life, that ineffable perfume of contradictions. I hoped she couldn't see the tears squeezing out of my eyes because I knew she wouldn't approve of them.

"You know I don't want you to come to my funeral," Grandma said, into the silence.

"Oh, Grandma, I can't promise you that."

"You'll be too pregnant, anyway," she predicted. "That's good. You know I'll be right here." She tapped herself on the chest and head.

I changed the subject. "Do you know, I was at a party with Julien's *tante* Chantal, she's about your age, a little younger—I think you'd like her so much."

"You wrote to me about her."

"Well, we were talking, and you know what she said? She said she was so glad to live to see the day when a young man from a French bourgeois Catholic family could marry a Jewish girl." I stopped short. This was, I realized, not necessarily the fate a Jewish grandma would wish on her only granddaughter. "Is it okay with you?" I asked. "Is it okay that I moved to France and married a goy?"

Grandma made an impatient noise. She reached around and smacked me on the bottom. "Mirandali, forget it. All that is in the past. You have to live your life *forward*. Go eat some lunch."

～

My grandmother died on September 19, 2010, the day after Yom
Kippur. I was, as she had foreseen, too pregnant to fly home. Our
daughter, Estelle Anna, was born three months later to the day, on
December 19, 2010.

On the eve of Yom Kippur, through fasting and prayer, you are
supposed to break your bonds with the physical world in order to
make yourself right with the Holy Spirit, in order to be sealed in the
book of life for another year.

I stood in a synagogue in Paris thinking hard about all the bonds
I had and hardest of all about the one I didn't want to break. I knew
Grandma was lying in her bed in Pearl River, with my mother and
uncle beside her, preparing to breathe her last breath.

I listened to the cantor begin *Kol Nidre,* the prayer that cancels
debts, vows, and obligations, and as the congregation joined in, I
broke my bonds with my grandmother. "You can go," I whispered
to her. "We'll be all right without you."

~

"What do I regret?" my grandmother wrote once, many years ago.

> *Looking back . . . I regret deeply only to have lived in a world which
> never replicated the simplicity and happiness experienced in my
> native country's villages. Seeking villages, when occasion permitted,
> I tried to see if they could replicate what I searched for, but it was in
> vain. Most probably the exaggerated feelings I thought I experienced
> as a child and teenager, meaning elation, happiness, hope, started
> to fade and [I found them] irreplaceable when I reached adulthood
> and the world around me started to disintegrate. And thus only
> living in the present—not looking back, or too much forward—made
> sense. I became the person full of awareness that the past can't be
> brought back and regrets are futile, impeding going forward.*

My mother says that on the day before she died, my grandmother's eyes flew open, and she looked up toward the ceiling, as
if she were being greeted by all the elation, happiness, and hope
that had faded when her world disintegrated. The last words she
responded to were my mother's telling her that Julien and I were
expecting a girl and that the girl would be named for her. When she
heard that, she smiled.

After our daughter was born, Julien and I moved back to Alba,
where we bought a medieval ruin of our own. (Which, inciden-
tally, was previously owned by the wife of John Ford, who filmed
the Nuremberg Trials.) And so I am writing these words from a
village—exactly the kind of village my grandmother longed for as
a young medical student; the kind of village that saved her and my
grandfather during the war; the kind of village she feared would be
lost forever to her family when she moved to America.

Now I know the house is not a rocky exoskeleton meant to hide
me from the pain of remembering; I can't come to La Roche to escape the past, to live smoothly among flowers and stones. Life here
is no less fragile, no less shattering. It is just like any other place
in the world: ugly, mundane, dirty, and boring, but also beautiful,
exalted, and full of love. That is the gift—the miracle—my grandmother made in buying the house: the opportunity for me to live my
life forward, even as the past swirls and eddies around me.

When I first arrived in La Roche, I believed in a fairy tale: Anna
and Armand fell in love, bought a house, and never spoke again.
Then I tried to tell the tale, and it fell apart on me. Maybe my
grandparents loved each other, maybe they didn't. Maybe both.
Maybe they would have divorced anyway, without the war—but
perhaps that's a moot point, since maybe they wouldn't have married without the war. And after all that searching, all those facts,

and all that doubt, I came home to La Roche and realized it really was that simple: Armand and Anna fell in love, bought a house, and never spoke again. The point of a fairy tale is never in the details. The point is that it's easy to remember, to carry, to tell. We'll continue telling until the stones fall down, and then we'll rebuild and start again.

ACKNOWLEDGMENTS

This book would never have made it to its current form without the steady guidance, good humor, encouragement, and understanding of my agent, Lydia Wills. Nor would it be what it is today without Miriam Chotiner-Gardner, in whom I found the thoughtful, smart, engaged, and rigorous editor every author dreams of. I am deeply grateful to both of you for your hard work and commitment to this project. This book has also benefited from an exceptional team of dedicated, gifted, and enthusiastic people at Crown, and I am thankful to each and every one of you.

My heartfelt thanks to my readers: Annelies Fryberger, eagle-eyed critic and tireless breakfast mate; Anne Chernicoff, Erin Fornoff, Keramet Reiter, Ria Tabacco Mar, and Rachel Taylor; and Matthew Quirk, for reading the most drafts and for the bicycle lessons.

This book also owes its existence and an immense debt of gratitude to the following people and organizations:

To the Harvard College Research Program, for early research support; to the Henry Russell Shaw Traveling Fellowship, for a postgraduate year to work on this project; and to the Harvard Hillel Netivot Fellowship, which encouraged me to grapple with the big questions that underlie the little ones in these pages.

To Patrice Higonnet, for teaching me how to write history, for encouraging me to write other things, and for giving me my first translating job. His personal insight and excellent graduate seminar on Vichy France helped me to lay the historical groundwork for this book.

To Mary Lewis, whose course on comparative citizenship in France and Germany helped me with certain knotty questions regarding my grandparents' nationalities (and my own).

To Rachel Taylor, for seeing my path and pushing me down it.

To Leslie Epstein, for his enthusiasm and encouragement before I had any idea of what I was doing.

To David Zane Mairowitz, for a room—and a bathtub, a library, and a workspace—of my own.

To the village of Alba, for taking me in.

To Marie-Hélène Frizet, for all her advice to—and patience with—my family.

To Grant King, with noble assists from Tom McEnaney and Forrest Richards, for braving the spiders with me; to Elizabeth Thornberry, for helping me paint the shutters; to Erin Fornoff, for being my shining star, for hoeing my garden, and for all the rules of engagement; to Elizabeth Janiak, for being there staunchly and always, and bringing me books. And appropriate shoes.

To Eve-Marie Cloquet, for another room of my own.

To Tomas Fitzel, for sharing his memories of my grandfather.

To Martha Zuber, benefactress, fairy godmother, cheerleader, maven, dear friend, and all-around mensch.

To Jonathan Zeitlin, Froma Zeitlin, and Daniel Mendelsohn, for their kind and enthusiastic support, and for leading me to Lydia.

To everyone at Moog Music, for standing by my family; to Mike Adams especially; and to Ian Vigstedt and Krystal Smith for help with printing and scanning.

To Christine Kane, for business advice that helped keep me afloat while I was finishing this project.

To Nikki Layser, for appearing with ideas and connections when I thought all was lost; to Nora Spiegel, for hard work, kind words, and meeting me in the rain; to Ben Wikler, for help with the title.

To the extraordinary staff at the EMS Les Marronniers, for taking such good care of my grandfather; to Michèle and François Fraiberger, for getting him there; to Jean-Philippe and Danièle Deschamps, whose hospitality, generosity, and affection got us through so many tough moments and created so many delightful ones.

To Hélène Deschamps, for giving us a roof over our heads when we needed it, for all the hours of grandmothering, for helping us to pursue our dreams.

To my four wonderful parents, for their love and enthusiasm throughout—Robert Richmond and Kathleen Mavournin: to both of you, for sharing your appetite for the written word from day one, and for reading all those drafts; to Dad, for help with the German translation, the broken rib scene, and countless other details. Robert Moog and Ileana Grams-Moog: to Abah, for more than I could ever say, even had there been more time to say it in; to Mom, for everything, really everything, and especially for being smarter than any pig.

To my grandparents, for all they were, all they endured, all they taught, all they remembered, all they did and didn't say.

To Estelle Anna, whose brightness, beauty, and determination bear witness to the star for whom she was named.

Last and most of all to my husband; for his unwavering support; for his wisdom, rigor, and kindness; for teaching me courage and helping me to be a better person; for making me laugh; for all the joy and love, every step of the way. *Doudou,* I think you know by now: it was never about the indoor plumbing.

A NOTE ON SOURCES

Below, for the reader who is curious to learn more, is a nonacademic and nonexhaustive list of sources I consulted to complete this book. I have included the works I found the most useful, informative, thought-provoking, and inspiring, so my list is divided by topic rather than by chapter.

All of the research for *A Fifty-Year Silence* was conducted in French and English (along with a little German, with help from my father, Robert Richmond); all translations in the text, unless otherwise noted, are my own. For the convenience of English-speaking readers, I have cited all French sources in their English translations, except for cases in which a translation is unavailable.

PRIMARY SOURCES

My main primary sources were, of course, my grandparents. In addition to my conversations and correspondence with them, my work would not have been possible without the sources listed here.

The Swiss Federal Archives in Bern: these archives contain some 45,000 personal files on the civilian refugees interned in Switzerland during the Second World War, including those of my grandparents and my mother (which may be found in Dossier No. 07130).

The Steven Spielberg Film and Video Archive at the U.S. Holocaust Memorial Museum: this extraordinary repository contains all kinds of information, including footage from the Nuremberg Trials in which I was able to observe my grandfather at work.

The Lillian Goldman Law Library at Yale Law School: complete transcripts of the Nuremberg Trials, available through its website, were of great help in reconstructing my grandfather's experiences.

Secondary Sources

World War II in France

BLOCH, MARC. *Strange Defeat.* Translated by Gerard Hopkins. New York: W. W. Norton, 1968.

BURRIN, PHILIPPE. *France Under the Germans: Collaboration and Compromise.* Translated by Janet Lloyd. New York: New Press, 1996.

FRY, VARIAN. *Surrender on Demand.* Boulder, Colo.: Johnson Press and the U.S. Holocaust Memorial Museum, 1997.

LEBOVICS, HERMAN. *True France: The Wars over Cultural Identity, 1900-1945.* Ithaca, N.Y.: Cornell University Press, 1992.

MARRUS, MICHAEL, AND ROBERT PAXTON. *Vichy France and the Jews.* Stanford, Calif.: Stanford University Press, 1995.

PAXTON, ROBERT. *Vichy France: Old Guard and New Order, 1940-1944.* New York: Columbia University Press, 2001.

ROUSSO, HENRY. *The Vichy Syndrome: History and Memory in France Since 1944.* Cambridge, Mass.: Harvard University Press, 1994.

Refugees in Switzerland

MUNOS-DU PELOUX, ODILE. *Passer en Suisse: Les passages clandestins entre la Haute-Savoie et la Suisse, 1940-1944.* Grenoble: Presses Universitaires de Grenoble, 2002.

REGARD, FABIENNE. *La Suisse, paradis de l'enfer? Mémoire de réfugiés juifs.* Yens-sur-Morges, Switzerland: Cabédita, 2002.

The Nuremberg Trials

GAIBA, FRANCESCA. *The Origins of Simultaneous Interpretation: The Nuremberg Trial.* Ottawa, Ontario: University of Ottawa Press, 1998.

GASKIN, HILARY. *Eyewitnesses at Nuremberg.* London: Arms and Armour Press, 1990.

KOHL, CHRISTIANE. *The Witness House: Nazis and Holocaust Survivors*

Sharing a Villa during the Nuremberg Trials. Translated by Anthea Bell. New York: Other Press, 2010.

RAMLER, SIEGFRIED. *Nuremberg and Beyond: The Memoirs of Siegfried Ramler from Twentieth-Century Europe to Hawai'i.* Kailua, Hawaii: Ahuna Press, 2008.

SONNENFELDT, RICHARD W. *Witness to Nuremberg.* New York: Arcade, 2006.

TAYLOR, TELFORD. *The Anatomy of the Nuremberg Trials.* New York: Alfred A. Knopf, 1992.

Miscellaneous

Sándor Márai's *Embers,* translated into English by Carol Brown Janeway (New York: Alfred A. Knopf, 2001), is the best literary exploration of a couple's long silence I have come across. Many thanks to Bertrand Deschamps for giving it to me. "Donal Og," my grandfather's mysterious poem, was written long ago by an anonymous poet and translated from the Irish by Lady Augusta Gregory. It appears, in a version slightly different from the one my grandfather had, in *The Rattle Bag,* edited by Seamus Heaney and Ted Hughes (London: Faber and Faber, 1982). Patrick Modiano's *Dora Bruder* (Paris: Gallimard, 1999; available in translation through the University of California Press), Daniel Mendelsohn's *The Lost: A Search for Six of Six Million* (New York: HarperCollins, 2006), and Jonathan Safran Foer's *Everything Is Illuminated* (New York: Houghton Mifflin, 2002) are the three books on remembering the Shoah that have stayed with me the longest and affected me the most strongly. Irène Némirovsky's *Suite française* (Paris: Éditions Denoël, 2004; available in translation from Vintage Books) is an excellent snapshot of the chaos of the *drôle de guerre.* Leslie Maitland's *Crossing the Borders of Time* (New York: Other Press, 2012) is a moving and meticulously researched family saga about two lovers separated during World War II, and I am deeply grateful to Ms. Maitland for her close reading and invaluable comments on my own work. *Iron Curtain,* by Anne Applebaum (New York: Anchor Books, 2013), provided precious last-minute insights into the aftermath of the war. Robert Darnton's *The Great Cat Massacre and*

Other Episodes in French Cultural History (New York: Vintage Books, 1985) helped me to think about fairy tales and how we read them. Michel de Certeau's *L'écriture de l'histoire* (Paris: Gallimard, 1975; available in translation through Columbia University Press) probably made this book harder to write than it otherwise would have been, but I am grateful for all the ways in which de Certeau's work deepened and complicated my thinking about history and memory. And Romain Gary's *Les cerfs-volants* (Paris: Gallimard, 1980) remains the best piece of writing, fiction or nonfiction, I have ever read about the Second World War in France, or about any subject, for that matter. I am currently translating it into English, but until I am done, it is worth learning French for.